DIAMONDS
AND
DIPLOMATS

Letitia Baldrige

ROBERT HALE · LONDON

Copyright © 1968 by Letitia Baldrige
First published in Great Britain 1969

SBN 7091 0875 3

Robert Hale & Company
63 Old Brompton Road
London, SW7

Printed in Great Britain by
Lowe & Brydone (Printers) Ltd
London, NW10

Contents

PART I
LA VIE PARISIENNE
IN THE AMERICAN EMBASSY
1

PART II
BELLA ROMA AND A LADY AMBASSADOR
45

PART III
"NO, MADAM, TIFFANY'S DOES NOT SERVE BREAKFAST"
89

PART IV
OFFICE ADDRESS:
1600 PENNSYLVANIA AVENUE
147

PART V
MATER FAMILIAS IN CHICAGO!
275

Introduction

THERE IS no message in this book. This is a simple recording of a happy life. Nothing more, perhaps a good deal less.

I do not look at life in chiaroscuro tones. For me, it is far easier to concentrate on the bright pools of light and to avoid the shadows. What such a philosophy loses in mystery is compensated for by delight.

If this book can give one moment of inspiration to a young girl on the threshold of life or one moment of creative impetus to a mature woman who cannot resist polishing all the facets, then it will be worth the effort. I myself hope to keep polishing away forever on these facets of womanhood.

Any woman would like to compare herself to a diamond. Yet a diamond, when it emerges from the earth, is a pretty cloudy, dull piece of rock. It takes a lot of work to make it brilliant.

L.B.

THIS BOOK IS LOVINGLY DEDICATED
TO MY MOTHER — WHO FROM HER PERCH
IN HEAVEN MUST SURELY BE EDITING MY
GRAMMAR ALONG THE WAY, FROWNING AT ANY
NAUGHTY WORDS I USE, AND DELIGHTING
IN ANY HINTS THAT PERHAPS I
GREW UP TO BE A LADY

Illustrations

facing page

The author in the drive of the White House. The author shows President Kennedy's office to a visitor — 150

President Kennedy, a military aide and the author, walking from the South Portico of the White House to a children's concert. On the steps of the White House after addressing the women delegates to 'The American Women in Radio and Television' convention — 151

The author checking the tables in the State Dining Room before guests arrive — 166

President and Mrs Kennedy at a State Dinner, standing in the State Dining Room with all the social aides — 166

The author signalling Mrs Kennedy in the State Dining Room while she talks with members of the Bolshoi Ballet. The author introducing dancers who had performed at a State Dinner to President and Mrs Kennedy — 167

Greeting the Girl Scouts on behalf of Caroline Kennedy and accepting a large doll for her — 262

Receiving Japanese dolls for Mrs Kennedy, from a UNICEF representative and Danny Kaye — 262

Greeting the ladies from a women's organization with gifts for the Kennedy's. Arrival at Athens airport; Mrs Kennedy with Prime Minister and Madame Karamanlis, and Chargé d'Affaires William Tapley Bennett — 263

In the ancient theatre in Athens. First row, left to right: head of Greek Theatre, Madame Karamanlis, Mrs Kennedy, the Prime Minister, Princess Radziwill, Chargé d'Affaires Bennett, the author and Prince Radziwill — 278

Party given by Mrs Kennedy on her last night in Greece. The author on far left. Princess Radziwill, Mrs Kennedy's sister, seated centre. Prince Radziwill standing far right   278

Dinner given by the Kennedys for President Ayub Khan of Pakistan in specially-decorated tent on Mount Vernon   279

The author chatting with a social aide at a military review held at the White House for the visit of the President of Tunisia   279

PART I

La Vie Parisienne
in the American Embassy

I

Paris after World War II had much the same exciting flavor of the post-World War I era so beloved by Ernest Hemingway and his colleagues. However, no one has written about the Paris of 1946 to 1956 with the nostalgic affection of the Lost Generation. Perhaps we young expatriate Americans of that decade had no style of our own. We were not flappers. We were quite serious. We drank as much as the Lost Generation, but we stayed out of the fountains, except when we knew the "flics" weren't around to jail us. The goal of the American student was to finish his education in France and then enter higher institutions of learning in the United States. The rest of us wanted to earn our living for a few short years in a respectable manner, to conquer the French language, and to add some valuable notches to our career sun that "would look good back home."

F. Scott Fitzgerald and the others would have found us very square. We were even bourgeois. Once we found jobs we did not haunt the cafés of the Left Bank; but we knew the cafés, and we enjoyed them. The difference was that we despised the long-haired, bearded, unwashed American students who frequented them for publicity's sake.

We preferred living in the XVIème or the VIIIème arrondissements on the Right Bank to the Quartier Latin. Toulouse-Lautrec would have found us pretty uninteresting. We were full of patriotic dreams and idealism and were much more prone to have bull sessions on the Marshall Plan, the future of the United Nations and NATO, than we were on the latest scandal in Montparnasse or the action at the Deux Magots.

It was always a pleasure to visit our artist and student friends in their uncomfortable walk-up apartments on the Left Bank. And there were, of course, those romantic *dîners à deux* in the little cafés, always smelling of pungent mixtures of strong coffee, cheese (very *bien fait*), fresh mushrooms and anisette.

One didn't have to be a beatnik to be au courant of what was great in the world of literature, painting, music or night-club acts. We listened to our Left Bank contemporaries and made note of what they recommended, but we always had some good suggestions for them, too, of concerts, lectures, and art shows. The two worlds criss-crossed neatly.

We all started off on the same foot, democratically speaking, in France in the post-World War II period. We finished our studies at the Sorbonne, the University of Geneva, Cambridge and Oxford. The boys had all been through the war and felt cheated of a knowledge of life they had to have. This familiarity with a civilized way of living is learned neither in a foxhole nor on a college campus. The perfect classroom is Paris. Before they settled down behind an executive desk, they wanted to savor a taste of something they might never have again.

The girls felt the same way, and I think we were right. None of us can ever go back again to our particular Paris, to live that same independent, inexpensive, carefree existence. It was a one-in-a-million chance. When one comes from Omaha, Nebraska, as I did, and has attended girls' schools all one's life, a strong thirst for the exotic, the unknown, the foreign, *l'autre côté de la rue* becomes both a psychological and a physiological fact.

Some of the young Americans landed jobs at the Economic Cooperation Administration (Marshall Plan agency), or American Express, the U. S. Lines, the House of Dior, Pan American — whoever would have us and wrangle a working permit from the French Government for us. I was considered the luckiest of all the female gypsies since I landed the job as Social Secretary to Ambassador and Mrs. Bruce at the American Embassy.

The job qualifications called for a female American citizen with full security clearance, completely bilingual, able to take dictation only in English but to type letters in both French and English. What the State Department did not stipulate on the job sheet is that the Social Secretary must be an expert in the Art of Bluff, have sturdy arches, a firm handshake, a superb memory, and an unceasing compassion for meddlesome old ladies. What I lacked in several of these qualifications I made up for in the Art of Bluff, which I have found is the most valuable instrument of policy one can possess.

Of course I never would have been able to put a foot through the Embassy door had it not been for a knowledge of secretarial skills. It is a hard lesson to learn, with a B.A. from Vassar and an almost M.A. from the University of Geneva, that one can still be unemployable. The transition to Temple Secretarial School from graduate work in Europe had almost killed me, but I had no choice. I was too young to go on relief.

Ambassador and Mrs. Bruce gave me a most unusual office in the Official Residence at 2, Avénue d'Iéna. They ensconced me in a reception room near the entrance. My desk was a magnificent Louis XV original, complete with elaborate bronze drawer pulls and corner reinforcements. The butler gently informed me my first day I must refer to such bronze trim as "ormolu." "Really, Mademoiselle, that is something *everyone* knows."

I had a lot to learn, more than just the nature of ormolu. The china mug Evangeline Bruce gave me to house my pens and pencils was a little treasure of Chinese export trade porcelain. So was the lovely bowl filled with paper clips that I could plunge my finger into, scrape away the clips, and thus expose the exquisite design of pink and green flowers at the bottom. I had no idea these practical desk accessories were precious antiques. I had it all to learn.

It was apparent, however, from the first day, that one cannot sit consistently surrounded by loveliness without being influenced by it. The eye suddenly trains itself to concentrate upon beauty of design and form. My office happened to be oak-paneled, with a rich oriental rug, magnificent damask-upholstered chairs and sofa, and a Napoleonic bouillotte lamp. One suddenly comes to take such a feast for granted, and to understand it. My passion for interior design thus began, day-dreaming in my office, when I should have been cleaning out the files.

The American Embassy in Paris was the perfect apprenticeship for a novice in the field of Social-Secretarying. First of all, my immediate boss, Mrs. David Bruce, was and is the smoothest pro in the entire Diplomatic Corps of any country. She was born and raised in the diplomatic service, spoke many languages by the time she was in her teens. She knew the art of flower arranging, could dash off menus *en français* that would inspire any Cordon Bleu chef, and could argue the finest points of protocol with any official Protocol Office in any country. She was a perfect hostess. There was never a moment of hesitation in her decisions. Evangeline Bruce always knew the right thing to do, what to say, what to wear, what invitations to accept, when to leave a party. If the feelings of a French official in the Quai d'Orsay had been ruffled; if the wife of a junior officer in our Embassy's Political Section were expecting a baby; if the American Guild charity operations in Paris needed jazzing up; if the

La Vie Parisienne in the American Embassy · 7

State Department's Foreign Building Operations did not come through with the money to refurbish the living room — no matter what the problem was, Evangeline Bruce moved with swiftness and professionalism. The entire American Embassy staff was her family — and the little gift sent with her handwritten note meant the whole world to a graduating eighth-grader or to a sixteen-year-old who missed the school dance because of an appendectomy. Her thoughtfulness and compassion consumed many hours of the week and devoured many dollars of the Ambassador's pocketbook. The United States Congress, when appropriating the trivial salaries and living allowances for Ambassadors, could well afford to look into the personal side of an Ambassador's life. The demands on his purse strings are enough to unravel a shopping bag.

I watched Mrs. Bruce write a personal note on her breakfast tray to each hostess who had entertained the Bruces at dinner the night before. There was always the fresh phrase, the enthusiastic marking off of little details of the hostess' house or dinner or special brand of hospitality.

The fine art of the thank-you note, which my own mother began to teach me at a very early age, was firmly impressed upon me by Madame l'Ambassadrice. I tried to memorize her fluid writing style, the light, humorous flattery. Alas, one *cannot* memorize another's style.

Everyone was struck by Evangeline Bruce's beauty. Tall and slim, she had a head of luxurious chestnut hair, subtly meshed with silver. Her hands moved with lightning expressiveness. She was forever on the International Best Dressed list. She moved with the grace of a dancer; and her voice was low, well-modulated, constantly punctuated with infectious laughter. The Ambassadress had so much style, so much taste, all her actions reflected it, and I kept trying to decide whether money was a necessary adjunct to all this elegance. With the passing of time, I can now say it is not. It is a flair and a verve that permeates the atmosphere around a woman; a sense of timing, and above all, a well-trained eye. It is *not* opulence. Living so close to the Bruces, I was struck with admiration, awe, and not a little jealousy because of this talented young woman, so sure of herself. There was no course for me to follow but to watch closely and to learn.

The Ambassador was a tall, silver-haired, distinguished scholar, whose wide knowledge ranged from history and international politics to fine wines and eighteenth century antiques. I worshiped him, too, and decided at the age of twenty-one there had to be more men around like him — single.

On weekends the Bruces sometimes took me along on their antique-searching jaunts to the Left Bank and to the more elegant shops in the VIIIème. I watched them appraise objects, detect repaired bits of new wood in furniture, closely examine the hallmarks on silver, discuss endlessly the merits of the shape of a small piece of Sèvres porcelain. They not only loved antiques, they knew them, and were treated with respect as colleagues by the dealers. I had never been exposed to such fine, beautiful objects before, and a pair of young eyes began to open wide. I began to understand the lingo of the trade. "Vermeil" was silver-gilt, not a skin disease; "Bergère" means shepherdess in French, but it's also a special kind of armchair Louis XV made famous. I heard this word so often; it had puzzled me greatly — why were people always sitting on the shepherdess?

I finally started going to little antique shops on my own, collecting small objects that were suitable to my handsome Government salary of $3,640 per annum. (One would require four times that sum today to live on the same scale, but it was still inadequate to appease my appetite for collecting things.) I always took a friend with me for moral support. On Saturdays, it was the little *antiquaire* on the Rue de l'Université or the Rue Danton; on Sundays it was the Flea Market at the Porte Clignancourt. For five dollars I purchased my first box — an enameled Napoleonic snuffbox depicting the Emperor in full battle regalia with his troops. For two dollars each, I could find dainty little demi-tasses, one of a kind, from the eighteenth and nineteenth centuries. We use them today for after-dinner coffee — a collection of twenty-four which depletes itself by breakage with the passage of time. Each one has a story. I cannot gaze at the coffee in any one of those little cups without recalling each time how I first found the cup in a littered stall, caked with dirt, lying apologetically on a dirty velvet piano shawl, or in a silver-plated flower bowl, or perhaps jostling in a cigar box with some old strings of beads.

Paris was a host of firsts for me. It represented my first job; my first taste of living in a large foreign city (student life in Switzerland was provincial by comparison); my first car (a patient little Peugeot 203, which looked like a snub-nosed beetle from the rear); my first apartment; and, of course, my first love. It had to be everything all at once.

The apartment was unique. It was the top floor of a woman's house in one of the chicest *quartiers* in Paris, on the Rue du Conseiller Collignon. To reach my abode, one had to walk right up through three floors of the poor lady's house which was inconvenient for everyone concerned. What she suffered from being awakened at odd hours of the night, she more than made up for in rent. The top floor had been a little concert auditorium, so my living room was half stage, half seating space. I took out a special insurance policy to cover the accidents of people falling off the stage at my cocktail parties and it was utilized twice by the victims. A tiny, almost non-functioning stove was set up in the back hallway, but my cleaning woman, a sturdy Bretonne named Marguerite, could turn out a fantastic repast on it with no trouble.

My dinner parties were rather successful. What I lacked in linens, china and flatware, I simply borrowed from the Avénue d'Iéna. If the china, crystal goblets and sterling silver all bore the official United States crest, no one seemed to mind. I quickly learned a trick that was always to enhance my dinner parties during Embassy years in Rome and during White House days: make good friends of the chef and he will do the dessert for your dinner parties. The butler was my friend, too. He would purchase the finest wines for the Ambassador at a low wholesale price and then sell some to me for my parties. (He probably resold the Ambassador's own stock, but never mind.) Not every twenty-one-year-old secretary can serve Château Haut Brion Bordeaux with her Rôti de Faisan and Dom Perignon champagne with her Profiteroles au Chocolat.

I became so accustomed to writing place cards and menus in French for each place at the Embassy lunches and dinners that I did the same for my own parties. Six people do not have trouble finding their places at the table but place cards look great, and menus listing the wines, as well as the major courses, never fail to impress. I still do it in Chicago, and if some of the guests look at each other with that silent "What the hell is this?" look, I ignore it.

A typical day in the life of a Social Secretary? One is always asked that. There is no typical day. Life is full of continuous crises, and the same one never returns. When I complained about this fact once to the fashion doyenne in Paris, Madame Jacques Bousquet of *Harper's Bazaar*, at one of her "Thursday afternoons with Mary Louise," she gave me some heartening advice. "My dear, don't ask for the same trouble ever to repeat itself. It's the new trouble that brings wrinkles to a woman's face. But they must be *fascinating* wrinkles. Just remember always to keep your wrinkles fascinating." I spend at least five minutes a week, at this stage in my life, analyzing the nature of my wrinkles.

Every morning I would report for work at the Avénue d'Iéna at eight-thirty sharp. My little car was always kept under the watchful eye of the guards at the entrance gate. I would first greet the French staff, which consisted of the effervescent housekeeper, Odette de Wavrin, the gardener, upstairs maids, butler, footmen, chef and kitchen boys. The noisiest members of the Bruce household were "The Boys," an ever-expanding pack of water spaniels, floppy-eared and lovable, all snowy white with chocolate brown patches on their curly manes. They would run down the stairs in perfect unison like a school of angelfish to greet all new arrivals at the front door, barking their pleasure at being the official welcoming committee.

The children, Sasha and David, would appear in my office next, with "Nursie" in tow. They were beautiful children, always meticulously dressed in French and English clothes, well-mannered, but full of life and vigor. Even the Bruce children were perfection. Then little Nicholas was born, a black-eyed, romantic Italian type. Evangeline went through her whole pregnancy at the brutal Ambassadress' pace without flagging a step. Christian Dior personally designed a series of evening clothes for her that were so stunning every non-pregnant woman in the room wanted one too. I made a mental note that it is easier to endure those nine months if one can sweep around in Dior at nighttime.

My morning was usually spent answering the incessantly

ringing telephone and coping with the great quantities of mail that flow in and out of an Embassy Residence. Invitations, requests for personal appearances at charity benefits, mail from the couture houses about the showings and fittings, requests from the French for "hand-outs," requests for the Ambassadress to make speeches, write articles, lend her name, complaints from members of the American colony who have not been invited to a meal, and on and on. The mail from America always spelled trouble. Friends would announce the arrival in Paris of friends of friends and would the Bruces mind inviting them to the Residence? In Embassy life, one's friends innocently and quickly can become one's enemies.

There was never time to finish any task. A telephone call would be interrupted by an urgent call from the Ambassadress' study upstairs. A letter being transcribed onto the typewriter would be interrupted by a seating chart to be done before lunch. Life in the pale green Louis XV salon was a mish-mash of dumped mail and packages, phones lying off the hook, people and dogs scurrying in and out, messages lying everywhere — including the floor — and worried-looking servants needing an answer before they could get on with their tasks.

Arranging an official dinner in an Embassy is a little like writing a script for a play. The prologue is the guest list, often the most difficult part of the whole creative operation. What guests would be appropriate to invite for the guest of honor? What hurt feelings in the official community can be assuaged by an invitation?

What balance can be attained between French Government officials, intellectuals, businessmen, and society? What other Ambassadors should be included? What members of the American community or important visiting firemen? If a stuffy official is sensitive about his precedence at the table, one removes from the list those of equal rank, to avoid a ticklish situation. And last, but certainly not least, one must have a sprinkling of attractive young couples, or beautiful single women. A balanced guest list of mixed elements is to a successful party what the seasoning is to a culinary triumph.

As I sit in my Chicago kitchen today, mulling over a guest list of those to whom we are grossly indebted and who must be asked to share a hamburger before they deem us totally ungrateful, I realize how fortunate we are not to have to face the problems inherent in every official party. However, a private little dinner in Chicago should be organized in much the same way. "Mix the guests" is the best rule. Have at least one stimulating conversationalist. Have people who do not know each other. Have some handsome faces shining around, regardless of their lack of importance, and above all, have someone on the same wavelength of interests as the guest of honor.

After Ambassador and Mrs. Bruce had approved the Embassy guest list, the invitations were handwritten by a French woman in the Chancery who had exquisite penmanship. Mrs. Bruce quickly arranged for this after noticing my own. The invitation cards were impressively engraved with the official United States seal at the top, embossed in gold or white. They were then mailed or delivered by chauffeur two to four weeks in advance, depending on the nature of the function.

Europeans are easily offended by errors in their titles or full names. Their exasperation is equal to that shown by Americans when the department store fouls up their bills. When one has to cope with a name like Le Comte de la Roche de Montereau de Grandmaison one should be forgiven an occasional slip-up.

One is not.

As I look back on my seven years of Social-Secretarying

abroad, it would require an electric computer to total the numerous times when, through carelessness or a lack of information, I omitted an "Excellency," downgraded a Count to a Baron, or reversed the family names in a seven-word title. It is all taken very seriously, and they are right. *Vive les vieilles traditions!*

Once the invitations are delivered comes the nerve-racking bookkeeping of acceptances and regrets. Here, too, slip-ups are easily accomplished in the endless juggling of names and addresses. One very haughty woman accepted for a dinner, but I inadvertently marked her as not coming while retyping the long list of names for the twentieth time. The butler could not find her name on the "Plan de Table" (a large piece of gold-embossed leather, shaped like the dining room table, with all the guests' names on little cards showing where they are to sit). The minute I saw the irate dowager in the front hallway, equally scarlet with rubies and with rage, I knew what I had done. The Bruces both tried to quench the fire, soothing her with charm and apologies. Another place was squeezed in at the end of the table, but the entire protocol seating was thrown out of whack — also the butler's service and the chef's numerical system for the roast ducks.

I had done it again.

I was fairly new at the protocol seating game when I seated a large dinner of several round tables, at which we were blessed with a plethora of important extra men. The Bruces did not have a chance to check on my seating charts before dinner. The entire dining room was suddenly lulled into stillness, as the guests became aware of my ingenuousness. I had placed an important French official next to his wife's lover. Everyone in Paris knew about their *situation d'amour* except the Social Secretary. Everyone in Paris also thought the American Ambassador was extremely daring and imaginative.

I had done it again.

The only word of comfort I can give to young girls starting out in this specialized field is that they should forget their errors. The more experienced they become, the more grievous grow their mistakes. Until a Social Secretary has almost single-handedly stopped traffic in the Suez Canal, she has not sinned effectively.

Once the invitations are out and the acceptances and substitutions are all nicely underway (no one must *ever* think he is a substitute for someone else on the original list — and do not think *this* does not require the fine Art of Bluff as well as Shakespearean drama experience), the party itself is planned, down to every last detail. Tasks such as doubly polishing the silver cigarette lighters and timing the admission of cold fresh air into the smoky drawing rooms become terribly important. The chef and the butler ride in tandem with the Social Secretary on these decisions. The menu must be balanced and distinguished as well. Choosing the proper wines is an exacting science. The logistics of ordering is the housekeeper's headache, but everyone keeps a check on the local markets. What is particularly fine and in season, what fishes are unusually delectable, what vegetables are especially tender — these, not someone's favorite gourmet recipe, are the governing factors for the menu.

Devising floral decorations for tables in foreign capitals is not a chore. Fresh flowers are plentiful and rather inexpensive in Mediterranean countries like France and Italy. Evangeline Bruce was adamant about the flowers on her table looking beautiful — and right. That meant that the containers, of porcelain, crystal or silver, were as important as the flowers in them. It meant that her choice of flowers always harmonized with the china pattern on the tables, or the pastel colors of the dining room. It meant above all that the flowers were kept low, so that guests could talk across the table at each other and see all the way around the table. Floral centerpieces on some tables are so overpowering the flowers seem to be creeping up on the guests. I remember a dinner party like that in Georgetown — a portly male guest was preoccupied with a heated argument and mistook a large flower stalk from the centerpiece for the celery on his butter plate. He munched halfway through the stalk before laughter interrupted him.

I learned another helpful household hint in Paris for the single working girl. After every large dinner or luncheon, when nothing else was scheduled for the immediate future in the Residence dining room, I took the flowers out of their containers and carried them home. They didn't look quite as well arranged by me in a seventy-five-cent glass bowl as they did when deftly grouped by Evangeline in a magnificent porcelain cachepot of cobalt blue and white, circa 1775. My friends were impressed by my imaginative choice of flowers, nonetheless. I purchased my first tablecloth on Saturday morning — in the Paris equivalent of the dime store. It was a rough-textured powder blue cotton, the exact color of one of the most beautiful embroidered tea cloths at the Residence. The purchase price was $2.35. Its success in my little dining room necessitated another trip to that store to buy six dinner plates that would pick up the same blue color. The "coordinated look" had taken hold in my embryonic decorator's soul.

The art of table setting is something that fascinates a woman or completely escapes her. Again, it is a finesse that has nothing whatsoever to do with money, but everything to do with taste. Through the years, after studying the artfully set tables at the Embassy in Paris, in the White House, at Tiffany's and in scattered parts of the world, the only conclusion I could draw is that the hostess has it or she doesn't. The young wife who dyes gunny-sacking royal blue to make a zippy tablecloth, runs up bright red cotton napkins on her sewing machine and arranges red, white and blue paper flowers in a shiny copper tea kettle for her centerpiece, has every bit as much verve and imagination as does the "Platinum King's" wife, Mrs. Charles Engelhard, famous for her dinner parties. They both see with well-trained eyes. They both understand color and balance, while abhorring the trite, the dull, the conventional.

As I helped lay away some of the Bruces' exquisite personal linens with the housekeeper, simply because I loved to look at them, I would mentally design my own table settings with the saucy flower prints of Mme. Porthault's tablecloths as the theme. Many years later, Evangeline Bruce was to remember these wild enthusiasms. She sent us as a wedding present a set of king-sized, custom-made, red carnation-splashed sheets and pillow cases. They can only be described as magnificent. We take them out and look at them proudly once a month. Sending them to the laundry costs more than purchasing half a dozen fine, new percale sheets.

Through the years, I have attended Embassy dinners, both American and foreign, all over the world. Almost all of them have been "beautifully appointed" ones — which is a polite way of saying the food and wines were expensive, the flowers lavish, the servants plentiful, the table accessories opulent. But some of them were dismal failures, from the point of view of enjoyment, spirit and warmth. They simply did not "move." This is the point where materialism stops — it can go only so far toward making a successful party. This is the point where the human element takes over. I could not help but notice the David Bruces at work at their parties. They looked relaxed, but they weren't. They were always working. The Ambassador from Cambodia, newly arrived, apologetic about his English, would withdraw with oriental melancholy — and out of the corner of her eye, Evangeline would notice it and immediately go over to him to make him laugh and feel part of the group again. A badly dressed American wife of a visiting official would be tongue-tied and embarrassed at a glittering dinner — Ambassador Bruce would sense her dilemma from across the room, bring her over to a group of guests who could speak English, and proceed to tell them what wonderful children she had, and what an important role in Washington life she and her husband played. No one was allowed to be a wallflower, no matter how large the group. When the party was oversized, the Bruces invited young Embassy couples whose specific job was to give individual attention to all the guests who might feel "out." The entire party reflected this spirit of total involvement.

Since those days, I have often seen young hostesses in small walk-up flats in American cities accomplishing the same thing at their own parties. Being a gracious host and hostess is not a question of high finance, nor just a question of the eye — the noticing of what is wrong. It is basically a question of the heart.

⁌⁌

I could not help but gloat to my contemporaries and college friends back in America. They were all sharing tiny apartments in Manhattan, learning how to cook in Pullman kitchens, and selling their souls to the accounting departments of Saks and Bonwit Teller. I had an apartment that was spacious, quaint and luxurious. I was giving Sunday brunches of Quiche Lorraine, piping hot with flaky crust, washed down with champagne, all cooked and served by my faithful Marguerite. I had a French car, which I could park absolutely anywhere on any street in Paris in those unusual days. With the top of the roof slid back, I would tear down to the Embassy Chancery,

La Vie Parisienne in the American Embassy · 19

singing French love songs at the top of my lungs, pausing to smile at the traffic policemen who waved me on with their batons, their capes swinging gracefully like matadors. Every once in a while I felt compelled to gaze up through the roof at the chestnut trees blooming exclusively for me on the Champs Elysées, or at the fountains dancing just for me in the Place de la Concorde.

Paris was mine.

I felt my wardrobe was equivalent to the famous, best-dressed Babe Paley's; yet I earned less than $4,000 yearly. True, I had a few emoluments she did not have. The haute couturiers all wanted to dress Mrs. Bruce, and they all curried my favor as well as hers, hoping I would influence her. Far from rejecting their warm friendship, I used it with enthusiasm, without exerting any influence whatsoever on my Ambassadress' wardrobe. I knew the late, great Christian Dior and Jacques Fath, and went to parties with towering, handsome Hubert de Givenchy. I followed every model off the drawing boards of Madame Grès, Jean Desses, Castillo, Nina Ricci.

I would buy exquisite material wholesale from the husband of a French girl who had gone to Vassar, Hilaire Colcombet of Bucol. The *façon* for making a dress or suit at my friends', the big couture houses, never cost me more than $40.00.

Now it would cost me at least $2,000 for a single evening dress.

Returning to life in the United States, having to buy clothes off the rack that never fit my tall frame, and which I see coming at me from every direction on the street, was one of the saddest readjustments of my entire existence.

Life was so exciting and full in those Paris days, it was normal — and really quite easy — to start the day at six in the morning, and to end it at three the next morning. Every day all summer I played tennis at 7 A.M. in the Bois de Boulogne, at "Le Racing," a club equally famous for its fine tennis courts, movie starlets and unbelievable nudity by the large swimming pool. By eight thirty I was in my office, and if I was lucky, and there were no functions at the Embassy, I was home by 6:30 P.M. Inevitably then came the cocktail hour at my apartment, or at a friend's, then dinner in a small restaurant noted for a special dish, then off to the Left Bank for coffee in the existentialist cellars, or for a *coupe de champagne* in a bar where a special entertainer was belting out a special kind of music. American singers were hot stuff in those days, and, of course, there was always Juliette Greco slinking around somewhere, Mme. Patachou cutting off the men's neckties while she sang to them, and the great Piaf tearing out the heartstrings. I worshiped Edith Piaf, and my landlady complained I was working to be her understudy, so many hours did she suffer through my overly-loud record-playing and my bathtub imitations of Piaf's "Hyme à l'Amour."

My French friends dragged me to off-beat plays, of which even they were hard-pressed to understand the dialogue. We would analyze the play for hours on end, over a *café filtre* in Fouquet's or seated on the uncomfortable little chairs in the Place du Trocadero. By the time I understood the French singers in the nightclubs, called *chansonniers,* with their brilliantly subtle political satire (which they improvised according to the news of the day), I knew my French was polished. It was my graduation certificate in the language. It took me over a year of straining, questioning and concentrating to achieve it.

I read *Le Monde* and *Le Figaro* every morning over my coffee and warmed brioche breakfast. One cannot understand — or love — a foreign country without speaking its language and reading its press.

I understood and loved France.

It is not popular in these times to be pro-French, but I shall be all of my life. I owe them immeasurable gratitude for their hospitality toward me. One cannot reject an entire nation because of the politics of its leader. When one lives in a country, grows close to its customs and its people — from all walks of life — only then can an attitude of respect and admiration, or hatred and rejection, be logically formed.

My years in France were not just fat, happy chapters from *Pollyanna*. I had some exasperating experiences, including having an entire, and very abundant, can of garbage dumped by some communist demonstrators on my head when I was walking innocently down the Avenue de Breteuil on a Sunday afternoon. I uncomfortably witnessed communist rioting on the Champs Elysées, when ruffians literally tore up pieces of the pavement and threw them at the police. I railed at French inefficiency, French ingratitude, and French stubbornness, with excellent volume and with amazing articulateness on many an occasion. The elevators and the telephone incessantly *ne marchaient pas*; the taxi drivers were inevitably so rude one learns new swear words more rapidly in France than in any other country; the gullible tourists (and how many of them ask for it!) are taken for a ride more swiftly and efficiently in France than in any other country.

But — if one lives in that country and shares the everyday life, then the picture is not an abstract of isolated incidents, daubs of aggravations and insults. The canvas is rather an impressionist's one, mellow and warm, with sunny colors.

The French make magnificent, loyal friends.

There is no substitute for the riches gained on a lifetime basis by the young American who studies or works abroad. No amount of money, nor graduate degrees, nor business successes can replace the lessons one learns in a successful adjustment to life in a foreign country. There are those who do not adjust at all — their letters home are full of complaints, they see the country and the people around them in their gloomiest context, as though they had extra-dark glasses that shade even the brightest spots. They should never leave home.

A foreign environment should be taken for the best it offers. If the local specialty is llamas, then the young American should become an expert on llamas. Those of us in postwar Paris were blessed with a thousand stimulations. Paris was a monument to an exciting past and a stimulating present. We were not preoccupied with its future. The theater — the concerts — the opera — all were available to young pocketbooks. For a few francs, on a moment's notice, one could go to the Salle Pleyel to hear a Rubinstein on the piano, a Heifetz on the violin, a Segovia on the guitar. There were, of course, the great museums of the Louvre, Les Invalides, Le Grand Palais, l'Orangerie, in which passing an occasional weekend morning of absolute rapture was a commonplace experience for every one of us. Such visits were carefully scheduled to avoid the tourist season. In fact, our lives were spent avoiding any contact with the tourists whatsoever, except of course, our own good friends. As one learns the small places and byways of a big city, the escape routes become increasingly more easy.

There was the Théâtre des Ambassadeurs near the American Embassy, where the plays of the great Henri Bernstein were elaborately produced with aging actors such as Jean-Louis Gabin exuding their own brand of sex appeal. For sentimentalists and over-grown adolescents such as me, these modern love stories were absolutely enthralling, so much so that I finally learned to take half a box of Kleenex with me to each performance. I would never laugh again at my mother's nostalgia for

John Barrymore and Francis X. Bushman. I gratefully knew my contemporaries were sitting in their New York apartments, praying for some man to save up enough money to take them to a "My Fair Lady" type of production, seats reserved six months before.

These contemporaries, however, were feeling just as sorry for me. I was missing all the reunions at the Yale-Harvard game.

In the summer and during the winter weekends, we would be off in our little cars for adventure in the countryside. This could range from driving all the way to Deauville for swimming and losing our hotel bill money at the gaming tables to hiking in the Vallée de la Chevreuse where we asked people to let us tour their private châteaux.

One Sunday afternoon near Dampierre, as we sat on the geranium-filled terrace of an inn, "St. Forget," I noticed a breathtaking old house across the road. We were lazy in the late sun, after a large *poulet rôti* lunch. The beautiful, lacy black iron gates kept beckoning, and finally I took leave of my friends and crossed over, down the long road to the front gates. An old caretaker answered me, and I identified myself as a *House & Garden* magazine editor. I was doing a story on the estates in the valley and, please, could I be admitted?

The caretaker called the owner, muttering, "*House & Garden*, qu'est-ce que c'est que ça?" The owner turned out to be a "Monsieur le Duc," a representative of one of France's oldest and most famous families. His house had belonged to a romantic hero of fiction, Cyrano de Bergerac, who had actually lived. The Duke took me through every inch of it, even allowing me to say a prayer (in repentance for my recent sin against Condé Nast) in the simple little estate chapel in which Cyrano de Bergerac had been baptized. The afternoon ended with his insisting I invite the rest of our group over to join his family for high tea. He also admitted that my story about the magazine editorship struck him as totally false from the beginning, but I was a *gentille Américaine* and he liked the Americans, and why shouldn't I see his house if I had had the "exquisite courtesy" to be interested in it?

When one is young and rather impudent, much is forgiven.

There were many customs in the life of the older French people that I could not espouse for my own daily routine, but it was a joy to observe them and to participate on a limited scale. There were the traditional "afternoon teas," with small amounts of orange juice, tea and dry cookies, coupled with large amounts of gossip and political diatribe. This is actually a very civilized and economic way of entertaining one's friends, but it will probably be dismissed in the history books as part of the nineteenth century.

Another old-guard method of entertaining was the "Musicale." One was invited at nine o'clock to sit on an uncomfortable chair in one of a series of drawing rooms, to listen to chamber music or a harpist. Again, orange juice or a white wine punch was served. At many points in the evening, laughter had to be suppressed as an old gentleman gracefully slid from his chair onto the floor, fast asleep, or as a buxom dowager heaved her bosom into a tremendous, irrepressible burp during a soprano's aria. My friends the Vaudoyers were even energetic enough to have a ballet dancer in a tutu perform in their living room, frisking dangerously about the antique furniture. Fifteen years later, such a gentle nocturnal activity could never be condoned in our televisionized culture.

The French sense of humor and intellect are famous, and rightly so. Off the Parc Monceau was one of my favorite *bistro de chauffeurs*, one of those inexpensive little restaurants tucked away in the corners of Paris in such an unpretentious way one does not even notice they are there. Two of us would often go there for dinner, order the menu for the day, and await the delicate aromas of the finest cooking-to-order. Out would come the most perfect of soups, a fragrant green salad, and the pink, tender garlic-scented roast lamb with white beans called "flageolets."

Naturally, of course, this "simple little dinner" was accompanied by carafes of red wine and a basketful of generously buttered bread. By the time we were savoring the Camembert or Port de Salut cheese for dessert, out from the kitchen would come corpulent Monsieur le Patron to join corpulent Madame la Patronne. She had been waiting on the tables and taking the orders. Her husband had been doing the cooking. With everyone *bien servi*, they would sit down to their own table, fasten white bibs around their necks, roll up their sleeves and enjoy an abundant repast. This was the signal for the conversation with the other dinner guests to begin. One first compliments Monsieur le Patron on his lamb. Especially good tonight, Monsieur. Merci, Monsieur et 'Dame.

The social amenities dispensed with, we were off. The news of the day came forth immediately. M. le Patron was continuously in a rage about *la politique*. His ire was vented equally on France, the United States, Russia and Great Britain. Occasionally he would probe into some Mexican scandal, a church event in Spain, or an uprising in Venezuela. Nothing escaped his notice, nor his wrath. With fat red fingers pounding on his white-aproned tummy, he would grab a large piece of bread, wave it in the air like a maestro's baton while he addressed the guests in the bistro, and then conclude that particular argument with an extravagant gulp of wine. The glass would be placed back on the table with such force, I always thought it would turn over. On the contrary, not even the remnants of wine left in the glass would spill during such acrobatics, so expert was Monsieur le Patron with his histrionics.

He was amusing. The show was never dull. The food was

superb. The amazing thing was this man's honesty, his earnest belief in his own opinions, and his great store of background knowledge of history and current events. He was an informed man. This was one of the great French mysteries to me, how a humble man, scarcely educated, could argue international affairs with the articulateness of a Washington news commentator. He was typical of that class of Frenchman who comes to mind whenever I hear the statement "The French are so intelligent."

I went on many hunting weekends with French friends and became an expert spectator. France was overrun by rabbits at that point, and all hunters were urged to shoot them in the farmlands, to help the farmers save their crops. At the Baron LeGuay's place in Normandy, we used ferrets to make the rabbits leave their underground labyrinths. The first time out shooting, I bagged nary a rabbit. The second day, I was still at zero, and everyone else in the shooting party had accrued an average of thirty rabbits daily. Roger LeGuay took me back into the farmyard where two rabbits were sleeping amongst the fowl. "You have to get at least one, Tish. For your own morale's sake, you *have* to. Aim steadily. Take all the time you need." He turned the other way, flinching at the unsportsmanlike behavior he was witnessing. I took at least three full minutes to address my sleeping targets, pulled the trigger, and succeeded only in completely pulverizing the rear feather assemblage of the proudest turkey in the place.

From that day on, I drowned my insecurity with the gun in an attempt at being the best-dressed lady on the shooting fields.

La Vie Parisienne in the American Embassy · 27

The first thing big brother Mac said to me when he passed through Paris a year after my arrival was, "Well, what have you learned, anything?"

Since I knew his question was directed at the art of living, rather than at a knowledge of museums, I answered quickly, "About men, nothing. About wines, a lot."

He could readily believe the men part, knowing his sister, but he could scarcely believe the wine part. I had always been a teetotaler, by choice. I simply intensely disliked the taste of any alcohol, wine and champagne included. Mac was very curious about how such a drastic change had come about.

The great historic city of Reims had been my undoing.

When I had first come to Paris and was working for the ECA Mission to France (shortly before our Chief, David Bruce, became Ambassador), there was a drastic shortage of French-speaking American officers. They had not yet been processed out of Washington. To prove how drastic this shortage was, John L. Brown, Information Officer for the French Marshall Plan, called me into his office.

"Tish, I have a big assignment for you. I've committed one of us into going to Reims to give a major address before this country's most active, loyal chapter of the France États-Unis organization. All stops will be pulled by the townspeople. There's a big banquet dinner. I promised them. None of us can be spared that day, so *you're* it." He broke forth in the widest possible grin, realizing the emotional shock the youngest and most inexperienced member of the Mission must be experiencing.

If I had known how many stops were really being pulled, I would never have had the courage to go.

A very lengthy, pompous speech about the Marshall Plan and France's hoped-for economic recovery was typed in French for me. It was equally weighted with stereotyped waves of the flag and boring statistics. The France États-Unis organization was informed that a "high-ranking Embassy officer, Miss Letitia Baldrige," was coming to make the address. If they had known that I was not even high-ranking among the clerk-typists at that point, the Stars and Stripes would have sagged perceptibly in Reims. After all, they were accustomed to the likes of General Eisenhower signing peace treaties in their town.

Driving down in a chauffeur-driven Embassy car, I practiced my *discours* with Betty Schasseur, a French-born girl in the Mission who had been sent to hold my hand. She winced as I stumbled over the impossible technical terms, which would have stumped me in English, much less in French. I grew increasingly aware of my inadequacies.

"Betty, I can't go through with this. I just can't."

"You've got to."

"I've never read a speech in my life I didn't know anything about. This isn't my kind of speech."

"Just think how much worse it would be for you if all this *weren't* written out for you. Relax!"

"But they think I'm an important official."

"You're tall."

I somehow did not see how height could turn someone into an important person.

"Look imposing," she continued. "Bluff it. I've seen you bluff before."

We both laughed at this, and I finally did relax — temporarily.

The Mayor, the President of France États-Unis, and the local Bishop met me with great flourish and formality in the main square of the town. They had been patiently waiting there for some time. I was ushered through the great Cathedral and

La Vie Parisienne in the American Embassy · 29

shown the art treasures and historic documents of the town. This part of the day was terrific, I decided, and I began to enjoy myself.

Then Betty and I were introduced to a handsome young man from the Taittinger champagne family.

"Reims is as famous for its champagne as it is for its Cathedral," said Monsieur le Maire. "Monsieur Taittinger will take you through his caves, which have been in his family for generations."

I felt an immediate foreboding. "Betty," I whispered, "I can't stand champagne. What will I do if they offer it to me?"

"Drink it," she whispered back, tersely.

"But I can't stand it."

"Drink it," she said, even more unsympathetically this time.

The handsome Monsieur Taittinger, who I discovered was a champion tennis player but, alas, also a happily married man, took us down to the lower levels and all the way through the caves, stopping to chat with the men in each room who turn the bottles lovingly on their racks and help the champagne along its bubbly way. In each room we stopped and sampled the wine, sipping from the wine master's silver tasting cups. I held my nose mentally, closed my eyes, and gulped, as I had done since childhood with medicine. Once the liquid was down, I would turn to M. Taittinger with a beatific smile and remark on how absolutely exquisite it was. M. Taittinger, I noticed, was becoming increasingly easy to smile at.

When we had inspected the entire operation, M. Taittinger sat us down in his plush office and pulled out a bottle of the firm's very best. Once again the glasses were filled, and I winced hard. I managed to down another glass and a half, under duress, and our visit to the champagne caves was over. Not our visit with the champagne glass, however.

The next stop was a *vin d'honneur* — champagne, of course — offered in my honor by the Mayor in City Hall. I managed two more glasses, while greeting the crowd, enthusing all the time, as I was expected to do, about the product of the gods that was indigenous to this extraordinary city.

By the time we reached the hotel and were seated for the banquet, I had had it. Champagne only, of course, was served through the entire meal. I was proud that I emitted only one little graceful hiccough, which Betty naturally noticed and remarked upon from across the table.

"It's terrible, what one has to do for one's country," she whispered.

The champagne no longer required me to hold my nose and gulp. It merely slid down, as the evening wore on. By the time the Pêche Melba was a rivulet of raspberry cream with a wisp of peach floating in the bottom of the guests' compotes, it was time for me to speak.

Betty Schasseur was the one who suffered that evening. I did not suffer, because I was well past suffering.

I listened to the glowing introduction of this *demoiselle charmante*, "so representative of her great country, so full of patriotic zeal for the world, so full of compassion for those in need, so full of love for the great country of France, and so blessed with an astounding intellect to be such an accomplished economist at her tender years."

I knew my economist's face was flushed. It felt as though I had been in a 400° oven for the last two hours. I was thoroughly baked. I looked down at the typewritten sheets in my hand. They were not only decidedly blurred, they looked even more deadly than they had in the car coming down from Paris. I could not possibly bore all these nice people with such stuff. They

La Vie Parisienne in the American Embassy · 31

didn't want to hear tables of hemp exports from the French colonies.

So I launched into my own discussion of American youth, how the French press did not understand them, how nobody outside of the United States really did. I explained what happened at football weekends at Yale and proms at Cornell, and what exact compositions of ice cream and sauces went into our beloved banana splits and black cows. I expounded on Vassar's Daisy Chain, hayrides in the Middle West, and why Frank Sinatra was the only one who made us girls — and our mothers — squeal simultaneously.

Betty Schasseur's face was hidden in both hands during the entire talk. She admitted afterward that never had she heard such a flow of perfect French from me, or from any American.

"You were absolutely plastered, Tish. You didn't give one word of the official speech. But your French was impeccable."

The banquet guests must have liked it. They kept me one extra hour on my feet answering questions about our college life and mores. I made a pact with Betty afterward to type up that month's monthly report for her back in Paris if she promised not to tell the ECA officials what had happened.

I have adored champagne ever since. And from champagne, it is not to utterly impossible to trade oneself down to a fine Burgundy or a Bordeaux.

+-+

Yes, I loved this country of France. Above all, I loved its people. After three years, a pair of worried parents who thought I would never be happy in my own country again, pulled me home to America. Perhaps they were right. I had left a part of my heart in France.

And I had forged a great friendship with David and Evangeline Bruce. Through the years, we have often relived those days in Paris. David Bruce went on in his distinguished career to become Ambassador to Bonn and to the Court of St. James's, the only American Ambassador to have done so.

Closing the book on the Paris chapter of my life was bittersweet, but without any sense of finality. I went back almost every year, even if for a visit of three days.

It is never the same, going back in the capacity of a tourist or businessman to a foreign city where one has lived. The only thing that remains constant are one's friends. Even the restaurants, cafés and boîtes open and close capriciously. New ones become the rage one year, shutter the next. The haute couture salons enjoy several great years, then eclipse in the shadow of financial failure. One stays in a hotel now, instead of heading home at night to a charming flat on the third floor in the Rue du Conseiller Collignon. One waves futilely for taxis day and night, instead of stepping into one's own little black Peugeot. One can follow no more the subtle political innuendoes of the *chansonniers*. The records played loudly and endlessly in the *maisons de disc* waft unfamiliar, jarring sounds into the sidewalk traffic.

Of course the most memorable of these returns to Paris had to be the Presidential State Visit to France in the first year of John F. Kennedy's administration. Ten years had elapsed between "Bruce Days" and "Kennedy Days." I had called Mrs. Bruce (it was now "Vangie") to let her be one of the first to know of my big new step into the White House.

I'm sure she did not know that without her patience in train-

La Vie Parisienne in the American Embassy · 33

ing me, I never would have qualified as Social Secretary to our Rome Embassy, nor to the White House.

She wrote me a letter, which is brief and very like her:

Saturday

DEAREST TISH,

When we had finished our telephone conversation, I felt I hadn't gotten down to the nub of what I wanted to talk to you about — namely, that I am so happy that you have started this new work. I know you can help and protect J. a lot, but also — I wondered whether you were feeling overwhelmed. There are so many moments when you must feel so, and I wanted to squeeze your hand down the telephone wire and tell you I know you are perfectly equipped for the job and it will be an enormous success.

All the better if the apartment (which you'll never have time to see) is fine, Christmas good and so on. But the big thing is in your pocket: you were made for it and can do so much.

Affectionately,
VANGIE

The second Presidential State Visit in the Kennedy administration was the one to France. The routine was now established. As Mrs. Kennedy's assistant, and in charge of her program, I had to fly with some of the President's aides to Paris one week in advance of their arrival. The work-load was inconceivably heavy and complicated. Before I left Washington, I already had two large black notebooks crammed with official papers. No sooner had I stepped off the plane, than I was whisked to the Crillon Hotel across the street from the American Embassy Chancery, handed the key to my room, and told to report to the Embassy in thirty minutes.

Thirty minutes! Working for the White House is inhuman at

times. I had been up on the plane all night and had been up all night in Washington three nights previously working on the background material and clearing matters with the Kennedys. There was no time to lie down for a quick nap, unpack, make a telephone call to say hello to my French godson James Vaudoyer, or even lose my sea-legs. I angrily picked up the phone in my hotel room to call the *valet de chambre*. At least I could get a dress pressed for tonight.

Instead of the hotel operator's voice saying, "Allo, oui?" I heard a familiar, very cheery voice saying, "Yes, Miss Baldrige, what can we do for you?" It was an unmistakable voice, belonging to one of the "Great Ladies of Pennsylvania Avenue," as we affectionately dubbed the White House telephone operators.

"What are *you* doing in Paris?" I queried.

"Oh, I'm not in Paris, Miss Baldrige. How are you feeling? Tired?"

"Where are you then?" I still could not believe what I was thinking.

"In the White House, of course," she laughed. "Can I get your secretary for you?"

This was my first direct experience with those incredible magicians called the White House Signal Corps. They make James Bond's tricks look elementary. That very morning they had casually installed a second telephone in my hotel room, as they did for all the arriving executive staff, connected directly to the White House switchboard. It was as though I were in my own East Wing office.

One of the other staff members said it was a ruse to keep us all on the straight and narrow on our official trips abroad. How could there be any shenanigans in our hotel rooms with the great long arm of the White House right beside the bed?

I was assigned a little office on the mezzanine in the Embassy, but before jumping into the Presidential fray, I managed a flying visit to all the old Embassy standbys, the local French employees left over from Ambassador Bruce days. I even found Tita Mendenhall, one of my greatest moral supporters, installed in Ambassador Gavin's office. There were some dear familiar faces in the Commissary; the White Russian was still running the elevator; and Marcelle Lecomte was still figuring out everyone's official travel schedules. Everywhere I received the wildest of Gallic grins, the most enthusiastic of exclamation points, *en français,* and kisses on both cheeks.

There was no time to see old friends outside the Embassy on this trip. The entire Embassy staff groaned and creaked under the extraordinary weight of logistical details, instructions, proposals and counter-proposals to the French Foreign Office. Minute questions of protocol became subjects of heated debate and lost tempers. I watched normally calm colleagues become prima donnas, then subside into a pout when they were overruled. If only there could have been a few more comments like "What the hell does it matter?" thrown around during that week, life would have been a lot easier for everyone.

A fortunate handful of us was chosen to stay in the Quai d'Orsay State Apartments with President and Mrs. Kennedy during the actual three-day visit. The Chief of Protocol, a handsome charmer named Baron Michel Pétiet, took the Secret Service and me through these palatial quarters my first day in Paris. It made the guestroom facilities of the White House look like a cozy country inn. The Secret Service were, of course, interested in the security aspects of the room dispositions. My mission was entirely different. Where would Provy, Mrs. Kennedy's maid, be housed so as to be readily available when needed? Where could the hair dryer be plugged in? Where was the nearest facility for an iron and an ironing board? How many hangers in the closets? (Never enough.) What kind of pillows on the beds? My own room, the largest for the staff and immediately off the Presidential suite, was a former salon, filled with magnificent antiques. I was to find out later the harsh disadvantages of this room assignment. Baron Pétiet told me the story of our historic furnishings that had come from the palaces of the French Kings and Emperors. What a pity there had to be injected into my historic boudoir an electric typewriter and cartons of office supplies. They offended my eye against the heavy damask draperies, the glistening crystal and ormolu chandelier, and the inlaid wood furniture.

I used that White House telephone in my Crillon Hotel room many times a day during that week. Madame de Gaulle would propose one new item on Mrs. Kennedy's schedule. This required Mrs. Kennedy's concurrence (not easy to obtain) and the subsequent detailed briefing of the Secret Service and the White House press office. The French side would be performing the same coordinating-briefing activities. Then Alexandre, the hairdresser, would complain it would take longer than the scheduled one and a half hours to do Madame La Présidente's coiffure for the gala dinners. Then the guest list for President and Mrs. Kennedy's thank-you luncheon at the Ambassador's Residence for President and Mme. de Gaulle would change again, and this meant constant calls back to Sandy Fox in my Social Office, who was in charge of calligraphy and protocol seating. When President and Mrs. Kennedy arrived on the big jet, they would bring with them for their luncheon all the menus, place cards, and *Plan de Table* beautifully lettered in script on White House cards, embossed in gold with the Presidential seal. I arranged for a case of an American wine to be put on board so that the American wine industry would not be affronted by the President's serving only French wines at his own luncheon.

Pam Turnure, the lovely-looking Assistant Social Secretary who took care of Mrs. Kennedy's press, arrived in Paris a couple of days after me. I had been loaded down with her work as well as mine before her arrival. The French press was carnivorous, insatiable, full of ruses and devious schemes. Mrs. Kennedy was beautiful and chic; she was the wife of the world's most powerful leader; above all, her father was French. They could not resist all of these factors and turned the coverage of the Presidential visit into a circus. They kept harping on Mrs. Kennedy's Bouvier cousins, who were to make a mass pilgrimage to Paris from their little village. The cousins were so far removed, it was difficult to trace any relationship whatsoever, but the Bouviers made headlines for days. The reporters followed me wherever I went, begging for tidbits on Mrs. Kennedy's schedule, her wardrobe, her comments on returning to Paris. One of the papers reported me as being "extrêmement sympathique," for which I was grateful, but then went on to say that Mademoiselle Baldrige was "a typical American career girl, talented, efficient, and the daughter of a millionaire who worked simply for the fun of it."

My father was glad to hear about his new financial status, too.

I was very glad when Pam arrived and took over Mrs. Kennedy's press. I was besieged enough as it was by the Ambassador's nervous staff, the perfectionists in the French Foreign Office, and the ten thousand "dear close friends" of Mrs. Kennedy's schooldays in Paris, who "felt it was just a clerical error they had been overlooked on the party lists."

At eleven fifteen on the morning of May 31, 1961, I stood on the balcony of an historic edifice and watched the Presidential cortege make its way slowly across the Seine from the Place de la Concorde. Président and Madame de Gaulle had met the Kennedys at Orly Airport and had driven into Paris with a motorcycle escort — which was subsequently changed for a mounted horse escort.

The trumpeters, with a precision worthy of the Rockette chorus, held their instruments aloft, blaring harmoniously. The open cars rolled slowly and silently through the streets, but the magnificently groomed black horses, mounted by the Garde Républicaine, beat a loud staccato on the rough cobblestones. The sun shot slivers of golden light through the trees lining the Seine to glitter on the trumpets and the brass helmets of the soldiers. The long red plumes on their helmets waved in unison with the French and American flags. Thousands of shouting Parisiens lined the streets, "Vive l' Amérique! Vive la France! Vive le Président Kennedy! Vive Jac-qui!"

"Vive Jac-qui" was to be heard more regularly and more loudly than any other chant during the visit, so much so that the President felt compelled to remark upon it. In his opening remarks at the Chamber of Commerce luncheon, he stated that he did not need to be introduced because he was "the man who had escorted Jacqueline Kennedy to Paris."

As we watched the horses and cars approaching the Quai d'Orsay, everyone must have been overcome with the same feeling — that America had two extraordinarily handsome, gifted representatives. There they sat, side by side with their elder French counterparts, an example of everything our country stood for that is right, youthful, hopeful and fine. They made every other official around them look tired. As the procession came closer to the Quai d'Orsay, I wept unashamedly with pride.

The Kennedys were just as awed and pleased by the Presidential Guest apartments as the rest of us. I think that the aspect that delighted them the most was the palatial marble bathrooms, which sent them into gales of laughter because they looked as though they had been designed for intimate meetings of the Roman Imperial Senate.

Those three days will never be forgotten. It was run, run, run every second of the day and night. The President and Mrs. Kennedy went on separate official schedules during the daytime, except for an official lunch. My office became the depository of all incoming mail and packages. The Secret Service checked these packages for possible explosives, then dumped them into my room for listing and disposal. The variety of gifts was incredible. There would be a pair of embroidered silk shoes made by an old peasant woman in Carcasson for baby John, a rosary carved of rosewood for the President's mother; a French child would send her school apron and notebook to Caroline, Mrs. Kennedy would receive books of poetry written in her honor and portraits of herself executed in colored yarn, marble pieces, silk embroidery, rug tufting, newspaper collage, or even hard candies. Mrs. Kennedy, of course, far outstripped the President in the number of gifts received, which he was quick to note. The French boutiques sent her the most expensive of perfumes, scarves, handbags, costume jewelry — all of which, much to our regret, we had to return forthwith . . . "Although your very thoughtful gesture is very much appreciated, we regret that the President and Mrs. Kennedy are unable to accept gifts of value."

Flowers arrived by the truckload, and I, suffering from hay fever, of course was the logical recipient for the overflow of these also. I redispatched them as quickly as I could to the children's wards of hospitals, but they kept coming. By four o'clock on our first day in the Quai d'Orsay, it was very difficult to find a piece of furniture in my large bedroom underneath the piles of odd-shaped boxes, packages, wrapping paper, cards and bouquets. The room resembled a nightmarish abstract painting.

I smuggled Alexandre the hairdresser and his assistants into the palace with the help of the Secret Service; and I smuggled them out again. Alexandre's little black mustache bristled with the excitement of a *roman policier* to be part of this intrigue. It seemed to me he brought enough hairpieces for Madame la Présidente to admire (part of "his art") to replenish the heads of every bald female in the world. At one point in the mad scurry of getting Mrs. Kennedy ready for a white tie dinner in the Elysées Palace, he looked at me down on the floor in my evening dress, my spectacles perched on top of my head, piecing messages and schedules together for the next day's activities.

"Mademoiselle Baldrige," he said sadly, zeroing in on my hairdo, "would I be indiscreet if I said — that — that you need me badly?"

"No, Monsieur Alexandre," I replied, still working on the floor. "I agree completely. Perhaps we will have time for each other — in the next world."

We all knew that if the press, lurking in the doorways, were aware of these hairdresser movements, this would be the lead of all their stories on the visit for that day. "Alexandre spends two hours fixing Mrs. Kennedy's coiffure" would be the headline. As it was, Mrs. Kennedy's wardrobe was the talk of everyone from the cheesemakers in Roquefort and the bar waitresses in the Yukon to the pearl divers in Japan. Her clothes were sensational, as they should have been for a Paris State Visit. For the gala at Versailles she wore a white satin Givenchy ballgown, with matching coat. The top of the dress was elaborately embroidered in colored paillette flowers. Her photograph, judging from the press clippings sent to us, made the front page of every gazette from Madagascar to Outer Mongolia. Her hair was worn in soft waves and curls in an upsweep hairdo, with the top hairpiece ringed with leaf-shaped diamond clips. The American press had a field day, noting her dress was by Hubert de Givenchy, and not by Oleg Cassini, her "official" designer. Every woman in Paris was beside herself, trying to catch a glimpse of Jac-qui on the street, or studying the newspaper photographs with magnifying glasses so as not to miss a detail.

I was glad I was big and strong, because I had to use brute force at times to help the Secret Service protect her from on-rushing hordes of women who would try to touch her in narrow corridors. At Mme. de Gaulle's favorite charity, the École de Puériculture, Mrs. Kennedy spent over an hour waving at the babies and presenting the older children with gifts. There was a little presentation ceremony when Mrs. Kennedy gave to Mme. de Gaulle some bright animal wall hangings and gay children's furniture I had obtained from Knoll Associates to furnish the dreary waiting room. People were knocked down in their eagerness to get closer to her; the French television cameramen knocked over small children and broke every rule we had laid down for press coverage; one hefty brute put the full force of his weight on my instep, as I was trying to wrench Mrs. Kennedy free from a woman who had latched onto her with a death grip, trying to intercede for her son who was in prison. The brute who almost crippled me, without apologizing, lived to regret it. I gave him back some of his own medicine. A secret serviceman, who had seen the trouble and was rushing over to rescue us, could not suppress a laugh, as he muttered under his breath, "Tish, we'll take you into the Service. Just any time."

Therefore, for Mrs. Kennedy's staff, even a ladylike excursion such as visiting a hospital or a museum was tantamount to playing a fast rugby game. Pam Turnure and I would count the number of body bruises after each encounter. As I rushed back to change clothes, it meant coping with new messages, changed appointments, cables to answer, lost baggage and whatever else might be waiting to bedevil me before rushing out the door again into the next official motorcade. Mrs. Kennedy, meanwhile, remained calm and serene, waving modestly at the cheering crowds. No one knew what lay behind the scenes as the poor staff lived a speeded-up caricature of a Marx Brothers film.

At night we would literally limp back into the palace, exhausted to the marrow of our bones. The French Chief of Protocol, Baron Pétiet, would lead us into the candlelit baroque dining room, where we found a sumptuous supper spread out for us: champagne, caviar, pâté de foie gras, three kinds of toasted French bread and rolls, green salad, platters of cheese, cold chicken and beef with aspic, dessert soufflés and fresh fruit.

Although we had dined with enthusiasm earlier each evening at the state functions, somehow that candlelight supper in the palace gave birth to a second appetite, and we all ate hungrily.

Around 1 A.M. the staff would be ready to retire for about five hours of sleep. I never got it. I would slip into my Louis XVI bed, with its gray painted wood headboard, and await my nocturnal callers. These callers were not — alas — bent on missions of the heart. In fact, they tried hard not to engage me in any conversation whatsoever. My bedroom had the great misfortune to be in the center of all the other bedrooms used by the Presidential staff. A State Department courier would rush through my room on his way to Secretary Rusk's room with a top secret dispatch; the Secret Service would change the guard and pass back and forth through the room. A Navy medical corpsman would report to Dr. Berkeley's room with medicines to be taken along for crowd emergencies the next day; the Signal Corps messengers came through, and McGeorge Bundy received, it seemed to me, a dispatch from the White House code room every hour on the hour. There was no way these gentlemen could get in or out without using my room. On my first night in the palace I had put on the usual hairnet and dry skin cold cream upon retiring. By 3 A.M., I had received untold snickering comments from my colleagues who by then had ceased to be embarrassed while using my room as the hotel lobby. The next two nights I dispensed with the hairnet and cold cream, and blamed my resulting hairdo and extra-dry-skin face on the U. S. Government.

The dinner given by Président and Madame de Gaulle in honor of our President at Versailles will probably remain the most memorable dinner in the lives of any member of the White House staff lucky enough to attend.

A long table was set up in the Hall of Mirrors, which was lit by an incandescent glow from the candles in the vermeil candelabra and by the newly illuminated frescoes in the ceiling. The entire table service was in antique vermeil, and the pinkish-golden glow cast by the candles on the surfaces was repeated in the pale peach color of the flowers down the center of the table. The women's jewels sparkled like colored fireflies on the great table — it was quite blindingly apparent that every Frenchwoman invited had borrowed the family treasures.

Four wines were served during the six-course dinner. I could not understand how they accomplished the miracle of keeping the cold food cold and the hot food piping hot without a kitchen and with that many guests. It continued to astound me, and I almost darted behind the screens into the makeshift butler's pantry to discover their secrets.

Afterward, we walked behind the two Presidents and their wives through the palace apartments over to the recently restored Louis XV theater. Small, perfectly proportioned, the theater was a confection of powder blue and white, trimmed with gilt. An eighteenth century ballet was performed, with the same costumes and musical instruments that were used in the time of the great French Kings.

We had turned our own lives back more than two centuries. It was pure magic, the entire evening, done with opulence, and yet with perfect taste and restraint. The French *know how*, I kept thinking, as I surveyed the ring of boxes, filled with magnificently dressed people who were witnessing a nostalgic return to the great era of Versailles.

On the ride back into Paris, we passed through acres of Versailles' illuminated gardens, with the fountains playing their own ballet in time to the music piped through the trees.

That music happened to be the two countries' national anthems.

The Kennedys stopped their lead car, got out and walked over to one of the main fountains shooting a diamond spray almost as high as the ancient trees lining the *allées* of the park. They just stood there in silence for a couple of minutes, hand in hand, listening to the music and savoring who knows how many precious impressions that would go into their book of good memories of the Presidency.

I had my own thoughts, too. I wondered what possible combination of elements had put me in Paris as a student, as a secretary, and now as part of an important moment of history.

There was no answer.

PART II

*Bella Roma and
a Lady Ambassador*

II

It was not the first time I had been accused of being too romantic. The old Italian gentleman sat in his antique *fauteuil* with the erect grace of the aristocracy he represented. "Letizia," he said, smiling apologetically, "I cannot understand you nor many of your countrymen. You love us too much some of the time. You forgive us too much most of the time. Siete troppo romantici."

—

One cannot leave romanticism aside in some cases. Rome is one of those cases for me. It grows a little more like a Tantalus apple every year. The city is like dope to a lot of us who have grown to know it well. A young girl who comes to live there finds that senses she never knew she even possessed come alive. In Rome people seem to love with more zest, murder with more imagination, submit to creative urges more often, and lose the sense of logic more easily than in any other place. I did not commit murder during my years at the American Embassy in Rome, but that was all I missed.

I try to be objective about the Rome of now. The whole country has changed amazingly since the 1950's. Labor is no longer plentiful, so the lovely luxury of domestic help is disappearing. The traffic is preposterous; one has to be either desperate or foolish to attack the rush hour mêlée. The jet age has catapulted some very unattractive tourists into one's favorite isolated corners of the country. Prices are high. Pride in craftsmanship is lessening, and the Big Beat has supplanted the dreamy aphrodisiacal music that used to permeate the air inside and outside the nightclubs.

Even taking into account these vast discrepancies between "my Italy" and "today's Italy," surely the Italians still retain their superior grasp on the "Arte del Vivere." They know *how to live*. The poor are happier, more full of smiles; the titled ones are snobbier and more appreciated for it; the nouveau riche are richer and more delightfully gauche about it; and the jet set is jettier and more noisily so than any other nationality I know.

⊷

After Paris I found myself home in Washington, working for the Central Intelligence Agency. It was increasingly difficult to readjust to the hum-drum existence of government service, even if my job in the Eastern European Division of CIA was fascinating. My bosses were all young, brilliant, experienced in heroic intelligence operations in the Second World War. They were all married too. My life *outside* the office was stultifying. With some gratifying exceptions, the men who took me out were justifiably impatient with me for always talking about Paris, and for sighing with nostalgia at a mere three notes of a French song. I also had the nasty habit of correcting an escort's French when he ordered dinner from a pseudo-French waiter. (In Washington pseudo-French means a Greek waiter who works for a restaurant with a French name.)

Actually, I am quite surprised any man took me out at all. I was not only suffering from a superiority complex, but I was on a different beat. I knew more about French writers, sports and Paris theater than about what people in my own country were discussing. Abroad I had been spoiled by everyone. Back home in Washington, I was spoiled by no one. None of my friends could even judge how good my French or my knowledge of current Parisian life was. They could not have cared less, and rightfully so. I was out of the mainstream, not they.

After two years of trying to readjust, I realized the only remedy was to get it all out of my system. My parents gave up the fight and, with resignation, agreed I should return. I took my two weeks' annual vacation from the Agency and flew secretly to Rome to job-hunt.

Ambassador Ellsworth Bunker and his wife Harriet, great friends of my parents, were getting ready to leave the post. They took pity on the state of my pocketbook and put me up at the official Embassy Residence, a beautiful estate called Villa Taverna.

Little did any of us realize that within a very short time, my rabbit's foot was going to work again, and that the room across the hall from my guest bedroom was to be my office.

The Bunkers tried to energize my flagging spirits, because they realized that every other American girl seemed to be doing what I was, looking for a position in Rome. The city was flooded with woebegone female job-hunters. The poor ones eventually had to go home on freighters, totally abandoning their dreams. The rich ones stayed on to paint, write or walk their dogs in the Borghese Gardens. The Italians, suffering from a severe unemployment crisis, naturally did not welcome foreign girls' grabbing the available jobs. A work permit for someone not in diplomatic service was almost impossible to procure.

The State Department had been honing down Embassy staffs in an economy push, so no American Embassy could hire U.S. citizens abroad. (Washington was recruiting only for the bush in Africa and the desert in the Middle East.) No Italian firm could pay me a living wage either; Italians girls by virtue of their sex earned so few lire they had to live with their parents to survive.

The only recourse was an American or international firm paying some of their salaries in dollars. I left my application with over fifty of them. None of them showed the slightest urge to employ me. One of the least inclined was the Time-Life Bureau on the Via Abruzzi, but at least I noticed they filed my application away with several hundred others. Then my two weeks were up and it was back to Washington for me.

The landing of the job as Social Secretary to the new Ambassador to Italy, Clare Boothe Luce, was like the successful climax of a love affair: a mixture of sheer luck and ardent preparations. On the preparation side, I had fresh experience with the "Art of Social-Secretarying." I spoke fluent French, bluffable Italian, and could handle Spanish. I knew my way around Europe and could toss off the names of aristocrats, diplomats and foreign ministers with ease. Mainly, I could pound a typewriter. This was my greatest asset and a talent I was forever having to defend before my fellow college graduates who sneered at such a lowly exercise.

On the sheer luck side, the Luces, in the meantime, arrived in Rome to find a most uncomfortable situation. Clare was the first American woman Ambassador to a major power; Henry Luce was the editor-in-chief of one of the biggest publishing empires in the world. Neither of them could even communicate with one member of their household staff. No one in the house spoke English, and the Luces, newly arrived, had not yet mastered Italian. Life at the Embassy Residence was one big beautiful impasse.

Then the Chief of the Time-Life Bureau, Bob Neville, remembered my job application sitting in his file drawer. The Embassy had no room for a Social Secretary on the staffing plan, which is a polite way of saying the State Department had no funds for one. Within forty-eight hours, I had been contacted, hired, and was packing to fly back to Rome, on a six months' trial basis, my salary to be paid by Time-Life in New York. Harry Luce was as anxious to get the house in order as his wife was, so he paid my salary gladly. He had moved his executive operations to Rome for her tenure of office, and he was used to a fast-moving, well-organized, efficient life, both at home and in the office. He was to find out, of course, that such a thing is impossible in Italy.

—

My job application form had read "Absolutely fluent in Italian," one of those little white lies that can be very incriminating.

I had studied the basic grammar and could bumble along in simple conversation. This was thanks to the enthusiastic efforts of the Contessa Sera in Washington, whose Sunday lunches of raviolis and pollo arrosto were a painless way to take language lessons. However, there is a great difference between a labored discussion of the Washington weather and a breathless discussion over the telephone about a plumbing break in Rome.

Besides, no matter how hard I had studied Italian in Washington, I could never have absorbed the proper vocabulary for a Social Secretary settling into an Embassy Residence. One had to summon words like radiator hood, plant food, copper scouring pads, mattress cover, lamp finials, tole planter, menu calligraphers, and furniture casters. Someone in the house also had to be able to handle the rash of incoming telephone calls. It was obviously me, and if I could not cope with it, there would not be even a six months' trial period for the job. If I did not understand what the caller said, then it was a question of making up what might be considered a logical summary of the call. The Luces never discovered the fakery of these conjectures. By the time four or five weeks of this had passed (Example: "Signorina Baldrige, mi scusi, I asked you to send me a sample of the curtain fabric in the bedrooms, not all the shower curtains in the house"), I had caught on to the lingo. The lingo had also caught on to me. One knows one has become proficient when the first reaction to something wondrous comes forth in an ejaculation like "Che bello!" instead of "Great!"; likewise when the first reaction to something annoying comes forth in the slang of the streets, accompanied by some properly vulgar hand and arm gestures. This method may not be Berlitz-approved, but it is still an excellent language test.

Someone once wrote, "As long as there are important people with loyal secretaries, slavery will not be abolished." The thought of becoming enslaved by this particular lady boss, Clare Luce, quite terrified me at first. I had heard a great deal about the force of her temper and about how she gave women short shrift (such as preferring the company of men after dinner and ignoring the ladies completely).

I reconciled myself to these constant criticisms soon after getting to know her. A temper is something any person working under extreme pressures has got to possess, in order to be normal. As to the second type of criticism, who *doesn't* prefer talking to the men after dinner?

Physically, Clare Luce was an enigma, very tiny and fragile, with porcelain skin as white as blanc de chine. (I suppose, after counting her achievements as a Congresswoman, journalist, playwright and political wheel, I had been expecting her to look like a lady pioneer fresh from pushing the wagon through the mud.)

Behind those deceivingly innocent Mediterranean-blue eyes, there had to lie a razor-edged mind, I realized the first time I saw her. She was working at her desk in her Villa Taverna bedroom, clad in a ruffly peignoir and pink ballet slippers. Except for the businesslike posture at her desk, she looked like an ad for the "Lady of Leisure Floating in Her Bubble Bath." It would not take me long to see the brisk efficiency that lay beneath those ruffles.

During those first few months, I found myself observing this famous myth of a woman very closely. I admired her attitude toward her difficult position as a lady Ambassador. She had thrown the Protocol Office into total confusion, and at first she was seated improperly — below her rightful position — at many functions. Her reaction was one of quiet amusement, not of pique. (One protocol official admitted, "We had to rewrite the book because of Mrs. Luce.")

There was much to learn from watching her patient, sure methods of coping with her staff and winning their friendship and loyalty. At first they had been cynical and nonreceptive. How much of her knowledge of handling people was born of her years of experience, and how much was born of her own intuition? These are the immeasurables in a successful woman's life.

She handled the men around her in the Embassy and in the Foreign Office with a dextrous skill that would be impossible to describe, much less copy. Surely, there was a bit of the actress in her too. She also handled her husband deftly, a man not easy to please. (Is there a man easy to please who is not also a bore?)

Clare Luce always saw to it that her husband was comfortable and well taken care of in the Villa. She filled their party lists with people who would interest and stimulate him. She engaged him in everything from rousing political arguments to avid games of Scrabble during their rare quiet evenings at home. His restless intellectual curiosity found a happy ground in this new diplomatic ambience. Henry Luce worked very hard during those years; his position gave him no other choice. He was close to the action in the European countries. He covered major foreign stories and handled interviews that normally would have been covered less well by the local foreign bureaus. There is no sabbatical for an editor-in-chief of his stature, even if he lives abroad. The executive operations were simply transplanted to Rome.

Henry Luce admitted many times that these were among the happiest years of his life, and his wife deserves recognition for this. She handled what could have been a very difficult, ego-shattering situation perfectly. Never once to my knowledge was Henry Luce ever made to feel outranked, overwhelmed and outglittered by his Ambassadorial wife. He had his own coterie of fans and worshipers; he was in demand as a speaker or as an honored guest at every major meeting of the leaders of European enterprise. The name of Henry Luce had enjoyed prestige in Italy long before his wife was named Ambassador. As one American journalist put it, "I hope the Italians realize what they have here. There will never be another Embassy like this one, with a 'double whammy.'"

When Clare briefed herself on an Embassy problem, she did not just read the homework prescribed by the State Department. Her large collection of briefcases bulged with papers given her by the Embassy staff and with research stemming from other sources. She knew how to get information. When I would walk in for my day's priority of orders, following the breakfast tray into the bedroom, there she would be sitting, propped up in a bed full of lacy pillows and beautifully embroidered sheets. A not-so-beautiful blanket of manila folders, reports, mail, newspapers and woven straw mail baskets covered the bed and the floor around the bed. ("Why are these boxes always 'In' boxes, and never 'Out'?" was her constant complaint.) Her life in journalism, literature and politics had trained her in shortcuts in briefing oneself on an issue. She could quote historical precedents with ease on almost every subject. Like John F. Kennedy, she was blessed with a mind that unfailingly registers and records what it reads.

The art of conversation must be one of the God-granted talents. Clare Luce is one of the fortunate ones. Her choice of the proper word is faultless. One can stumble around searching for a precise word, or one that is vivid, amusing or sharp, without ever finding it. "If you have to search for it, don't use it," was the advice of one of my college English teachers in a discussion on word use. The famous women of other centuries practiced the art of conversation in their "salons," but the conversational habits of most of us today could best be described as sloppy. Women have an excuse, at least. We have to be involved in domestic chores so many hours of the day.

Clare Luce had no domestic chores to worry about. Her rhetoric was good enough to give me an inferiority complex, not just impress me. Even her little instruction memos, which were left scattered around my office in snowstorm formation, were perfect in grammar and varied in vocabulary. I tried Scrabble as an antidote to my own language problems, because the Luces played it so often and so well. Unfortunately, games were not the answer.

If the Ambassador's conversations were witty, direct, to the point and scholarly if the occasion demanded it, her manner was always completely feminine. She had a disarming way of outmatching her conversational opponents, yet leaving them amused. If feminine wiles were needed to get the job done, she used them deftly. Her male adversary would never know what hit him. (A female adversary is a different story.)

These were all valuable lessons to anyone like me, of the female gender, starting in the business world. One should never let the men, associates or competitors, forget for one minute which sex one belongs to. Just as it is the one thing that can hold a girl back in climbing the ladder to success, so it can also be her greatest asset. How she "plays it" will be her most important choice, and one is not referring to boudoir tactics here.

One of the Foreign Office officials told me one night at a reception, "Your Ambassador is like a marvelous notebook." When I asked for an explanation to the puzzling allusion, he explained, "Clare is full of serious and memorable contents, very important to refer to, and all encased in a magnificent binder."

⁌⁋

Italian compliments will always be one of the major reasons why tourism in Italy is so successful. It was obvious that the lady Ambassador took great pains to dress beautifully and to look well in public at all times, which is an effort for someone under pressure and too busy ever to relax. More business was transacted in forty minutes under her hair dryer than occurs in a full day in many offices. She did not have time for beauty treatments, but her face and skin were always exasperatingly perfect. (The late Elizabeth Arden once said, "A beautiful woman's look comes from within, not from without. The more interesting she is, the busier she is, usually the more serenely beautiful she is.") Mrs. Luce's evening dresses were properly showy, yet fashion-right; her jewels were eye-filling, and an aroma of expensive perfume wafted over her head in an ever-present halo wherever she moved. A stag dinner party of diplomats and officials — at which she would obviously be the only woman present — was always played to the hilt. It must have amazed those rather sophisticated, staid gentlemen to sit listening to a pastel blond, lighting up the sea of black dinner jackets with her jewels and with the flashing paillettes on her dress, as she discoursed with animation on the latest international political development.

Alas, in comparing those days with the present, one realizes that Clare Luce is Clare Luce and that Italy was Italy. The climate for women in the business world today is vastly different. In our crisp American business-life, femininity is not even recognized, much less appreciated. One feels that if one were to make a grand entrance in a conference room, swathed to the floor in velvet and jewels, one could not even cut through the cigar smoke to be noticed. This is the price of our "emancipation."

An American Embassy in a major capital is like a junior Washington, D.C., in many respects. The government employees reporting to Ambassador Luce stretched into almost every branch of the American system, because Italy was such an important part of the Western European anti-communist community. The Departments of Agriculture and Labor had their representatives on her executive staff, each with the rank of attaché; the Treasury Department had its own attaché on her staff, as well as a crack group of agents working to break up a large Mediterranean narcotics ring. The Commerce Department had its attaché. There was a burgeoning organization for the economic aid agency. The Central Intelligence Agency had its people represented on the staff. The Military was represented not only in the regular military, air force and naval attachés, but in a large military assistance group, and in liaisons with NATO and the Naples naval command. The United States Information Service with its library, traveling exhibits and press office was another large, important arm of the Embassy. So was the bustling consular section handling visas, passports and other business affecting American citizens abroad. There was a Veterans Affairs Officer, a Budget and Fiscal section, a large General Services and Personnel section. There were First, Second and Third Secretaries, a Political and an Economic Counselor on the Ambassador's executive staff. Put them all together under the Ambassador and her Minister, and you have an official family that would frighten any family-planning commission.

Although my office was not down in the Chancery (Palazzo Margherita), and although I was not on the government payroll, I was considered a regular member of the Embassy. (The greatest emolument involved, of course, the use of the commissary and the purchase of non-taxed liquor and cigarettes.)

My own domain was the Embassy Residence, five minutes from the Chancery. It was most certainly a working challenge. The Villa Taverna was a big, old, impractical house. Its handsome, rosy stucco facade, overlooking acres of disciplined gardens, was the result of a nineteenth century architect's deft addition onto the sixteenth century remains of the original structure. One could walk through rose gardens, down alleys of gnarled, intertwining ilex trees, or through Renaissance walkways of box hedges and fountains, without realizing this was the heart of the busy residential section of the city. Bits of ancient statuary lined the paths. They had been uncovered by blasé archeologists and left there as reminders that life is very transitory. The Villa even had its own catacombs, which I found exceedingly romantic, and which Mr. Luce, with his practical turn of mind, had hoped to use as a wine cellar. On an early foray into the musty, caved-in substructure, he was locked in. The big door swung shut on him, and he was not discovered for some time. The Time-Life staff in New York dined out on that one for some time, too.

The Villa was comfortable and grand at the same time. Pastel damask walls, frescoed ceilings, mosaic tile floors and large windows overlooking the gardens made the interiors seem very cool and spacious. The furniture was luxuriously upholstered in Italian silks. What was lacking in antiques was made up for in comfortable, well-made reproductions. The house really sprang to life when the Luces brought their art collection over from New York. The entire downstairs became a museum; the Villa almost seemed to have been designed as one. There was even a gallery between the two drawing rooms, which was soon filled with Matisse, Chagall, Fantin-Latour, Dufy, Modigliani, and the like, each self-illuminated. The success of having their art collection on view to a grateful public later sparked a whole new movement in respect to our Embassies. In conjunction with the State Department, an ambitious program was launched for the loan of art from museums and private collections in America to our Embassies all over the world. We were not, it seems, the "cultural clods" some countries made us out to be.

I loved that house — there were so many things to feast the eyes upon, such as the oversized, rosy marble fireplace on which Mr. Luce's Ming and Tang horses pranced; the vaulted ceilings in some of the rooms; the beams painted in a mosaic pattern of the Renaissance period in other rooms; the great iron torchères standing like stiff sentries in the front hall; and the intricate lacework designs on the borders of the eighteenth century Venetian glass mirrors. My office was outside the Ambassador's sitting room. I had a tiled floor and a view of the rose gardens and the American flag hanging over the front door. I also had a framed sign hung over my typewriter by an anguished employer which read, "A Dirty Desk is the Sign of a Dirty Mind."

The real challenge of the house was the staff — fourteen totally diverse individuals, requiring separate loving care, and sharing only one common bond, their Italianism. Mario, the butler, was in his sixties and inordinately proud of having been in the Bersaglieri (the crack troops who traditionally wear long feathers on their helmets and who always run, never walk, in formation). When the Trieste issue was solved, he ran around the house for twenty-four hours, wearing his old helmet, doing everything "on the double" for old time's sake. He needed constant approbation and demanded an hour of my time each day with his problems and reminiscences. I had already learned in Paris how to continue typing a manuscript while listening sympathetically to someone on the staff. Every five minutes or so, one had to stop typing and make the proper sympathetic comment to the outpouring of Latin emotion.

Ubaldo, a very fine first footman, needed his ego reduced every so often. He wore his inevitable success with women like a badge on a conceited, handsome face. He smoked constantly, even while working, through a long, silver cigarette holder. After he dropped some ashes on the hors d'oeuvres without noticing it, and passed the platter to the guests, I was able to issue an edict. Even Ubaldo had to admit that ashes scattered on mayonnaise sauce is not aesthetic.

Beppe, the youngest footman, had a head of blond, undisciplined curls, freckles, and a continual Huckleberry Finn grin. Lecherous older women were always trying to get their hands on him; he was young and innocent when he came to us, but I was convinced, after one year of casual observation, he could have authored the Kinsey report all by himself. The upstairs maids were like a flock of twittering, giggling birds, complete with love problems I had to listen to and attempt to unravel. I tried to ignore the amount of pinching occurring in the house between the young boys and the upstairs maids. Since all of the protagonists seemed to enjoy it, it was better not to interfere. Fernando, the gateman, was full of ailments for which I was supposed to suggest remedies. For Nicola, the gardener, I had no reply; he was the master breeder of the place, producing one child per year through one Ambassador's tenure after another. "No, Nicola," I would say dispiritedly each year, "no, not *again!*" as he announced his glad tidings.

Wernon, six feet tall and the house chauffeur, looked like a matinee idol with wavy black hair streaked with silver at the temples, and eyes that were like two shiny ripe black olives. Rocco the cook was an imperturbable silent genius, who could hardly write, but who could turn out an exquisite Filets de Sole Normande. He could make a platter of Melone con Prosciutto look as though it had been designed by Ghirlandaio. His young assistants were always at odds with the footmen, the laundresses were always at odds with the upstairs maids, and queen of all the turmoil was Gretel, Mrs. Luce's German-born maid. She reigned as the Grand Duchess in the kitchen, sitting at the head of the staff dining table, always being served first and treated with the greatest respect. She understood no Italian; they understood none of her guttural English. Yet, everyone talked constantly with everyone else, and she seemed to know all the Villa gossip by osmosis.

Our daily household life was not exactly routine. Little spices were constantly being thrown into the boiling kettle. One evening, while Mr. Luce was in New York and the Ambassador retired early, she was aroused by masculine shouts and terrified feminine screams from the servants' quarters above her room. She ran upstairs in her dressing gown, brandishing a small unloaded pistol. This instantly broke up a nasty fist fight between two of the younger footmen. Screaming can also be an effective defensive weapon — I once arrested a knife fight in the kitchen with the power of my lungs.

When our first butler, beloved Capitani, died before our eyes of a heart attack, we all agonized through a three-day wake that featured him laid out on a bed, clad in a dark suit of Mr. Luce's, in a cottage on the Villa grounds. He was grandly flanked by four enormous sterling candelabra lent by the Luces. A covey of wailing nonstop mourners kept up the noise level day and night. Over a hundred of Capitani's friends and acquaintances trooped through the gates to pay their last respects, much to the consternation of the security guards trying to maintain strict surveillance over the grounds.

It was never a quiet household. The constant stream of house guests, the heavy entertaining schedules, the last-minute changes and additions were hard on everyone. The staff took it all in stride. With them, nothing was impossible. It was the perfect staff. I was to find this marvelously comforting situation only once again in my life, at the White House. Undoubtedly, I will never come across it again.

✦

The Rome job differed from the one in Paris in many respects, although the job title was the same. The menus, the types of food, the wines, the protocol were completely different. In Paris I followed the orders of Mrs. Bruce; in Rome, Mrs. Luce's orders were only of the most general nature. She was busy at the office, so I had to be the creative executive, not the sub-lieutenant. I was to manage the house well, keep it clean at all costs, serve a distinguished cuisine, provide a handsomely set table, and see to it that beautifully arranged flowers filled the house. Of great assistance was our housekeeper, the Duchessa Lante della Rovere, "Nelly" to us, who was of such blue blood she descended from Popes on two sides of her family. My greatest support, however, was a minute dynamo named Dorothy Farmer who worked in the Ambassador's Chancery office for a year, then returned to New York to handle the Luces' private affairs. Since Dorothy had been Clare Luce's right arm since the 1940's, she was always able to predict, console, and advise on our employer's moods, peeves and pleasures — no small feat in our fast-moving life.

Entertaining turned out to be effortless and inevitably a success. The Villa lent itself to large groups of guests with ease, because of the series of spacious rooms overlooking the beautiful gardens. All summer long our dinners were held on the marble terrace in what seemed like a chapel of ilex trees. The travertine tables and benches were illuminated by wax burning in iron pots on the ancient stone walls flanking the terrace. We placed lights strategically in the trees overhead, and the hurricane lamps on the tables cast mysterious shadows on the old walls, tree trunks and bits of Roman statuary.

In the winter we used the large dining room and placed extra tables in the art gallery when necessary. Since the staff was adept, the service was fast and smooth. Because of the Luces' vast acquaintances in the worlds of politics, the arts and journalism, the conversation was always exciting, and the atmosphere warm and cordial. Serenading musicians were available at a snap of the fingers. They would play and sing for three or more hours for the large fee of $15.00 each. Many of the best ones, whom I knew from my trattoria and nightclub wanderings, tended to be less than well groomed. They finally realized the Signorina Letizia was very demanding about matters of soap and water, and they learned to arrive at the Villa with washed hair, polished shoes and a clean shirt. Often they would compose subtle political parodies about the leading guests, which they made up as they went along, to the refrains of the "stornelle Romane."

Our menus, place cards and seating charts were written in beautiful script by the Poor Clare Sisters who lived in a cloistered convent only two blocks away. They were proficient calligraphers. I would talk to them through a heavy grill and slide the lists of names to them under a screen. I could never see their faces, only their shadowy forms, but their voices were filled with laughter. They were always happy, and they loved to hear about the outside world and our glittering parties. I knew they subsisted on almost no food; it never failed to upset me to pass the draft of the opulent dinner menus to them. The food served to each of our guests at one sitting would have lasted a Poor Clare for a whole week.

The food in Italy can only be described as magnificent. Succulent fresh fruits and vegetables, savory soups, amusing delicacies such as squid and octopus stewed to perfection, subtle combinations of hot pasta and sauces, mellow cheeses, and unusual treatments of lamb, veal and chicken, made every meal an experience to be joyfully anticipated. After French wines, I found the Italian ones younger, cruder, but amazingly good and varied. In my estimation, only on the question of dessert does the Italian cuisine fall short of excellent. Their *dolce* are often contrived, heavy and overbearing. At the Villa we served only fresh fruit and cheese, light soufflés or fruit sherbets, which seemed to round off any repast with proper bravado. The first thing the returning American regretfully notices is that with a few exceptions, like Romeo Salta's in New York, there is hardly any similarity between real Italian cuisine and that served in the "Italian restaurants" in our country.

I made my usual gaffes — a tradition already established in Paris — in preparing the menus for the Ambassador's official and private meals. The first great dinner of diplomatic note I organized turned out to be entirely white, from the creamed soup to the fluffy dessert. Rocco and I had to perform emergency therapy on the platters by quickly garnishing them with every bit of color we could find in the kitchen. The platters ended up looking like a psychedelic experiment. I also arranged to have a great Italian dish served with bits of pork in it to the Arabs (their forbidden meat) and to feature Florentine beef at the Indian Ambassador's dinner (against the Hindu religion). When President Eisenhower's Secretary of Agriculture, Ezra Benson, was guest of honor at a large dinner, almost every single course was flavored with alcohol. The fact that the Bensons are Mormons, do not touch alcohol and therefore could not eat any part of the dinner made me somewhat aware of my fallibility as a Social Secretary.

However, in spite of the disasters, menu planning was easy in Italy. There is always such a variety of fruits, vegetables, and pastas to balance the usual basic dishes. Table settings were also a delight to design in a country full of amusing objects in silver, porcelain, and earthenware, as well as imaginative linens. I had fun spending the Luces' personal money on buying accessories for the tables. There were none in the house when we arrived, another proof that an Ambassador's job is not for the poor.

Dinner was always at 9:00 P.M., and guests arrived on time. They sat down to dinner no later than nine-forty, and everyone went home by eleven thirty or midnight. No one became bored, tired, or over-inebriated with this short entertaining schedule. I often long for Roman habits in this country, as the cocktail hour drags on unmercifully, and as the guests arrive at the dinner table over-martinied, un-hungry, and just plain exhausted. Many a potentially exciting dinner partner has been lost to the lady on his right because of the sloppy timing system at American dinner parties.

⁕

Another responsibility of mine was to cope with a raft of non-official mail which flowed into the embassy. Both the Luces had been famous figures in the eyes of the Italian public before the Ambassador's appointment was announced. As a team, they were considered to have an unlimited supply of money, influence, and jobs to dispense with ease around the Italian countryside. Every day the Ambassador would throw piles of letters onto my desk, from Italians asking favors and from Americans announcing the arrival of tourists. She would slug at the top of each letter one of our code phrases, "SMAT" (see me about this); "PBO" (polite brush-off); "VFN" (very flowery "no"); and "T-I" (throw-in to one of the big receptions). It seemed that everyone in the world who was traveling came to Rome, and because the Luces seemed to know everyone in the world, they all expected to be entertained at the Villa.

Our "Throw-in" party list for a Friday reception, 7 to 9 P.M., might consist of only ten names on the preceding Monday. By the day of the party, the list would have swollen to 350. Since I had complete charge of the guest lists, I "threw in" many of my own visiting firemen and contemporaries. I myself was receiving about twenty-five letters a week announcing the arrival of friends and friends of friends. School acquaintances whom I had not seen since fourth grade suddenly appeared on my doorstep, pledging firm allegiance to our undying friendship. The Ambassador was wise to my infiltration technique, but she permitted it to continue. She knew that those summer parties would be lugubrious without some bright young faces around to pep up the proceedings.

A large party of the mail with which I had to deal was asking for favors and money. Famous people of affluence are inevitably candles around which the begging moths fly in constant formation. I was unused to such a volume of tragic mail, shed many a tear over it, and plied the Ambassador with little notes attached to certain letters: "Can't we do something about this one?" or "This is just terrible — can't we help in any way?" The requests, of course, were all couched in the most dramatic terms. No wonder all the heartrending operas were written by Italians.

The Ambassador finally took me to task over the issue. "You mean," she said, throwing a pile of "can't we help?" letters back onto my lap, "can't *you*, Mrs. Luce, help? You're not really suggesting a joint charity project, are you, with you contributing, too?"

Having gotten the point across that it was very easy to be generous with other people's money, she explained patiently how a majority of these letters were phonies, written by professional beggars. If the Luces were to answer each appeal, she added, they would have to possess the entire funds of the United States Treasury. They neatly solved the problem by having their own private foundation make a large annual donation to the National Catholic Welfare Conference in Rome, which would investigate the needy cases, weed out the fakers, and somehow manage to help everyone in serious need.

The Ambassador had X-ray eyes and could see through a phony letter immediately — an art I would have to learn before

White House days began. Even when Mrs. Luce responded affirmatively to these tear-jerking communications, she would sometimes use a phrase I considered, at first, cynical. "No good deed goes unpunished," she would say with a smile. The first proof of the axiom arrived when I diverted twenty dollars of the Embassy's monthly petty cash account to send to a poor woman in southern Italy, who wrote dramatically that she needed money to buy food.

By return mail came her poorly scrawled thanks, blessing me a thousand times and entrusting my life forever to our Lady of Pompeii. I basked in a feeling of philanthropic satisfaction. One would almost have thought the twenty dollars was my own. Unfortunately, the letter continued on another page. There were four paragraphs requesting: a) Mrs. Luce to adopt her daughter's forthcoming illegitimate child; b) new shoes for four children; c) eyeglasses for herself; and d) an American education for her brightest child.

I did not answer the letter. A week later, the entire family, seven strong, pregnant daughter included, was waiting for me at the front gate of the Villa Taverna. They thought a face-to-face encounter would produce results. It took me two whole hours of listening to weepings and wailings to get rid of them. I gave them a basket of food from our kitchen and enough lire to get them home on the bus or train. This was a good ground lesson in "No good deed goes unpunished."

―――

When Mrs. Luce moved into the Villa, it was sorely in need of basic repairs. The great old house had construction problems, plumbing breakdowns (usually on a Saturday night, when we had someone like the Secretary of State as a houseguest), and gardening projects to be implemented. A new ceiling was needed in the Ambassador's bedroom. New draperies were a necessity. There were no table linens nor any terrace furniture. Since outdoor dining is a way of life in Rome five months of the year, this had to be corrected.

I had been through scrimmages before with the Foreign Buildings Operations during my Paris days. The FBO is that branch of the State Department that decorates, equips and maintains all our Embassy and Consular properties abroad. It is dependent on the United States Congress for funds, and the Congress appropriates about one-tenth of what is required to do the job properly. Therefore, one must practice the art of gamesmanship with the Government. I had watched Evangeline Bruce plead with them in theatrical despair about the United States making such a poor face with our supposedly prestigious Paris Embassy. It worked.

Clare Luce used different tactics. She simply went ahead and ordered everything needed for the Villa, paid for it herself, and then asked the FBO for reimbursement. The expenditures were so logical and necessary, the FBO had to find the funds somewhere. I often wondered whether our successes meant that the Helsinki Embassy was deprived of its new plumbing or that the garage plans for the Ambassador's house in Tunis had to be abandoned.

The FBO, of course, never fully repaid Mrs. Luce, but she left behind a considerable inheritance for the Embassy, including a hi-fi system, china services, flower containers and linens. Here was yet another lesson for young eyes and ears to comprehend: One must become rich before entertaining aspirations to be an Ambassador to a major power. When I saw the out-of-pocket expenditures of the Luces mounting up to thousands of dollars each year, I gave up any idea of heading my career ambitions in this direction.

In Paris, my duties had been completely divorced from the Ambassador's official work. In Rome, there were secretarial duties of a classified nature, simply because Mrs. Luce worked late at night and all through the weekends. Cables would be dispatched at night, speeches and memoranda for the State Department drafted at any hour. There simply were no office hours, and my departure from the Villa could be at 8 P.M., 10 P.M. or midnight. It was fascinating to watch the vacillations of Italian politics. The governments rose and fell, with ministers playing musical chairs to a dizzying beat. Analysts and columnists gave up trying to predict the government's actions.

The Italian Communist Party was the largest communist party outside the Soviet Union, which made Rome a diplomatic hot seat as far as Washington was concerned. One of the most effective weapons to help the Italian Government keep the country from becoming a Russian satellite was the American economic aid program, under the Ambassador's overall authority. It was called FOA in those days. (It suffers from alphabetitis, having been called ECA at birth in 1948, AID at present, and having had other sets of initials in between.)

There were some juicy riots, too, during this period, but Minister of Interior Mario Scelba's crack "Celere" squad moved their jeeps into trouble areas with startling efficiency. One anti-American riot occurred in front of our Embassy, and was stopped only when the petite female Ambassador, against the advice of her worried staff and of the Italian officials, calmly walked right into the fray. The jeering, screaming students in the Via Veneto stopped cold. Their sense of chilvary must have overcome their bellicose sentiments, proving they were more Italian than communist. They sent a delegation to talk to her at her request, and then disbanded the crowd. The police made such disturbances literally more colorful by spraying the protagonists with an unwashable dye, so that the guilty ones could easily be rounded up later in the streets.

The settlement of the Trieste question — a subject rousing the strongest emotions in every Italian — was one of the greatest coups in which any diplomat could have participated. Ambassador Luce played a major role in the triumphant negotiations, and her stock with the Italian people rose because of it.

The role of an Ambassador has never been more clearly drawn than it was in the secret arbitrations concerning this matter. It is an Ambassador's duty to interpret American foreign policy to the foreign country, to explain that foreign country's policy back to our own government, and to contribute in any possible manner to the betterment of understanding between the two countries. A knowledge of history, acute observation, accurate reporting, a strict sense of security, and super-tact are not always part of a brilliant man's makeup, much less a woman's. True diplomacy is that rare and wonderful gift that brings the Churchills to the history books.

As far as the Trieste issue is concerned, people in the United States had no idea what a barrel of explosives it was for both the Italians and the Yugoslavs. Several unsuccessful negotiations for the control of Trieste had taken place beginning in 1946. The two countries had exchanged shots several times, and every time an attempt was made to sit down at the conference table, the glare of national publicity fired up nationalism in both countries to a boiling point. It was obvious that the typical UN debate in a transparent, illuminated goldfish bowl would accomplish nothing. Each side stood firm on its sovereignty rights, and the press reports would only stimulate the stubbornness. National pride can make an impenetrable fortress out of a small bunker.

This is where Clare Luce's role in secret diplomacy began. As a new approach to a tired and desperate situation, the British and Americans persuaded the Italian and Yugoslav officials to let them act as mediators in total secrecy in London, a capital far removed from the source of irritation. It began to be part of a James Bond story when the American Ambassador to Vienna, Llewellyn E. Thompson, whose post was momentarily tranquil, was chosen to head up the negotiations in England. His absence from his post was not newsworthy; he checked into a small out-of-the-way London hotel. Then began the private meetings with the British half of the negotiating team, former Minister to Moscow Geoffrey Harrison, in places far removed from the official world of the British Foreign Office or the American Embassy. The Yugoslavs and Italians refused even to sit in the same room with each other, so the American and British representatives shuttled back and forth between the two parties, carrying word of the latest progress on settlement, and attempting to force agreement on each laborious point. Lengthy reports of each meeting were relayed to our Embassies in Rome and Belgrade, so that our Ambassadors could influence the governments in both countries to accept the terms of each point of litigation.

Many of the urgent top secret telegrams came into Rome in the middle of the night. They were long and complicated. The lady Ambassador would have to "sell" every point in them to the Italians before the meetings in London could proceed. Our code room was on continuous alert duty, and many of the young American code clerks stayed at their post for twenty-four hours at a time, undertaking the arduous, delicate task of decoding and preparing the long messages in from London and back out again from Ambassador Luce to London and to Washington. I ran into one clerk hiding her bloodshot, exhausted eyes behind sunglasses. She had not been to bed for two days and nights, but she could still manage a laugh. "It's a good thing I'm not a man," she said, her hand shaking so hard that coffee sloshed out of the paper cup and onto the floor, "because think of the beard I'd have. And then the Congressmen would start to investigate the Foreign Service beatniks again."

The Ambassador and her staff, in the meantime, were treading a roundabout, delicate path to the Palazzo Chigi. Her arrival at the Italian Foreign Office to make her reports would have caused suspicions in the press — the one thing she wished to avoid — so she transmitted the reports that had arrived in her Embassy to the Italians through Aubrey Casardi, the brilliant Special Assistant to the Foreign Minister. Aubrey would drop in quietly at the Villa Taverna after lunch, or come to Minister Elbridge Durbrow's apartment, to be joined by the Ambassador — sometimes well after midnight. It was Aubrey's job to get a quick reaction from the Italian Government the next morning, and to feed it back to Mrs. Luce and "Durby" Durbrow for transmittal to London and to Washington at once. There was synchronized panting going on in Rome, Belgrade, London and Washington.

Mrs. Luce, having done her homework better than ever, and being thoroughly cognizant of both the emotional and historic nature of the Italians' feelings on Trieste, always found some sort of face-saving quid pro quo for the Italians when they had to capitulate on a point. For about a year her briefcase was swollen with reports and documents on every aspect of Trieste. Her woman's intuition must have been a factor in handling the fuming Italian officials. She kept the pot from boiling over, and calmed them down — no small task when it concerned a government in an emotional flap. The Deputy Chief of Mission in Belgrade, Woody Wallner, sneaked privately into Rome to discuss with Mrs. Luce and Aubrey Casardi his own problems with the Yugoslavs, and Assistant Secretary of State Robert Murphy flew to both capitals as the plot began to thicken.

After seven months of almost daily haranguing without the knowledge of the press, the agreement was reached. "We can step off the platform of eggs now," one Embassy official sighed with relief. Neither side had had to freeze any of its positions because of publicity leaks. It was a masterful stroke of diplomacy, and the security aspects were downright miraculous for a Latin country. Simultaneous press conferences were held in London, Rome and Belgrade so as to give the entire detailed story equal importance for both Italy and Yugoslavia.

The Ambassador held her dramatic press conference for the American and British press at five o'clock on the warm autumn afternoon of October 5. To a man, the correspondents were astonished that not one word of these protracted negotiations had leaked for seven months. One of them kept pressing the Ambassador on whether she had given her editor husband some hint of the negotiations. She replied, "No, I could not, because as a newspaperman and under his rules, he would have had to cover the story in some way." (This was very revealing to me — a proof that a woman can respect the exigencies of a strict security matter as well as a man.)

When the journalists kept pressing about how no one had suspected what Tommy Thompson was doing in London or why the American Ambassador was seeing the Foreign Office so often, she gave a few details of how she, Durby and the staff had operated. Then she announced, with a typical Luce-ism, "Gentlemen, contrary to the lofty idealistic principle announced by President Wilson of 'open convenants openly arrived at,' we settled the Trieste problem by open covenants secretly arrived at."

Bella Roma and a Lady Ambassador · 75

There was something about Rome that caused intrigue, violence and mystery to bubble in the lifestream of the city. Crimes of passion were commonplace and imaginative. Front page newspaper stories related how a broken-hearted young buck had tied himself to the railroad tracks because of his spurned love; poison was swallowed in public places, to allow for maximum drama in the death throes; and ladies of all ages seemed to wield firearms against husbands and lovers with amazing accuracy. Even Americans who had lived in Rome for some time suffered from this "pazzia del sole"; we lived through some vivid scandals in our own colony that probably would never have occurred in an Anglo-Saxon climate.

Late in the second summer of Mrs. Luce's tenure, I was busy fixing the files in my office. The Luces were in America on an extended summer leave. They would be back in a few days, and I was trying to organize everything for the forthcoming deluge of confusion that always accompanied their return. An officer of the Embassy brought two serious-faced men who had just flown over from Washington out to meet me. Sitting on straight-back chairs that had been heaped high with my files, they began telling me a tale in terse phrases that made me feel I was going to be actively ill. I could not grasp the meaning of their words, and I kept touching my desk and fingering the telephone to reassure myself that this was reality and not a nightmare.

"It has been discovered that Mrs. Luce is suffering from arsenate of lead poisoning," they said. That was the first sentence of the conversation — succinct and to the point. The two men from Washington were an agent and a doctor dispatched by the CIA. The situation was extremely delicate, they explained, as I struggled to gain my composure and make an appropriate comment. Everyone at the Villa Taverna was suspect. I was suspect, too, but they had to gamble on someone, and so they were gambling on my being innocent, since I was the only American-born member of the staff at the Villa. (Gretel, the maid, had become a citizen only recently.) I was the only one attached to the American Embassy, other than perhaps two senior officers, who was to know about this whole matter.

Because I was an alumna of the CIA myself, I did not interrogate them as to the whys and wherefores of the case during the entire time they stayed in Rome. I knew better than that. As the investigation got down to the fine points, I did ask them technical questions about arsenic poisoning per se. I saw a lot of those gentlemen for several days. They put me through a third degree about the staff, about possible enemies of the Luces, about all the events of the preceding year. These interrogations left me exhausted and depressed.

It was true that Mrs. Luce's health had deteriorated during her first year in Rome. When she arrived, she was a chronic colitis sufferer, which was already a big strike against her being able to withstand an extra intake of arsenic. She suffered from chills occasionally, and so slept with very little fresh air in her bedroom. She worked so hard, she never had the time to get any outdoor exercise whatsoever, not even a walk in the gardens. She traveled to and from the Villa to the Chancery on the Via Veneto in an air-conditioned car. Her life was indoors, in a closed-shut environment — and in the meantime, her bedroom ceiling was flaking down a constant stream of powdery dust and grit. On the third floor above her room and my office the domestic staff did laundry, pressing, shoe-polishing and other personal chores for both the Luces. Their constant footsteps and the moving of ironing boards, furniture and other equipment made a continuous muffled sound above us, but we learned to ignore it. Because of the traffic overhead, the painted frescoed ceiling, freshened up in the nineteenth century

Bella Roma and a Lady Ambassador · 77

with its Renaissance motif of square mosaics and garlands of flowers, showered down an arsenate of lead dust.

We, of course, knew nothing about the arsenate problem in the ceiling. We just knew about the dirt. The maids were under orders to dust Mrs. Luce's bedroom twice a day, and we beseeched the FBO to fix the ceiling. A whole new ceiling was required, they stated, costing several thousand dollars, and they told us they would have to await the following January, when Congress would reappropriate their budget. There were absolutely no funds with which to do the job at present.

The FBO had been out to check the ceiling dust several times, but they inevitably made their check after a thorough dusting of the rooms, and could never see the damning evidence. Mrs. Luce and I fixed that situation — I went to the CIM department store, bought some inexpensive black cotton fabric, and stretched it over her desk, coffee table, and other parts of the room that contained electrical equipment (radio, record player, tape recorder and dictating machine). This equipment was constantly going on the fritz, which, in order to absolve myself from any blame, I attributed to Italian electricity and electricians. The powdered dust and pebbles were assisting the crisis, too, beyond a doubt. Even my typewriter outside her room received daily showers of dust and was constantly clogging and chugging to a breathless stop.

After a weekend of no dusting in the Ambassador's room, I called the FBO to come survey the dirt that showed up so brilliantly on the black cloth. They took one look and placed a new ceiling at the Villa Taverna as one of the first priorities for Western Europe on next January's budget. Our battle was won; we recommenced the constant dusting of her room and forgot about the ceiling. It would be taken care of in due time.

No one could realize then what the continuous downfall was doing to Mrs. Luce. Her colitis grew much worse. Then it obviously became something else. She had difficulty keeping food down. She grew weak and listless. We canceled every social appointment we possibly could. Mr. Luce went alone to social functions to represent her, and she stayed in her room, working on papers, signing cables, and carrying on her Embassy work in bed. We all knew she was obviously a very sick woman. The doctors in Rome continued to diagnose the trouble as acute colitis. The Navy doctors in Naples then began to study her illness with grave concern. Mr. Luce firmly took her back to America for a summer vacation. She felt she should not go, because she had been ill so much that spring.

We were relieved to get reports almost immediately from America that she was feeling better. The change was doing her good.

Then the Embassy official brought the investigators from Washington to me, with their startling announcement that a Naples U. S. Navy doctor's report showed Mrs. Luce was being poisoned.

The Luces arrived back in Rome within a few days of this staggering piece of news. There was no one with whom I could discuss it. I was instructed to be very offhand in my conversations with the Ambassador, so as not to frighten her or give her any sense of alarm. I was not to speculate on who was involved. The whole subject was frightening and terrible.

The bottom drawer of one of my well-secured safes became a repository of syringes and hypodermics for the doctor to use in case Mrs. Luce went into a bad reaction from the poison. (The amusing sequel to this little phase of the story is that one Sunday Mrs. Luce was looking for something in my files. She opened the combination to this safe and found the syringes.

She did not have the slightest clue they were for her, but instead had a sinking reaction that her secretary was engaged in illegal dope traffic, or was hopelessly hooked on narcotics!)

Those were three nightmarish days — something one would find in a thriller movie, but not in real life. The Ambassador's food trays would be brought to the door of her bedroom by Gretel or the butler. I took it from them each time with some excuse. Then the agent in the dressing room would take the tray and give me another set of dishes, with perfectly safe food in them. The contents of the first tray went immediately to a lab, where it was checked for traces of arsenic. None was found in any of the food she was being given.

She then stayed down at her office for two whole days, and did not come back to her room, according to instructions from the agents. They locked themselves in her room, saying they were workmen, and proceeded to make samplings of everything in her environment. They took a sample of every pill, perfume bottle, powder box, lipstick, hair rinse, soap, cigarette lying around in her room or bathroom. I was fascinated by this, and it was at this time that I learned we all take in a certain amount of arsenic in our daily lives with our food, cosmetics and so on, but it is too small an amount to harm us. If, however, all of this is accumulated and held in the system, and then is topped by an intake from another source, the level of tolerance is passed. The investigators found a somewhat higher than normal percentage of arsenate of lead in my own system, but I was not feeling the ill effects. I was playing tennis, dancing all night, living out of doors, and generally ridding my system of the poison. Mrs. Luce was not.

I watched the men take scrapings from all over the ceiling, putting the samples in carefully marked jars which went immediately to some mysterious lab for analysis. This was the day of the discovery. This was the gold letter day. The findings came back immediately — the ceiling fall-out was loaded with arsenate of lead. So this was the answer. Mrs. Luce, in delicate health with colitis, staying in a closed room, had breathed in a continuous veil of dust. She had retained it in her system and gradually came down with a good old-fashioned case of paint-poisoning. There was no bogey-man, no foreign spy trying to do away with our famous lady diplomat.

I have never been so relieved as when the results of the investigation were final. The agents went back to America, and the FBO fixed the ceiling with unbelievable rapidity. All there was left for us to do was to keep our mouths shut about the entire inflammatory incident and pray for the Ambassador's prompt recovery.

A couple of years after this amazing episode, which was known only to very few people in the entire world, the story came out in the press, was picked up and magnified, garbled, and reprinted in such confused detail, everyone, including the Italians, became angry. Those of us engaged in the investigation had sealed lips — it is only now, many years later, that I feel free to discuss it with ease. Columnists, especially, had a heyday poking fun at the story for being implausible, impossible, and silly. We sat tight; to have made any further comment only would have kept the case floating in the public eye in a distorted manner for a longer time.

✦✦

We Americans in Rome lived well in those days. In fact we lived too well for someone as young as I who would subsequently have to watch her standard of living plunge downward back in her own country. My splendid furnished apartment had a living room with an illuminated wall niche I had always thought went only in movie stars' homes, and a dining room full of superb Directoire furniture. The kitchen was medieval, but since the extent of my cooking was to boil water three times in almost four years, this did not depress me. My maid-cook-laundress, an elderly but strong peasant called Brandina, was as noted for her ardent Fascism as she was for her size 52 bust. She was such a great *cuisinière,* no one minded when she entered bearing a large platter of *saltimbocca* garnished with tender little artichokes, and delivered herself of a five-minute diatribe for the political party of her choice. She refused to take a day off, went out of the house only for marketing and for mass, and earned a stipend of $28.00 weekly. To replace her in my present life, I would need a staff of four.

My little car received the same elegant care in the garage across the street as my neighbor, Ingrid Bergman's husband (Roberto Rossellini), received for his fleet of four custom-made sports cars. A handler of champion French poodles gives his charges no greater grooming care than my little black auto received from the handsome *garagista.* All of this service came to $15.00 monthly, including the flirtatious attentions of the *garagista.* It was all worth a great deal more.

My made-to-order wardrobe, from hats to shoes, was lavish. As had happened in Paris, I purchased Italian fabrics wholesale, and the Roman couturiers made my clothes for practically nothing. My closet was filled with showy originals — including evening gowns that were hand-embroidered to perfection, costing $75.00. Today such a gown would cost closer to $2,000.00.

In order to know the Italians well, one should be single and female. In order to know them in all classes of society, one should be young, single, female, and attached to an Ambassador. The invitations to other Embassies and the palazzi of the *aristocrazìa* is the frosting on the cake. It is an undeniable pleasure to dine in a tiny trattoria on *lasagne verde,* fresh fruit and a big *fiasco* of white wine with attractive, impecunious Italian friends. It is also an undeniable pleasure to dine on a seven-course feast in a tapestried chamber of a seventeenth century palace, illuminated by burning torches on the wall, and with a liveried footman behind every chair. I was realistic enough to know that I was invited to the latter not for my charm, but for my potential in having my hosts put on an important Embassy dinner list. I have to chuckle when I hear an actress or lady of fame saying to the press, "I want to be accepted for myself, to be loved for myself." If I had operated on that theory all my life, I never would have gotten out the front door.

The Ambassador used to wonder at my staying power — when I would work hard until 9 P.M. and then rush home to change into the little black dress, apply the new face, and launch an attack on Rome by night. I tried to explain to her that subsisting efficiently on four hours' sleep a night is not a question of youth — it is a question of Roman air. She never quite accepted my explanation. Every morning she would interrogate me about what I had done the night before. I could never quite tell whether she was acting in a motherly capacity and striving to keep me on the straight and narrow, or if she was envious of my freedom and wished to partake of it vicariously. Her own life was full of stiff, official formalities. There was no other side.

There is more to do in Rome at night than anywhere else in the world. There is good food to eat — at a reasonable price, which always makes it taste even better, somehow. The atmosphere in the small trattorie is always inviting. There is music — everything from the strolling minstrels who peer appreciatively down one's décolletage as they croon Neapolitan love songs, to swingy, groovy combos beating out the latest tribal rhythms. When one dances with an Italian, one knows he is there. After the proper amount of dancing by oneself to the latest rhythms, two bodies meet like two facing sheets of contact paper. A couple can last all night in a nightclub on one drink apiece, something not to be attempted in New York City. If there is absolutely no money in the till, then there is a nighttime sport guaranteed to please any female, regardless of her feelings toward her escort. It's called "Piazza Walking." If one is passionately in love, then the walking is executed passionately. (Italian men are athletes who can make two people walk as one.) If one is disinterested in the escort, then there is much to gaze upon in the streets, much to listen to, to smell. The creature at one's side can become inconsequential. The street lights cast stripes of amber across the incredibly rosy façades of Old Rome; its rough stones echo nostaligically with sounds of ancient footsteps; the cadence of the ever-present water fountains makes poetry for the ears. The different hours of night mean different colors and forms to the lights and shadows on the great carved facades. Everywhere one looks there is serendipity. A leering gargoyle perched on an apartment house ledge for no apparent reason; an unexpected ancient inner courtyard with its own bubbling fountain, dotted with vestiges of the present (a baby carriage and some bicycles); and a pair of massive wooden doors with bright brass rings, in an elaborately carved stone frame. The door is proudly crowned by a Cardinal's hat to proclaim its original owner.

The perfect evening, in those golden Roman days, after a pleasant dinner, was to discover all this while strolling and listening to the noises of the piazza. There was an irresistible urge to partake of the life of the streets, whether it be filling out the football scores for next Sunday's games in the noisy tobacco shop, listening to the water in the fountains, or buying ice cream bars on sticks to give to a ragged band of *ragazzini*. This part of Rome hopefully will be around forever.

Hopefully, Italian men, too, will be around forever. They

manage to convey the impression of total dedication to womanhood. They happen to love big blonds, and I happen to be a big blond. When an Italian man vocalizes his feelings, it is the sweetest music of all. That those feelings may be very transitory or too universally dispensed does not matter. The moment of truth is always far enough away not to detract from the pleasure of the present.

⊷⊶

Living in a tourist's paradise was unsettling — because within easy reach at all times were the places and people featured in travel posters all over the world — the dreamy waterways of Venice; the crenellated towers of Florence; the toasted beaches at Formia and Viareggio; the white-frosted peaks of Cortina d'Ampezzo and Sestriere; the fragrant blossoming trees of Sicily; the energetic business centers of Milano; the tanned, sinewy fishermen of Capri. The Ambassador was a tough taskmaster, and since she worked about eighteen hours a day, she considered her staff should be able to work at least twelve. When I finally managed my first vacation to visit the Attolico family on the island of Ischia, off the Bay of Naples, the Luces' rented yacht tracked me down after only two days of peace. The Luces were due in Naples unexpectedly, to visit the Admiral in command of the Mediterranean fleet. There would be the Mayor of Naples, the Bishop of Naples and all the military brass with which to cope on a protocol basis. I was needed, and like a killer shark cruising silently in the darkness, the yacht found me.

On my one day of rest — Sunday — I would drive my little car out to the country for lunch, either to the mountains of the Castelli Romani, to the rolling hills of Abruzzi or to the fishing villages on the sea. The Ambassador had a secret radar system in her limousine, I was sure, for her chauffeur found me on many occasions, and S.O.S.'d me back to the Villa for some crisis.

In spite of a slight persecution complex in regard to these interruptions of my private life, I managed to work in some totally memorable trips all over Italy during the Ambassador's absences from the country. There are not many secretaries who can say they gave an unsolicted midnight guitar concert in the piazza at Positano, slept on a glacier on Monte Rosa in the Alps, and won honors in a local wine-drinking contest near the Pope's summer palace in the Alban Hills — all in two weeks' time. As I look at the boot on the world map right now, there is precious little of it I have not explored. It would, unfortunately, take me the rest of my life to say that about my own country.

It is important when one is single, living abroad, and able to travel with a sense of humor about one's living conditions, to investigate all corners of the country. There is a vast difference between what the tourist holed up in a youth hostel or in an Excelsior Hotel suite sees of a country, and what a young person who lives there sees of that same country. The two perspectives are totally different. To know the language, the customs, the habits, to discover the hidden spots, to taste the subtle pleasures of local life is to come to love a country.

To know Italy is to know when to cheer at the "futbol" games, and when to whistle at an opera performance. It means knowing where to buy a handmade bag from an old craftsman in a fourth-floor walk-up. It means knowing what to serve with the *formaggio bianco* purchased at the neighborhood dairy, and when to avoid the Via Veneto as if it were the plague. It means reading and laughing over the want ads in *Il Messaggero* with morning coffee, and arguing with the plumber over why hot water now comes out of the cold water faucet and vice versa. It means showing up at an Italian home for the first time automatically armed with flowers, and knowing all the latest musical hits to request from the musicians who stop by your table at a restaurant. It means knowing how to fight for a rightful place on the bus, and when to give money to a beggar. It means understanding and appreciating the unequalled commercials at intermission in the cinema, and understanding and appreciating the role of Italian art in everyday life. Above all, it means understanding the people, and taking them, like the marriage vow, for better or for worse, for richer and mostly for poorer.

True familiarity with a foreign country and its peoples is such a precious, personal and emotional experience, one carries it deep in the heart all through life. It is comforting to pull it out of the sub-conscious, to savor it, to live it again. Those who know that country only as a tourist are not so fortunate.

But the most important advantage in serving one's country abroad is the personal satisfaction rendered by that service. No matter how unimportant his job, an American who is attached to a government staff in some capacity has the ability to influence hundreds of people with whom he is in daily contact. The young Embassy clerk who volunteers to serve a nutritious breakfast to the slum children in Trastevere; the Marine guards who teach the orphanage children in an all-communist section of the city how to play baseball with equipment donated by an American Legion post in Connecticut; the code clerk who teaches a painting class for indigent aged on his weekends; the junior officer who gives a speech on democracy in fluent Italian at his child's eighth grade commencement exercises; the Embassy wife who visits her building's janitor in the hospital, bringing gifts of good cheer — all of these people reach out in waves of strong affirmative influence that can do more good on America's behalf than millions of dollars of economic aid.

There is thus a sense of power in representing one's country abroad. Every American's action is magnified and generalized, and the bad behavior exhibited by some summer tourists is happily offset by the Americans living there who understand their responsibilities.

There is a delicious confusion of incidents in the memory collection of my years at the Rome Embassy. I can never forget the reaction of the entire country when we needed a nursing mother dog for the Ambassador's two toy French poodle newborns. They had become orphans at birth. The Italians responded by bringing nursing animals of every variety to the Villa, from pussy cats to braying donkeys. Everyone tried to be of help; it was considered an international emergency. We finally purchased a flea-bitten mongrel in the dog pound who took on the job with the greatest of diplomatic tact. When Mrs. Luce christened her "Signora Snackbar," and her two adopted babies "Romulus" and "Remus," all of Italy rejoiced that an Italian had solved an American crisis for a change. (One newspaper headline: "Once again, Italian Mothers' Milk Proves to Be Best.")

I have memories of telephone lines constantly going dead; of the electrician singing opera while making the electrical breakdown worse instead of better; of introducing the Parkistani Ambassador to everyone at a reception as the Indian Ambassador; of sitting on the hill overlooking Rome in the moonlight with a group of friends, singing Italian songs, with a guitar and a bottle of wine; of becoming so emotional at a soccer game that I found myself hitting an objectionable fan over the head with my purse; and then there emerges a very proud and serious thread of reminiscences that will probably always affect my life. I am proud to have witnessed Clare Luce's triumph over the problems of her job, and over the prejudices against her becoming a United States Ambassador. She raised her head above Congressional and press criticism, and concentrated on the problems ahead. There is only so much time in the day for one's own thoughts, so when the going gets tough, perhaps a system of priorities in one's worry habits is the answer. I watched her fret over the future far more than the reverses of the present. It is an excellent mental discipline to adopt — if one can.

Above all, she guided me and helped me at every turn. To watch her handling Italian contacts, visiting officials, journalists and intellectuals of every walk of life was in itself a course in public relations.

And always, there was the presence of Henry Luce, the man with the endlessly inquiring mind, the perfectionist, the kind philosopher. The casual conversations between the Luces, their arguments and intellectual games were the quickest of verbal tennis matches to observe. Above all, one knew they needed each other. Clare Luce often said that a woman who has important responsibilities in a man's world needs the right kind of man by her side — more than does a woman with only domestic responsibilities. A career woman does not steer a difficult course easily by herself; another hand is needed on the helm. That Clare knows what the late Henry Luce meant to her life is apparent. In a recent letter, ripped off in her usual unstudied speed, she wrote:

> ... *For the truth of the matter is, women need to love and to be loved, for life without love is crippling at best, and meaningless at worst. It's just a pity that a woman is asked so often to sacrifice her personhood in order to fulfill her womanhood.*
>
> *Only men who are of large spirit and who are really superior are, perhaps, capable of loving a woman enough to permit her to be altogether a person. My Harry was a man like that.*

PART III

"No, Madam, Tiffany's Does Not Serve Breakfast"

III

THE BRONZE GIANT holding the clock on his bowed shoulders is one of New York's most beloved and most practical landmarks. Tiffany's long-suffering Atlas, which surmounts the big marble doorway, is the only way most Fifth Avenue travelers know whether or not they are late to work. This morning the giant's clock registered eight forty-five, as I slipped past it and around into the trade entrance on 57th Street. The huge Fifth Avenue doors would not swing open until the much more civilized hour of 10 A.M.

I was just another employee, and our automatic elevator near the trade entrance was crowded, hot and uncomfortable. I was to report to the executive offices on the fifth floor. There was no glamour in this part of the emporium — only bulletin boards and metal employees' lockers.

The fact that today was April first, April Fool's Day, did not help my peace of mind. I knew no one in this store, except for fifteen minutes' acquaintanceship with its owner, Chairman Walter Hoving. I knew nothing about the jewelry business, except for what it does to husbands' dispositions when the bills come. I was going to be Tiffany's first woman executive, its first publicity director and director of public relations. And just what does a publicity director do?

There was one naked desk — obviously reserved for me — in the oval space already filled with men and women typing, working adding machines and writing reports. I sat down at that desk. Everyone around me smiled, came over to shake hands and introduce themselves, and returned to their labors. I could tell from their expressions how curious they were as to my raison d'être; I was not about to inform them I was equally curious. I had no orders, no guidance, no supplies, nothing but a clean desk, a chair and a telephone. I had bluffed my way into this job. I would certainly have to exhibit something other than bluff at this point. My first inspired official act in my new position was to approach the large office dictionary in the Accounting Department and look up "public relations." I understood the term in reference to one person — Clare Luce. She was a master of personal public relations with her deft handling of press contacts. But the dictionary was a great help in giving me a more specific and clear understanding of my new trade: ". . . The activities of a corporation, union, government or other organization in building and maintaining sound and productive relations with special publics such as customers, employees or stockholders and with the public at large so as to adapt itself to its environment and interpret itself to society."

Great. It was obviously all clear to me now.

And thus began four happy years of living, breathing and often rocking to its very foundation the great institution of Tiffany & Co. As time went on, some of the old-timers (such as Felix Ullman, a silver engraver who had only been with the company sixty-three years), would shake their heads as I passed, because they were historians at heart and sentimentalists at soul. They knew that Charles L. Tiffany, who opened a "Fancy Goods Store" in New York in 1837 with a borrowed capital of $1,000, must be ready to burst forth from his grave in horror at some of the deeds wrought by his store's first Publicity Director.

As usual, Lady Luck had held me by the hand in landing this job. Ambassador Clare Boothe Luce, back from Rome, sat next to Walter Hoving at a dinner party. He told her of his recent acquisition of Tiffany's, how the store was dying on its feet and had become stuffy and outmoded. There had never been anyone doing public relations for the store — indeed, management had discouraged, even forbidden, free publicity. The new Chairman of the company would have to change that at once. By the time the demi-tasses were being served after dinner, Clare Luce had convinced Walter Hoving that there was only one person in the entire world capable of doing the publicity job he needed, and her name was Letitia Baldrige.

The fact that Clare Luce understood nothing whatsoever of the duties of the job did not deter her enthusiasm nor lessen the effectiveness of her salesmanship. I flew from Washington to New York and was offered the job during a quick interview. My time with Mr. Hoving was spent in ironing out the logistical details of salary, starting date and the like. Nothing about the nature of my responsibilities was discussed. I felt in my heart that two factors would pull me through — how could any Tiffany crisis be worse than the diplomatic ones we had all survived abroad? Also, there had been no one in the job ahead of me, no brilliantly successful career woman to live up to. The job was mine for the making. For the present, bluff would be the only course of action to take, until enough time had passed for me to learn the business. Learning about diamonds, gold and sparkling crystal would not be, after all, such a horrendous chore.

Next I headed for a newsstand, picking up any magazine or newspaper that had anything to do with home furnishings or with fashion, including trade publications. I brought them all back to my desk, staggering under the load and causing several colleagues to mutter that I must have some tough job, to be able to sit and read papers and magazines all day. I made a card index on all the editors of these publications, who might deal with Tiffany merchandise, and began to call each of them for an appointment. Their reaction was unanimous — one of warm welcome and total disbelief that Tiffany, the cold marble bastion of the carriage trade, was coming around to realize the value of press promotion. Doors opened automatically to me. I was treated with respect bordering on awe. It was basic economics — my company possessed the magic of a great name.

Those first days I also spent a great deal of time interrogating some of the gentlemen on the fifth floor who had been at Tiffany's all of their working lives. These men spun such tales, it was like reading an absorbing novel to listen to them; yet it was all history, not fiction. Charles L. Tiffany must have been the greatest merchandising genius in the entire nineteenth century world. In thirteen years he had raised the prestige and profits of his little store to such an extent, he was able to open an elegant Paris branch. By 1852 he was telling the United States Government they should follow his company's example by adopting the English sterling silver standards for American-manufactured silver. Because of this, a federal law was soon passed regulating the silver content in all metal bearing the word "sterling."

By 1886, Charles Tiffany had launched a new way of setting diamond solitaires in raised prongs for rings. It forever after was known as the "Tiffany Setting," even in foreign countries. He knew how to seize an opportunity. When the first great Atlantic Cable was laid under the sea in 1858, he purchased all the leftover pieces and had them made into every possible kind of

"No, Madam, Tiffany's Does Not Serve Breakfast" · 95

bric-a-brac and souvenir. Riots ensued when New Yorkers by the thousands stormed the doors to buy them. All available police were called into action to handle the crowd. He then purchased the enormous "Girdle of Diamonds" in France that had belonged to Louis XVI's young queen, and broke it up into small pieces. He knew full well that a little lady "way out west," whose husband was making millions in the mining business, would like nothing better than to be able to fondle the necklace of stones around her throat and say, "Why, thank you, yes, these were Marie Antoinette's diamonds . . ."

My elderly colleagues on the fifth floor showed me correspondence between President Abraham Lincoln and the store concerning his order of a pearl necklace for his wife Mary Todd. They reminisced about how Diamond Jim Brady used to stop in after lunch, puffing on a big cigar, and buy several diamond bracelets as party favors, and maybe one fine $5,000 oriental pearl with which to delight some fortunate damsel that evening. An admirer of Lillian Russell's had a ten-foot-tall carved sterling silver mirror made, to enable her to admire herself properly framed. One of Sarah Bernhardt's admirers commissioned the store to make a diamond and ruby-studded bicycle to titillate her imagination and, I suppose, make exercising more pleasurable. A Frenchman ordered a sterling silver bidet for himself, but an actress upstaged him by ordering a 24-kt.-gold chamber pot. The Directors of the New York Central Railroad gave J. P. Morgan a handsome Christmas gift every year. Those were the days when payola really counted. One year it was a $50,000 set of three hundred gold-plated dessert plates for J. P.'s intimate entertaining needs. In those good old days gentlemen who felt a little racy or perhaps a bit contrite would stop in the store on their way home to pick up a $2,000 jeweled garter to please their ladies; at the turn of the century, it was not even unusual to write up daily orders of natural pearl necklaces for $750,000 each. How fortunate were those generous men never to have known a Bureau of Internal Revenue.

Louis Comfort Tiffany, the founder's son, also brought fame to the family line. He was a famous artist and interior designer in his own right. His lovely "Tiffany Glass" creations at the turn of the century sparked the whole movement of Art Nouveau in the decorative arts, a trend that has enjoyed an amazing revival in recent years. His glass dining accessories, lamps and desk sets of Favrile glass became so popular, he opened his own studios, separate from the store. He was called to Washington to design the entire wedding of President Grover Cleveland from the gowns and wedding cake to the decor of the East Room. As I sit writing this chapter, looking from my Chicago window to P. K. Wrigley's red stone mansion across the street, I see a house of another era, another life. The entire interior architecture and design were executed by Louis Comfort Tiffany. All in all, they were quite a family, those Tiffanys. When Chairman Hoving took over the company, two of Charles Tiffany's direct descendants remained as integral parts of the team —William T. Lusk in the role of President, and his bachelor nephew, Harry Platt, in another top position. Bill Lusk had been given an added education far different from his Yale classmates — he was trained from early youth to be a diamond expert. Harry, a champion racing sailor, was to become vice president in charge of the gold and diamond jewelry, proving that a man has almost as many facets as a diamond.

The store fought through the Civil War by turning itself into an arsenal for the North. Charles Tiffany, smart merchant and convinced abolitionist, grabbed the French catalogues of guns, ammunition and officers' uniforms, rushed to the White House, and promptly became the import commissionaire for these items with President Lincoln's government. The factory stopped making luxury items, and made officers' swords and uniform buttons instead. In World War I, the company patriotically ceased setting precious gems once again and turned their talents to making surgical instruments. In World War II, the government called upon the specialized skills of the workmen yet another time. In utmost secrecy, the "red castle" (as the nineteenth century ivy-covered, turreted, red stone factory in Forest Hills, New Jersey, is called) became the scene of the manufacture of classified precision airplane parts. General Doolittle's raids on Tokyo could never have taken place without the handmade parts supplied by the company's jewel-setters and silver-spinners.

The new Tiffany of Walter Hoving was fresh, young and exciting — and probably unpalatable to some of the conservatives. Favored traditional china patterns were eliminated from the stock, profitable though they might have been, because they did not conform to the new standards of design.

Diamond rings for men would no longer be sold — the store felt they were not in good taste.

A certain air of tongue-in-cheek crept into the ads. A shimmering two-hundred-thousand-dollar diamond necklace would be shown, for example, with tiny print reading at the bottom of the copy: "By mail if you wish." The store began to sell such items as sterling silver frying pans, sterling garden shovels, and 18-kt.-gold golf putters. At the same time "leaders" (or "traffic pullers") appeared on each floor. These items in silver, china or crystal cost from $2 to $10, a good counter-balance in the public's mind to the store's luxury image. After all, if a young man starting out in the business world from college buys his first piece of jewelry for a girl at Tiffany's (perhaps a twenty-dollar gold pin), then that young man feels at home behind the marble facade, and will logically return for the engagement ring, wedding anniversary presents, and bigger and better baubles according to the expansion of his wallet.

There was so much to learn about the intrinsic nature of our merchandise that this became a "back to school" period in my life. I had never stopped to think about the difference between earthenware and basalt, or between 14-kt. gold and 18-kt. gold. It was difficult enough remembering that karat is for gold, and carat is for gemstone. One cannot promote or enthuse over something that is not understood. Columbia University offered a night course at the Metropolitan Museum on eighteenth century china, silver and glass, which proved to be a far more stimulating way to spend my evenings than with the neurotic bachelors I knew at that point. There were excellent books to read on the decorative arts, and shops like The Antique Porcelain Co. to browse through and ask questions of the salesmen when they weren't busy.

Van Day Truex, former head of Parson's School of Design and an accomplished artist and interior designer, joined the staff to give a whole new look to the China and Glass Department. Van edited or restyled all the merchandise, and within months, the floor was alive with delicate bone china flowers, eighteenth century reproduction chinoiserie monkeys, outsized heavy crystal bar glasses, and English bone china, hand-painted exclusively for Tiffany's in France. The merchandise of the entire store was edited by experts with a fine-tooth comb, angering the old guard customers, the old guard salespeople and the penurious stockholders alike — until the store profits began to zoom upward. The funeral parlor "wake slabs" used to display merchandise in the center of the aisles on all floors went to the scrap heap. New lighting, new combinations of paint colors, fresh cotton prints, plush carpeting on cold marble floors and entirely new merchandise picked up the spirits and the morale of the entire sales force, including the previously shocked skeptics. The store began to pride itself on being able to offer a customer as a wedding gift idea anything from a $2.50 ashtray to a $5,000 one-of-a-kind table centerpiece, or a gift of jewelry from a little gold charm at $5.00 to the Tiffany Diamond at about a million dollars. This was a whole new image for Tiffany — but it was the right one for the temper of the times.

Jean Schlumberger, a soft-spoken Frenchman and a fantastically imaginative jewelry designer, was brought into the firm as a vice president. He was given his own niche on the mezzanine, complete with multilingual salesmen and a special air of chic to his salon. Schlumberger used to amaze me, as he sat in a tiny room which was his private closet overlooking 57th Street. He would make lovely minute drawings of animals, sea life, fruits and flowers (which would be translated by his engineer partner, Nicol Bongard, using precious gems), all the while giving avid attention to the daily soap opera serials on the radio. If he did not like the idea of making a jewel a customer particularly wanted, he would refuse to do it, regardless of the remuneration involved. His designs were known for their realism, movement, and three-dimensionality; he was honored by being the first jeweler to receive a Coty "American Fashion Award," presented at the Metropolitan Museum. I did research on the history of jewels, had colored slides made of museum pieces and of the greatest of his pieces; then I toured the country giving lectures on "The History of Jewelry Design" in twelve museums in major cities. It was on one of these tours that I came to my future home, Chicago, for the first time in my adult life. It was not a fortunate visit. I began to writhe in pain on the lecture platform and finished, bent over double against the lectern, suffering from acute appendicitis. Not every lady lecturer can claim to finish addressing five hundred fashionably dressed females on the glories of Sumerian B. C. gold jewelry and proceed to the operating room for a quick shot of sodium pentathol.

One of the emoluments of my job was being able to borrow anything I desired from stock. The prerogative was exercised constantly, particularly with Schlumberger pieces. Occasionally, I would worry about being hit over the head in my apartment some night, if the neighborhood realized what I was constantly carrying around with me. I always covered up any jewelry while riding on the buses or subway, or while pushing a grocery cart. I was left alone. After all, a girl who is arguing over the price of a box of spoiled peaches is not logically wearing half a million dollars worth of diamonds.

One extremely hot summer night, I borrowed a necklace worth just under $400,000 from Johnnie Schlumberger to wear to a posh dinner party. The necklace was called simply "The Morning Glories." Luscious morning glory blossoms, executed in sapphires with diamond centers, hung flexibly on a choker of prickly gold branches, which were accented with small buds and leaves of diamonds. It was made for a much smaller neck than mine, but I wore it anyway. It was a sensational piece. By the time the black tie dinner party was half over, agony had set in. The choker was truly choking, and the branches were scratching my neck. I felt blood being drawn on my skin. The necklace would simply have to come off. It had a very complicated clasp at the back that looked like the inside of a miniature office computer. I could not possibly reach it. Then I made an unforgivable mistake. I turned to my dinner partner, who looked as though he had played professional football, told him my problem, and asked him to remove the necklace for me. His huge hands began to grapple clumsily with the clasp, and the result was, of course, a totally sprung clasp that could not be opened by anyone. The dinner guests went into consultation on the matter, and decided that rather than risk wrenching it off and strangling me in the process, plus breaking the very delicate and expensive mounting, I should suffer in silence until the next day.

Suffer I did, including in my bed all night, with the necklace choking me more every hour, as my neck swelled under the pressure. I tried to insert a chiffon scarf between the necklace and my skin, with little success. The next morning, it was almost 100°. I walked to Tiffany's to work as usual, wearing a little red cotton dress, the sun pouring down on my bloodied neck. The sun's rays cast magnificent reflections of light as they hit $400,000 worth of sapphires and diamonds. The blasé New Yorkers I passed looked at the apparition without showing any emotion whatsoever; I was just another kook passing by on just another kooky day. My first stop was the Diamond Office where one of the men donned a pair of magnifying-glass spectacles. Using a small blowtorch, he managed to disengage the clasp without ruining the necklace, and without adding third-degree burns to my lacerated neck. There is no moral to this story other than it is difficult to be a woman at times. One could also add that jewels, like shoes, should fit or else not be worn.

―•―

Gene Moore became another very important new member of the Hoving team. He was Bonwit's display director and window designer, but now he had an additional assignment: Tiffany's windows. The windows on the Fifth Avenue and 57th Street sides were reconstructed like tiny stage sets, so that he could go to work, wielding his lights and stage effects like the zaniest of Broadway's set designers. Instead of actors and actresses, however, he was staging jewels, china, silver, glass, clocks and even stationery. His windows quickly became the talk of

New York, and suburbanites made a pilgrimage to the city every two weeks or so when the windows were changed, to see what he was up to now. Gene would drape jewels over a pile of noodles, or on top of a mound of dirt being excavated by a tiny truck. During one terrible New York cold spell, he had a miniature pot-bellied, black-iron stove spewing forth rubies. He set up a ballet performance of ice cream cones alternating with crystal goblets. He used original pieces of art, miniature furniture, balsawood toys, bubbling fountains (using gin one time when New York had a desperate water shortage), styrofoam, aluminum foil, egg cartons or anything that struck him as having a good texture. Sometimes one had a difficult time finding the merchandise.

The windows were meant to attract attention, not to sell merchandise. The windows especially attracted the attention of a highly professional gang of thieves, who used pickaxes in broad daylight one August Sunday morning. They got away with all the diamonds in the two main Fifth Avenue windows, supposedly burglar-proof, much to the chagrin of the New York police force. That unsolved robbery gave us all a bit of excitement for a long time. When the glass company, after long hours spent in the laboratory to improve their product, sent their top executives to present the store with new, absolutely unbreakable windows, Mr. Hoving personally tested them out with a pickaxe in the basement. His stroke shattered right through again, so it was back to the drawing boards. To penetrate the glass resulting from the final studies would probably require a two-ton truck ramming through at high speed. In my early flounderings in the job, I was to find that protecting the good name of Tiffany's was as important as promoting it. A major soup company persuaded me to come to Rockefeller Plaza with almost a million dollars worth of diamonds before I knew ex-

"No, Madam, Tiffany's Does Not Serve Breakfast" · 103

actly why they wanted them. They wanted to drap them over a fountain temporarily filled with consommé instead of water to promote the drinking of "consommé on the rocks," as a cool summer drink. (The double play of having the soup bubble over Tiffany's "rocks" was just too adorable.) And once an underwear manufacturer was bringing out a new line of rhinestone-trimmed evening bras, and tried by subterfuge to arrange for the loan of five hundred loose diamonds to sew on one as the star presentation piece for the market buyers. Fading actresses tried to borrow our jewels for public appearances in order to feed some badly needed personal publicity to the columns.

I had much to learn — and in Tiffany's kind of business, one never stops the process of education. The nature of gemstones alone is a science. One has to know what makes a diamond just a "fine white one" versus the best quality in existence, called "a triple extra-river." There are all the gem cuts to learn, from baguette to marquise, all the colors of semiprecious stones to memorize, from peridots and opalines to malachite, hematite and tourmalines. What is the nature of fine lead crystal? What makes the etching or cutting of crystal particularly fine? Why is sterling silver sterling? How is a piece of flatware designed for good balance? What is the difference between earthenware, faïence, porcelain, bone china, ceramic, and matte bisque? When do you say "vase" and when do you say "vahse"?

One of my biggest challenges came four weeks after I began the job. I arrived at the weekly luncheon conference as usual three minutes late, so as to assure that all the men would be there and would have to stand up for me. (My first day, they were so nonplussed to have a woman around, they forgot to acknowledge my presence and rise at all, so I remained standing; the problem never reoccurred.) The day's discussion centered on Tiffany's forthcoming introduction of "vermeil" to

America — a permanent silver-gilt finish to sterling silver. It seems that in the days of the Louis' in France, the "gold look" was such a rage, no one who was anyone could live without it. When the Kings began to seize their subjects' gold to save the Royal Treasuries, the courtiers had to turn to something that would give them the gold look without being pure gold. So they began applying the vermeil finish with mercury to their silver objects. The fashion spread over all of Western Europe, and remained popular well into the nineteenth century when a humane Louis Philippe outlawed the process. Too many workers had gone blind from mercuric poisoning. Tiffany's process was not causing anyone to go blind. They had worked for over a year in the factory on a process that applied the gold electrolytically and achieved the same silvery effect without mercury. Now that the firm was finally ready to introduce it — at great cost — the publicity department was to come up with a detailed, powerful program of promotion, including a major in-store exhibition and the production of consumer material to explain the heritage of this art in simple layman's terms.

No one in America knew what vermeil was or cared. The antique pieces were hopelessly expensive, and our pieces were not going to be cheap either. No one could even pronounce the word. There were no books on the subject. My days spent in research in the library were futile. The only references to it were in very technical trade books. The name itself, of course, was often used (without any reference to the process) in museum listings of fine silver pieces. Then the Metropolitan Museum came to my rescue. They knew of three collectors of vermeil — Cornelius Ruxton Love, Jr., Ronald Tree, and amazingly enough, a man named Ambassador David Bruce. They suggested I interview these men. I did, and not only did they provide some very interesting historical details about how ver-

"No, Madam, Tiffany's Does Not Serve Breakfast" · 105

meil became fashionable and who used it in the great courts of the world, but they all three agreed to lend me some of their prized pieces for an exhibition in the store.

There it was — the major in-store exhibition problem solved. We would have a museum display of the great old pieces in conjunction with our new ones. Lady Luck smiled again in the form of Mrs. Eisenhower's gracious response to Mr. Hoving's request — that some of the Margaret Thompson Biddle vermeil collection willed to the White House be lent to Tiffany's. I rushed to the White House and spent an entire morning with the Chief Usher, J. B. West, going over each piece on the floor of the room where the Biddle vermeil collection was stored. The Biddle collection had arrived at the White House in one large unidentified jumble. There had never been a proper inventory made, listing the country of origin, date and maker. Nothing had been researched.

I took all of the pieces to Professor Carl Dauterman at the Metropolitan Museum, where he lovingly examined them and prepared a provenance for each piece to be used for the White House files. There were masterpieces by Paul Storr and Odiot, but the greatest discovery of all was a priceless and historic Louis Philippe tureen. The Biddle list had called it "covered tureen, English, probably nineteenth century."

In an old French book I found a reference on how to keep vermeil clean — it should be washed in soap and warm water, or, "if preferred, a light white wine or a champagne." This little item was bound to appeal to young homemakers. I knew we had a hit, because who would not gladly replace detergent with champagne for cleaning purposes?

The public loved the museum exhibition and flocked to it. We had items like King Charles tea caddies to gaze upon, German seventeenth century pilgrim bottles, and a traveling *nécessaire* of a lady of the royal French court of the late 1700's which included a saucepan for brewing her cosmetics, an espresso coffee maker and a toothbrush. There were all the great French and English pieces from the White House to exclaim over. The new Tiffany vermeil began to sell vigorously.

In the euphoric heights of my success, I took the best museum pieces to a television studio to show on a program in color. The cameramen started to spray the pieces with paraffin wax, before I stopped them by throwing my body in front of the table like Pauline of the Perils rescuing a small child from the villain. They wanted to take the shine off the surface, so there would be no hot spots for the cameras. When I explained that this was a life-long historic sheen that would be completely ruined when removing the wax coating, they let me alone. Then another worker raced across the cement floor, carelessly carrying several pieces. He dropped Napoleon's chocolate cup and saucer, among other things, and when I shrieked in hysterics at him and picked them up tenderly myself, he walked off the set. I had broken a strict union rule protecting the prop carriers in major studios. The rest of the crew had to walk off in sympathy; the program went off the air, and I walked off from the world of television for a goodly length of time, by mutual consent.

My duties and responsibilities quickly outgrew my capabilities. The press was growing more and more enamored of Tiffany's merchandise — and the pull of its name. I was now ensconced in what could best be described as a pale peach closet on the fourth floor. A typical morning would find me wrestling endlessly with the telephone while six people waited: a *Harper's Bazaar* editor in need of coral and diamond jewelry for a colored fashion photograph; an advertising account executive who wanted Tiffany's best bar items for a liquor ad; a television give-away program producer who wanted to make a deal on giving away Tiffany jewels; a *Wall Street Journal* researcher who needed help on a story on Christmas business; a suburban club president who wanted a lecturer on Tiffany table settings for the club's annual benefit program; an editor from *Vogue* who wanted three or four items for the "Shophound" column.

Mine was hardly an efficient operation. But soon providence intervened, the crisis was solved, and two ladies wafted into my peach closet — a secretary and an assistant. The latter was a dark-eyed, creamy-skinned brunette, Chandra Donnels. She was as calm and shy as she was lovely looking. Working in exactly the opposite pattern from me — noiselessly, without emotion, interruptions or hysterics — she complemented me at every turn. She was an artist, and soon taught herself photography layout and styling. She even learned the art of retouching photographs (removing a tired line on a model's mouth, or bringing up the outline of a crystal goblet), which would save us about twenty-five dollars a photograph. If anything needed sewing, drawing, gluing or improvising, she did it. My secretary, Georgie Palmer, soon defected to the altar, but I hired in her place a pretty Vassar graduate, Duane Garrison, who was known as "Miss Bubblemouth." Duane chattered incessantly, knew everyone's trials and tribulations, and was a walking gossip center. IBM should have electrified her, because everyone loved to "turn her on," from the leading executives to the back hall cleaning man. She could hold a busy, bored, affected fashion editor spellbound with her conversation while picking out men's cuff links for the forthcoming "Christmas Present Ideas" section of the magazine. She was an expert on all gossip columns, knew the day-to-day activities of Elizabeth Taylor, Princess Margaret and Tony, Princess Grace and Rainier, as well as every local member of the jet set. She had her finger on every degree of employee morale, and fed us valuable information about who was griping on the sales staff and why. She was also highly efficient. Our office was a happy team, overworked, loyal to each other, and totally feminine in its best and in its worst aspects.

I received an annual budget from the boss for taking pictures hopefully to place in the women's pages of the New York papers. This budget had to cover everything from a close-up of a new peanut-shaped silver pill box to full-scale room settings and to fashion photography. The latter I enjoyed most of all. It meant trips deep into the heart of the better houses of the garment district to select beautiful evening clothes, furs and hats to show off our jewels. I quickly discovered that by paying the top price of Eileen Ford's best models, the pictures would turn out better and be placed in the press with a higher degree of success. It was a false economy to skimp on the model's fee. In a close-up, only the blasé pros really knew how to turn on that "I've always been used to the best, and these diamonds are really *it*, dahling" look. It made me feel better to see these absolutely glorious creatures arrive at the studio looking like something worse than my worst mornings. Their hair was usually in tangles, their skin mottled, their overall aspect tubercular. After an hour's attention to makeup and hair, they, of course, metamorphosed into the most incredible of cool, poised beauties. Another affectation of the models was that they always arrived on the job carrying either a dog or something highly intellectual like a volume of Proust. The dog was always miniature and well behaved, the intellectual treatise was always unread but impressive looking.

When I found all the sketches in the old Tiffany files of the diamond headache bands of the pre-World War I era, I thought what great fun it would be to revive the fad. Chandra with her

"No, Madam, Tiffany's Does Not Serve Breakfast" • 109

deft fingers sewed diamond necklaces, clips and bracelets from the diamond counter onto velvet ribbons. The jewels looked terrific on our headache bands, nestled in short, soft, fluffy hairdos. Our pictures of Anne St. Marie and two other top beauties were picked up by three hundred and sixty papers on the wire services, as well as numerous foreign magazines. We did launch a revival fad, because rhinestone headbands popped up in stores across the country.

We revived jeweled garters, too, using again the Tiffany order sketches from the past, and sewing loose stones or small clips onto pretty garters that were custom-made for us. Shooting photos of the models decorously stepping from foreign sports cars, with the glimmer of the jeweled garter showing beneath the short skirt, stopped traffic in New York for several blocks around the area in which we were photographing. Jack Paar had me bring them down to his nighttime show, and in discussing them said, on the air, "this opens up a whole new field for pickpockets."

We took on a lot of very difficult photographic assignments, from the point of view of logistics. When we shot diamonds on lavishly dressed models in the "Diamond Circle" of the old Met, to appear a week before the grand opening of the opera season, we had to reshoot the picture on four different days, the lighting problems were so vast. We decided to shoot, for a Christmas promotion picture, a model in a white shantung jump suit hugging her two white Russian wolfhounds (Lord and Lady Wolfschmidt) and a slinky white Persian cat (Nicodemus). The model and the animals were all decked out in a half million dollars' worth of diamonds. The animals were professionals and used to modeling, but our human model was very late. By the time she got there, the animals, like children, were tired and irritable. So were the two armed guards we were paying to guard the sitting. We gave tranquilizers to the animals to quiet them down, whereupon the Russian wolfhounds went fast asleep. It was almost impossible to keep their eyes open for the snapping of the photographer's shutter. The cat in the meantime was giving the model an atrocious case of hay fever (she later admitted she was allergic to all cats and never should have accepted the assignment). There we were, all of us laughing, whistling at the dogs, chirping at the cat to stay in place, while the harassed photographer yelled "Quiet please! Get the damned dogs to open their eyes! Put Nicodemus back in his place — Stop sneezing, for God's sake, Jessica . . . Your mascara is running again . . ." Our trials paid off — a nice big picture ran in the *Herald Tribune* ten days before Christmas.

One can never foresee certain success with a publicity photograph, no matter how much work and thought goes into the whole project, including the selection of the photographer, the model, and the background. I soon discovered that the magic of Tiffany's merchandise solved three of the four basic problems of successful publicity, but the last one was always a question mark. Our Tiffany products made news in the fields of fashion and decorating; they were beautiful and luxurious; and they bore a good name. The other necessary element, the "just-right-photograph," was not so easily assured. The greatest press release could flop completely if the accompanying picture was not right. Tiffany's had its own small photographic studio on the sixth floor — presided over by Lee Prescott and his assistant, Lee Cook. They never shot live models, just merchandise. One could wander in there at any hour and find them bent over their table, as though they were studying something under a microscope. Instead, it was a two-hundred-thousand-dollar stone nestling in a piece of velvet for a catalogue shot, or perhaps a dangerously fragile pyramid of champagne goblets for a *New Yorker* ad, or a still life of holly around a sterling eggnog bowl for a Christmas card scene. They worked painstakingly on their close-ups like a couple of fuddy-duddy professors with new theories. The lately formed publicity department, with its frantic deadlines for newspaper pictures, made them very unhappy and insecure in their safe little nest. We yanked them away from their studio at odd hours to shoot table settings on location all over New York. We made them lean over high terraces to get the best angles for outdoor shots. There was a constant battle against the elements in this kind of photography. Rain would spot the silver and crystal; winds would flap the edges of the tablecloth or disrupt the centerpiece. Occasionally, we would lose a napkin or a goblet from a windy terrace down into the street. Eventually, no request we made of the photographers surprised them.

They particularly disliked our bringing sand into their studio. We were constantly using sand as a background, for jewels or picnic table setting ideas. After every such project, they would walk on sand on their floor for weeks at a time before they could get rid of all of it.

The outside photographers we used fared no better. We borrowed an elaborate fish aquarium and asked Kal Weyner to shoot our jewels suspended in the tank on invisible wire, while the fish swam around them. The splashing of water as we kept rearranging the clips and earrings shorted all of his lights and plunged the studio into darkness for a long time; then two of the prized fish jumped out of the tank, and we had to stop everything for another half hour to search for them on the floor. (They survived.) Finally, bedlam broke loose when someone from the Schlumberger department happened to look in on the sitting. He registered horror at the sight of his priceless 18-kt.-gold flexible fish, reclining on its tail on the bottom of the tank and observing the proceedings through a pair of ruby eyes. "My God!" he shouted. "You've ruined it! Our cigarette lighter. You've ruined it!" We had thought it was just a fish. It had to become just that, because its intricate lighter insides had to be thrown away after two hours of immersion. The photographer took four hours to shoot, but it was beautiful. The fish even seemed to enjoy circling the emeralds, diamonds and sapphires, which proves they're not such dumb creatures after all.

Perhaps the most fun of all was photographing babies for our Tiffany baby presents publicity. When I had made all the elaborate arrangements through the Ford Agency to have a baby and her older brother on hand as models, including a supply of diapers, baby bottles et al, we waited and waited for our protagonists to arrive. Finally, the mother reached me on the telephone. The little boy had come down with measles that very morning, so none of her family could come. We had already arranged an elaborate crib and a mobile of dangling sterling silver gift items that would not hold together for longer than another hour. I made a hurried call to a friend, Nancy Rees, and down she rushed with Liberty (two and a half) and Camilla (six months), to save us. They acted like pros in front of the camera and in the hot lights, their eyes glistening with excitement at the moving mobile of shiny objects. Liberty made the picture salable by her costume alone — she was clad in her own peignoir, a Jean Harlow model of pink silk trimmed with pink ostrich feathers. I had no trouble placing that picture in the papers.

Fashion photographers are notoriously careless with props in their intense concentration to get the job properly done. When the props happen to be expensive jewelry, it is a serious matter. At the beginning of one sitting, a diamond clip clattered to the cement floor because it was not fastened properly on the model's shoulder. The mounting was bent, and two large diamonds were missing from the setting when I picked it up. The Tiffany guard, Chandra, the photographer, model and I got down on all fours and searched for the better part of an hour. The floor had obviously not been cleaned for a year or two, as evidenced by the blackened state of our knees and hands. The model had another sitting across town at the end of the hour; she left us to keep her appointment, but we had to pay her without one flick of the camera's lens. The expensive sitting was over without a picture. At least we had recovered the stones. Mr. Hoving failed to be impressed.

The fashion magazines infuriated our jewel designers and our Diamond Department by the manner in which they photographed the pieces. They would take out the biggest jewels of our stock and tie them up for days at a time while shooting on location. This cost the store hundreds of dollars in special insurance coverage and in paying extra armed guards. Three months later the photographs would appear — and there would be our Tiffany jewels, absolutely invisible. A model would be caressing a monstrous-sized diamond and gold clip on her coat lapel — caressing it so effectively that her long, tapered fingers completely covered it. A large sapphire and diamond necklace, bracelet and earring set would be shown on a model in a swirling chiffon evening gown — swirling so vigorously she was a complete blur in the photograph. The reader was unaware she was even wearing jewelry.

It took a lot of persuasion to talk President William Lusk into letting the Tiffany Diamond go out of the store for the first time in its life, to be photographed by a fashion magazine. The editor-in-chief of the magazine and I spent several sessions talking him into it. The stone was treasured by him and the Tiffany family. It was a museum piece in its special display case, a kind of shrine set up on the first floor which generations of people had come to see since the latter part of the nineteenth century. Finally, reluctantly, he let it go. We all waited breathlessly for the picture of it, a full page in color. None of us had been allowed to go to the sitting, only armed guards, and they would not tell us how it was photographed. The magazine finally reached the newsstands. There was the Tiffany Diamond, dangling from the antler of a hairy deer. The photograph looked like an exhibit of the American Museum of Natural History gone amuck. Bill Lusk did not speak to me for days. At the same time, Jean Schlumberger's prized new diamond necklace, which he considered his finest museum-piece design, appeared in a fashion magazine draped around the skinny calf of a model, above a weird shoe. On days like these our publicity department achieved great popularity with everyone.

The Controller, Ellsworth Hyde, tried to keep us in line with the strict insurance regulations concerning taking jewelry out of the store. He lived in constant fear of the publicity department because of the raised premiums we could incur by losing jewelry, or because of the lawsuits we came so dangerously close to bringing on the store. Once while we were shooting a table setting in a New York hostess' apartment, one of our photographer's lights crashed down onto her collection of eighteenth century porcelain snuffboxes. In photographing a Christmas story for the papers, we used a great beauty for a model, and posed her wearing a new Schlumberger diamond necklace next to a large white candle. The necklace looked like a delectable Christmas wreath. The photographer kept saying "Closer, closer," to the model, so that he could gain the proper reflection on the stones from the candlelight. The model put her head so close, her coiffure caught on fire. Since the girl's stock in trade was her beautiful hair and face, the photographer said worriedly after her departure, with the smell of burned hair and skin overcoming us all, "I sure hope she doesn't sue you." When I passed this on to Ellsworth Hyde, he went into his office and softly closed the door. He was too much a gentleman to communicate his thoughts explicitly. Luckily, our singed heroine was perfectly all right.

For every target we hit in our publicity efforts, we scored many more zeroes. I finally learned never to tell anyone in the store in advance of something that should be a success. Let them be happily surprised — and let them never know the terrible misses we scored constantly. When we took a million dollars' worth of jewels to drape around a famous singing star on her hour-long television show in color, the credit line at the end read "Jewels by Cartier." When we lent four cartons of beautifully washed, polished and wrapped merchandise for a food company's national ad, it appeared in fourteen major magazines without a mention of our name. When we made the Diamond Office gold-plate the mounting of a very expensive diamond solitaire ring, because the fashion magazine shooting it in color insisted on a "gold look" for the page, it took one man three hours of intense work to accomplish the plating job. A week later, after the ring had been returned to stock with the gold-plating removed, the magazine asked for it back again. They had to reshoot the entire picture. This gold-plating had to be done yet one more time before the editor was satisfied with the picture, totaling in all eleven hours of plating and unplating the ring. When the picture was finally published, it was in black and white. Platinum and gold look identical in black and white.

Nonetheless, the fashion and the shelter magazines were our life's blood. We had to keep cooperating, and the fashion editors were our fast friends. Every once in a while, a model would be shown in *Harper's Bazaar* wearing a $2,000 diamond-studded gold bracelet, which peeked out from under her mink-lined raincoat — and the store would receive four orders in one week for the bracelet. *Vogue* would show a page of our silver boxes, and customers would write in from all over the country. Good publicity is not only *free* advertising — it is often more effective.

⁕

I am forever inscribed as an offender in the files of the Treasury Department. In fact, I was asked about my crime when I was being cleared for the White House post later, and the Secret Service agents at 1500 Pennsylvania Avenue teasingly never let me forget it. It all came about because I decided to assemble a $5,000 jeweled money clip holding a $10,000 bill "for the woman who has everything" as a Valentine's Day stunt. I knew I could get the picture on the wire services, if the details came out well. I took a large and beautiful gold chrysanthemum clip, flashing with diamonds, and attached it to the top of a perfectly plain gold money clip. The caption would not even mention the size of the bill — it would just be there in a very understated manner in the photograph. Then I set about finding a ten-thousand-dollar bill. The first bank thought I was in need of psychiatry and would not even discuss the matter with me. Two more banks refused to help me. Finally, a friend in the investment business asked for the Federal Reserve to send him one, c/o The New York Trust. The wheels of bureaucracy began to turn, but it took several weeks. Each ten-thousand-dollar note was numbered and registered with the Federal Reserve, and obtaining one was tantamount to one of the chores of Hercules. Patience won out. I went down to the New York Trust with

"No, Madam, Tiffany's Does Not Serve Breakfast" • 117

an armed guard, picked up my little green note, and returned to the store.

The next day, with the bank note safely returned to the New York bank, I was going over the glossy prints of the money clip just made by Tiffany's own photographers. The pictures were stunning. The effect was just as I had wanted it. The bejeweled money clip was elegant, luxurious, quite plausible. The money bill, folded over, was a blur except for the $10,000 figure in one corner. We would have great success with the press on this item, I felt sure.

Then two tall, very good-looking young men stepped into my office, flashed their Treasury badges and sat down by my desk. Within five minutes, they had all of the glossies and all of the negatives of my picture, plus sworn statements from me and both photographers that there were no more prints or negatives in existence. I had committed a heinous crime, photographing a United States currency bill. It was so ludicrous, I could scarcely believe it.

"But why?" I protested.

"Photographing bills is against the law, because it enables counterfeiters to make their plates."

"But how could anyone make a plate with a folded-over bill and only one corner of the bill showing? And, surely, you could never expect someone to counterfeit ten-thousand-dollar bills," I said, "I mean, wouldn't anyone have a little trouble just cashing a real ten-thousand-dollar bill, much less a fake one?"

"M'am, the law's the law. And you've broken it. You should have known better."

Evidently, if I had used silver money in my photograph or play money, it would have been all right. But that would have been meaningless for my picture. I was liable to punishment in prison or to a fine for my actions, but fortunately, I was excused.

The photograph had not appeared in print. I placed in our files a gentle reminder of my criminal behavior — "Receipt for Counterfeit and Contraband." That year Tiffany's managed to survive without a jewel story in the press for St. Valentine's Day.

✢

One of our department's major responsibilities was to think up new exhibits and promote them. Everyone in the store worked hard on these shows, from the Advertising to the Display departments, but we ring-mastered them. Every fall we invited New York's top interior designers to do table settings — and they built entire vignettes of dining rooms or dining areas as the proper background for their tables. They would bring into the store anything from a white painted swan-boat to a $15,000 French *guéridon table*. Each year they tried to outdo themselves and their competitors. There would always be something traditional, like Billy Baldwin's "Maryland Hunt Cup Breakfast," William Pahlmann's "Coral Beach Club Party," or Jimmy Amster's "19th Century Easter Luncheon."

However, Mallory and Tillis' "Dinner in a Treehouse," Sister Parish's "Sunday Painter's Picnic," and Gene Moore's "Supper For Two in a Moonlit Forest" provided an innovative touch. The public reacted with wild enthusiasm to these table setting shows. Just as the decorators came every fall, the leading New York hostesses set up their tables every spring, bringing in their own linens, and often their own antique accessories for the table. The names most familiar to the New York public starred in these shows, like Mrs. Vincent Astor, Gloria Vanderbilt, Kitty Carlisle, Mrs. Lytle Hull, Diana Vreeland and Mrs. Albert Lasker. Two matrons, surveying Mrs. Gilbert Miller's parade of eighteenth century porcelain cabbages down the center of her table were awed by it all. "Jeez," one said to the other, "I

"No, Madam, Tiffany's Does Not Serve Breakfast" · 119

can't get ahold of those china things, but I could coitanly put fresh cabbages down the center. Do you think Harry would mind the stink of fresh cabbages with his dinner?"

"Not if you give him boiled cabbage for dinner at the same time, honey," was the reply. "The whole joint will smell like a big cabbage anyway."

"You don't think that's overdoing it?"

"Naw, honey."

"I'll try it tonight."

I had to tell Mrs. Miller her own taste was definitely raising the taste of New Yorkers.

Mrs. William Paley came in to arrange a table called "Breakfast at Tiffany's." Her designer assistant just had to be, of course, author Truman Capote. He was very gracious and helpful with everyone on the floor, and Babe's table setting sold just that many more copies of his book for him.

Mrs. Howell Howard brought in her priceless collection of eighteenth century Neapolitan crêche figures, and designed a Christmas table around them. Three years later I would be greeting her at the front door of the White House, as she came to set up that same crêche against the yellow satin drapery in the East Room, in a tremendous bank of green fir trees and white flowering plants sparkling with tiny Christmas lights.

The interior designers were completely professional about setting up their vignettes. They came and went on the appointed day, working quietly and performing miracles with backdrops, borrowed rugs and antique furniture, and fresh flowers or fake plants. By contrast, some of the hostesses put themselves and us into a state of nervous apoplexy. Occasionally, one of them would finish her table completely, leaving Eleanor Pompili of the display department totally exhausted from hauling up stock, washing and shining all the day's choices in china, silver and stemware, only to have the lady decide her colleagues had outdone her. Said hostess would start afresh an hour before the exhibition began and change everything. Of course, her table already had been photographed and the picture released to the press.

Learning how to write press releases on these table setting exhibitions was another education in putting the imagination to work. One simply could not state, "Mrs. La-ti-dah set a lovely dinner table for six, using her own antique Meissen plates, Tiffany's Waterford goblets and the Hampton silver pattern." The editor would have gone to sleep in the first sentence and thrown the release away. I soon learned to write such sentences as "Mrs. La-ti-dah has set a magical table, bathed in the warm hues of pink and blue, and touched with the golden glow of vermeil. Her pink and blue flowered antique Meissen plates star against the rich sheen of a pale blue brocaded cloth." An editor reading this kind of description may feel slightly ill, but at least she will not go to sleep.

Perhaps the exhibition that delighted us all the most was Renato Signorini's show of gold, silver and vermeil portrait sculptures. The Roman artist arrived in the store dressed in an impeccable manner and gave every woman he encountered, customer or employee, a long, smoldering, appreciative glance over the smoke from his cigarette holder. He mesmerized the ladies all over New York, and had several of them coming every day to his exhibition, just to gaze at him. Each morning when he arrived in the store, he would gallantly raise the hand of the Irish elevator girl, Nora, to his lips. I am sure he was well repaid — for Nora added him immediately to her prayer list, and Nora was always praying.

Renato's art was unique — the small jeweled busts of famous women he carved and chiseled so exquisitely out of gold and silver were something that had never been seen before in

America. It took me two weeks to get his objects out of customs, because they insisted on classifying them as "jewels" and placing a hefty import tax on the value of the metal. We finally won out in classifying them as original works of art, which come in duty free, but not without letters from the Ministry of Fine Arts in Italy and our own Government officials. I accused the customs men of delaying us on purpose, just so they could look at the sculptures some more. I found every piece of Renato's work lovingly spread out on their desks; they admitted they liked to examine them during the day, because they had never seen anything like them. Fortunately, the sculptor taught his unusual art form to a beautiful young apprentice, Elizabeth Jones, who will carry it on for many years to come.

Renato and I spent one whole day taking his twenty-eight-inch-tall vermeil statue of Queen Elizabeth over to her suite at the Waldorf Towers. She was going to be using the suite for one day only, changing her clothes for official functions. She had asked to have the statue left there, so she could view it. Renato had previously offered it to her as a gift, but it was of too high a value for her to be able to accept. The statue portrayed the Queen on her throne in official robes, wearing her crown jewels, and holding the symbols of her office. While Renato made sure it was properly lit in the living room of her suite, I toured the bathrooms and bedrooms, which the maids were busily readying for Her Majesty. Once a Social Secretary, always a Social Secretary — I called the hotel housekeeper and told her there was no facial tissue in Her Majesty's bathroom. Also, the regulation hotel soap wrapped in paper was an affront to the hospitality of the house. There were too many flowers in the suite. Her Majesty would be asphyxiated. Most certainly my comments were not welcome, but I could not resist making them.

Renato's show was an outstanding success. People saw the

little portrait busts set into illuminated velvet shadow boxes, and the profile plaques framed in velvet, and commissioned him to do members of their own family. I got him on every television show in New York, and each time, the women telephoning the studio about "that Italian sculptor" would tie up the switchboard for hours. When he went back to Rome, the store seemed to settle into a gray, depressed cloud. His gallant courtesy to women and his incredible kindness toward the store's staff were far removed from our commercial mores. When Renato Signorini died of leukemia in Rome the Christmas of 1966, sadness struck many hearts in many countries.

→←

I had been to Newport, Rhode Island, several times in my life. I had never seen it through the eyes of a working girl, however. Now, because the first "Tiffany Ball" was held there, I knew Newport through many different pairs of eyes. The gala ball meant a lot of fun and frivolity for a lot of people; for my department, having had the responsibility thrown squarely at us with a force that knocked us right off our chairs, it was a tremendous amount of work. Tiffany's, as the sponsor, picked up the tab for a goodly share of the expenses. I was required to oversee all of the publicity for the ball and to help on the national publicity for the ball's beneficiary — The Preservation Society of Newport County. I had no idea at that time what the Society was preserving, but I soon found out. They labored to save not only the greatest of the "summer cottages" (huge mansions built on the sea in the "Mauve Era" by the "Robber Barons" in the late nineteenth century), but they also saved an amazing number of lovely colonial dwellings of the seventeenth and eighteenth centuries. Newport was a lively town in George Washington's days, and there are over four hundred dwellings extant from that period to prove it.

The scene of our ball was to be the stately "Marble House," built on Belmont Avenue for William K. Vanderbilt in 1892. It had everything from twenty-one kinds of marble and massive French eighteenth century portraits to Gothic stained-glass windows and a Chinese lacquered tea house. It had never before been on view to the public, and was owned by the William Wood-Princes of Chicago who lent it to the Preservation Society for this occasion.

The ball weekend was to include tours of other great mansions like "The Breakers" and the colonial shrines like Hunter House, and the Touro Synagogue, the oldest in America. The weekend would also mark the restoration and reopening of America's oldest tavern, the White Horse Inn. My first release for the July ball was sent out in January. It piqued the interest of society reporters, feature writers, fashion editors, and preservation journalists alike. Here was a weekend comprising many points of interest — and was snobby old Newport really opening her doors to the public for a charity ball?

We were besieged with requests for information during the whole seven months' period, and we found ourselves spending as much time in research on Early American architecture as we did in promoting our regular Tiffany merchandise. Investment broker Ralph Carpenter, Jr., became my steadfast cohort; he was one of the spearheads of the restoration activities in the Newport colonial area. He also happened to be an extremely attractive, stimulating man, which made preservation and restoration so much more palatable. There were stories of great interest to the press to research, such as the clothes and jewels worn by Consuelo Vanderbilt at the debut party given by her parents in Marble House. Just a description of the several hundred hummingbirds released in the front hall to welcome the guests and the expensive French antique favors given everyone at her party was enough to convince me they did indeed lead the good life. What would Who wear to the ball became a matter of grave importance in the New York fashion world. The ball began attracting society from all over the country, and requests for permission to cover the ball began to come in from leading papers in many major cities. We conjured up raffle prizes for the ladies, got a cigarette company to donate a package of their new brand "Newport" to everyone at the party and White Horse whiskey to help out with the opening of the White Horse Tavern. I found myself promoting just about everything but jewelry.

If the weekend was not hitchless, at least it was full of zip. I shared an air taxi from the Providence airport to Newport with the young John F. Kennedys who were coming to stay with Jackie's mother, Mrs. Auchincloss. We spent the entire time talking about Clare Luce and Walter Hoving. (If I had been carrying a Ouija Board on that plane, it would have jumped right off my lap.) Newport was quickly filled to its tiniest nook and cranny with press, the overflow of out-of-town guests from the big house parties, and luminaries in the work of restoring America's historic shrines. We reopened the White Horse Tavern amidst enthusiastic speeches from officers of the National Trust and Historic Williamsburg. We launched the daytime tours of Newport's old houses to the tune of the fast tinkling of coins in the Preservation Society's coffers. We even obtained weekend privileges for the visiting press corps at Bailey's Beach Club, an innovation that shook the old elite to the core. One of the ladies accosted a ball committee member to complain, "But they'll eavesdrop and write down everything I say." The committee member shot back the perfect squelch. "Darling, I'm sure nothing you might say will be of the slightest possible interest to them."

The night of the ball, as Lester Lanin and his men tuned up

in the great rose marble ballroom hung with huge gilt mirrors, the heavens opened up. It was imperative that the older generation keep its cool. Ena Prochet stood in her Balenciaga ballgown on the terrace, watching the water flow over her beautifully set pastel tables placed all over the terrace and outer lawn. Katherine Warren tried to reassure her, "Never mind — they'll have a good time anyway." And they did.

The LIFE reporters and photographers began setting up their ladders and elaborate equipment to shoot indoor color pictures without flash light, when a committee member came over to me with eyes smoking with anger. "Those men," she stammered indignantly, "those men don't even have dinner jackets on! They can't stay — please get them out of here."

My heart sank. Getting LIFE to do a long article was one of the greatest of my publicity coups. "But they have to," I protested. "They're so important — this coverage is priceless. We have to let them stay."

She demurred. "Out!" she said to them, "and don't come back unless you are properly, decently dressed," which in her language meant black tie and dinner jacket.

The guests for the ball had started to arrive. I made a telephone call to the home of the man who ran the Navy store in downtown Newport. I pled my case with such desperation, he met me with the LIFE men at his store, opened it up, and we outfitted them in Navy stewards' uniforms (which have black bow ties, of course), and rushed them back to the scene of the party. No one knew the difference about their attire, but I am sure the LIFE accountants must have questioned somewhere along the line the reimbursement claims for four Navy stewards' uniforms.

Town & Country magazine photographed the dining room in color, fortunately before the guests descended upon it. I had brought up crates full of Tiffany vermeil tureens, candelabra, serving platters, flatware and elaborate goblets. The whole buffet table was aglow with vermeil in the candlelight, and Newport's Charlie Paterson and Anthony Kloman designed a magnificent baroque fresh fruit centerpiece that ran the full length of the forty-foot-long table. We served a midnight supper, but some of the guests could not wait for the witching hour. By ten-thirty there was not even one grape left of the beautiful arrangement.

No one seemed to care about the rain. However, some of the old dowagers cared a great deal about the behavior of some of the guests who, as one of them sniffed from the sidelines, "should never really have been allowed to come to Newport." It was a swinging party, and the ball committee was delighted with the whole atmosphere and the amount of money being made. Perle Mesta added to the glitter by wearing every diamond she possessed with her blue-gray tulle ballgown. I felt she needed an armored truck guarding her, not just an armed guard.

The Honorary Chairman, Mrs. Sheldon Whitehouse, reigned like the most regal of queens, wearing the famous Tiffany Diamond around her neck. It was the first time in its history it had been actually worn; it swung perkily from a choker of perfect round diamonds, each one of them large enough to make an impressive engagement ring. Danny Dugan, one of Tiffany's most adept, senior diamond salesmen, was along for the evening to help guard the guests' jewels. In other words, he had a gun. He followed along behind Mrs. Whitehouse muttering softly, hoping someone would hear, "The Tiffany Diamond, found in South Africa in 1878 and purchased the next year by Tiffany. Containing 128.51 metric carats of golden sunlight and flashing with ninety facets, this is the largest and finest canary diamond in the world." Danny is a human adding machine, as well as being the kind of diamond expert with an inbuilt jeweler's loupe in his eye. He estimated the value of everyone's jewels that evening, and toted up the total for my amusement every hour or so. It was high enough in the millions to make any insurance company extremely nervous. Tiffany was nervous anyway about having its famous diamond worn in public. Two gunmen stuck to Mrs. Whitehouse like Saran Wrap wherever she went all evening long. They would have accompanied her into the powder room had we not intervened just in time.

When the Preservation Society suggested a few months later that, because of the incredible success of the first Tiffany Ball, there should be another one next July, we silently cheered when Mr. Hoving said no. Although it had been a great experience, our department had much more to do during the forthcoming year than work for the Newport Chamber of Commerce.

Everyone was skeptical over my proposed stationery exhibit. Admittedly, stationery is difficult to promote, and my budget was very small. However, my idea to utilize famous love letters to showcase our writing paper was not considered very sound. I had perused books of famous letters of famous people to each other and had found a staggering number of passionate love letters, everyone from George Sand to Elizabeth Barrett Browning. Reproducing some of these letters on different samples of Tiffany stationery would at least be a method of making the note paper come alive. We could make people look at it. Blank stationery looks so cold and lifeless lying in the case.

My staff and I set about finding people who could imitate other peoples' handwriting. We found someone with a big bold flourish resembling Napoleon's. One of our own calligraphers imitated the Elizabethan script to perfection in recreating Queen Elizabeth I's handwriting. All in all, we garnered about twenty love letters from famous people through history, received permission from the publishers to reproduce them, and rewrote them on a piece of modern Tiffany stationery. Farnham Lefferts, the bright young head of the Stationery, Clocks and Watches departments, and later to become Tiffany's president, thought the whole idea slightly offbeat, but amusing. He was curious to see what would happen.

Gene Moore mounted the letters for me on standing bulletin boards covered with bright red felt. He placed them in a line on the first floor, starting by the semiprecious stone cases and continuing over the full length of the stationery department. By noon there was a long line of customers patiently waiting to read each letter. Some of them went back and got into the line a second and third time. The noontime traffic, sprinkled with Wall Street men who had come uptown for a quick errand or lunch, had swelled the waiting line right out of the store onto Fifth Avenue. The day after the exhibit opened, the *New York Times* had a column on the editorial page that ran the full length of the page. The exhibit was described in detail; readers were urged to visit it and to recapture some of the art of expressing oneself on paper as practiced by great personages. The newspaper lamented the fact that in our era of quick communication, we have all forgotten how to write. This was the first and possibly the last time in Tiffany's history that the store made the editorial page. We sold a lot of stationery and tickled the fancy of people who hadn't known, as one visitor phrased it, "that Napoleon along with everything else was really a sexy old guy, wasn't he?"

✦✦

During my Tiffany years we had bird trouble — not once but twice. The first invasion of birds was brought on by the intro-

"No, Madam, Tiffany's Does Not Serve Breakfast" · 129

duction of a new sterling silver flatware pattern called "Cordis," which means "of the heart" if one remembers one's Latin. The name was derived from the fact that the handles of the pattern were heart-shaped. We needed some publicity-attracting display to launch this new silver pattern. At the mention of the word "heart" the romantic sap in me began to flow. I set up a large table on the Silver Floor right by the front elevators, which every customer would be forced to view, whether she liked it or not. The setting was all pink and white, with everything hearts-and-flowers in the most sentimental way. Labar Hoagland, the good-looking vice president in charge of the Silver Department, watched the table go up, not knowing whether to laugh or cry. His sense of humor told him it was ridiculously funny; his Yankee masculinity told him the whole idea was nauseating. On a pink, rose-splashed tablecloth, I used pink and white flowered china and pink stemware. The sterling ashtrays were, of course, heart-shaped to match the design of "Cordis." I purchased a birdcage from the dime store, had it painted pale pink, and plopped it in the center of the table. Chandra wove pink and white flowers around the bottom of the cage. We rented two snow white doves to put in it, whose names happened to be Bill and Coo, and christened the masterpiece "The Love Dove Table."

About three nights later, I was working late at my desk at 6 P.M. the only one still left on the executive floor. The night watchman telephoned me from the second floor. "Come quick, Miss Baldrige, come quick to the Silver Department!" From the urgency of his voice, I knew that disaster had struck the birds. I found him standing next to the cage on the darkened floor. There inside the cage were one calm and one very agitated white bird. There on the floor of the cage were two lovely pale pink eggs.

Neither of us knew what to do. Would the mother die because of lack of pre-natal care? Why was the father acting in such an aggressive manner? Or was it the mother being aggressive? I will never learn how to determine the sex of a bird, that is clear, but both the watchman and I knew something must be done. We called several pet shops and, of course, they were closed for the night. Finally, I reached an all-night pet shop in Brooklyn. After finishing his fit of laughter, the shop-owner managed to give some instructions.

"You've got good packing excelsior in that emporium of yours, don't you?" he asked. I could tell he was one of our customers, because he knew about our excelsior.

"Yes," we both chimed in.

"All right then, get a Tiffany box a little larger than the underside of the mother bird. The mother bird, by the way," he said, "is not the one who is raising the fuss. The angry one is the father. He's just jealous, so ignore him."

"Oh," we said, beginning to feel a delicious wave of relief in our hearts.

"Put some tissue paper in the Tiffany box, put the eggs in it, and place the mother gently on top of them. She won't neglect them. But stuff some excelsior on the floor of the cage, turn out the lights, and leave them in peace to build their nest in the box."

We did just that. I rushed home and into my evening clothes, arriving late for a black tie dinner at the Jock Elliotts'. My dinner partner on the left was a distinguished gentleman whose name I did not catch. I began telling him our bird story, and how nervous I was that we had jeopardized the lives of our doves by not being properly equipped for a blessed event. My dinner partner laughed and said he would help me out, that he knew just the man to solve all our problems. I turned to the man on my right and asked for the other's name. "Why, that's Fairfield Osborn, the head of the Brooklyn Zoo," he said, in a tone of wonderment. Everyone knew who Fairfield Osborn was.

The next morning the Brooklyn Zoo Chief Bird Keeper arrived by subway. He was in his snappy uniform and was bearing a very professional-looking bird's nest. He took one look at the nativity scene in the pink birdcage and stated he would not dream of disturbing the mother bird. She was glowing with contented maternity from her turquoise Tiffany box. He also expressed some amazement that she had kept so faithfully to our pink color scheme in the colors of her eggs. The birds had shredded the bits of excelsior to the tiniest of pieces during the night and had cushioned the eggs with a very neat nest, on top of the folded tissue paper. It was an excellent piece of engineering, and marked the first birth inside the store in the history of Tiffany & Co. The store began to cope with added crowds of children coming in after school to see the eggs being hatched.

We had to return our love doves to the pet shop before the incubation time was over, but "Cordis" was launched with memorable publicity.

Our feathered friends came into prominence again when the Publicity Department organized a major exhibition of the porcelain works of New Jersey sculptor Edward Marshall Boehm. The large portion of the exhibit was comprised of his very delicate, expensive bird figurines. We arranged them in a corner room on the China and Glass Floor, and I placed, as an added enticement for the show, a six-foot-tall, antique Spanish wire birdcage, rather dilapidated, but attractive. This was to house a collection of live birds.

Helen Boehm, the sculptor's wife, arrived on this particular cold and rainy Columbus Day morning with the back of her station wagon filled with small tropical birds in various carrying cages. These were not ordinary birds. They were Ed Boehm's prized specimens from his aviary outside Trenton. Most of them were rare and had been bagged by the sculptor himself in Africa and in South America. Inadvertently, one of the cages in the station wagon had not been closed securely. As Helen Boehm opened the back door to remove the cages, eight little birds pressed against the door of their cage and escaped. Out they flew into the frigid dampness; off Helen flew in hysterics to seek aid in relocating them. Thus started a bird hunt in blasé Manhattan. The gallant policemen directing traffic in the area began to help look. The doormen at the Plaza Hotel, Bergdorf's, Bonwit's, Tailored Woman and Henri Bendel's searched like boy scouts in all the trade entrances of their blocks. People began combing the scraggly little trees on the sidewalk. The news went out over the radio, and before we knew it, the Tiffany switchboard was tied up with incoming calls of inquiring newsmen and people who claimed to have sighted the long-tailed, brilliantly colored little birds.

A longshoreman called us from the Brooklyn pier, saying "I think I saw them boids." The description did not fit, alas. He was, instead, in possession of one crow and one pigeon. We received calls from all over Long Island and Connecticut. Children began bringing dead birds in paper bags into the store by five o'clock that evening, and continued doing so for several more days. We saw quantities of deceased sparrows, wrens and robins that were clutched in saddened children's hands. In respect for the solemnity of the occasion, I gave each child a blue Tiffany box to give his bird a proper burial in someone's backyard, or in a vacant lot. Helen Boehm also arranged a mass burial for the remaining little creatures collected by the children. The lost Boehm birds, of course, either could not survive

"No, Madam, Tiffany's Does Not Serve Breakfast" • 133

the cold of this hostile world or, as others from the Central Park Zoo stated, they might have been snatched up by marauder hawks hiding in skyscraper crevices before they could reach the sanctuary of the park.

That same afternoon, Gabe Pressman and his NBC television news crew came to the China and Glass Floor of Tiffany's to report on the story. They began to film the exhibit of the Boehm porcelain birds and the cage of live birds.

In order to lend proper background sounds to the bucolic scene, as the camera turned, I turned on a record of bird calls. Unbeknownst to any of us, in the middle of the record came the call of the screech owl, a bird of prey terrifying to these little imprisoned birds. They began to grow very agitated, and two of them, right in front of us and the camera, managed to squeeze through the narrow metal bars of the cage to freedom.

This was the last straw. As the cameras ground away, the two long-tailed whydahs circled the ceiling in real terror, crashing into the mirrored pillars of the floor, swooping down over $3,000 figurines, and into the store's most expensive crystal stemmed goblets and gold-decorated plates. One was quickly bagged by Helen Boehm; the other eluded capture. The customers began flailing their handbags and hats in the air, trying to catch it. We tried dust mops and large boxes. Nothing worked. Pandemonium reigned on the floor, with everyone screaming suggestions and voicing sympathy for the frightened little creatures. I called the A.S.P.C.A., but their "net man" was on his holiday for Columbus Day. The office was officially closed. Fortunately, Helen Boehm seemed to know her birds. She placed food in a fine crystal fingerbowl borrowed from a display, and we awaited darkness — which fell, of course, at closing time. We turned off the overhead lights one by one, and slowly the bird circled toward the remaining comforting beams of light and the food. Finally, the only illumination left was a flashlight, and the bird flew down to this source of light. As it did, Helen captured it with her handkerchief and put it back into the cage. I immediately gave the bird call record away to a saleslady on the China Floor who lives alone with a cat.

By now, management had had enough of live creatures in the store. "Tish," they asked in tired voices. "Would you mind doing us a big favor? Would you mind sticking to inanimate objects for a while? That is, after all, what we sell."

As an addendum, it must be admitted that at the same time our birds got loose, a Brahma bull escaped up Broadway from the Madison Square Garden rodeo. He ran amuck in the heavy but thoroughly startled traffic, and was finally lassoed by a cowboy on a horse. The charging bull was eligible for several traffic tickets, because he was even charging up a one-way street in the wrong direction.

For most New Yorkers, however, it was just another Columbus Day.

Something unexpected always seemed to happen when I worked on projects with Helen Boehm to promote her husband's porcelain sculptures. During Queen Elizabeth's and Prince Philip's visit to the United States in 1957, President and Mrs. Eisenhower gave the royal pair as their State Gift Edward Boehm's statue of "The Polo Player." We managed to arrange for Mrs. Boehm's appearance on Dave Garroway's "Today" show to show the television audience the one existing replica of the porcelain piece. This extremely fragile statue had several hundred interlocking pieces, and it was packed with loving care at the pottery in Trenton. The morning of the show, we had to arrive at the studio at 6 A.M. It then took Helen Boehm and me one whole hour to open the crate and free the statuette from its wrappings. Enormous bags of popped popcorn — minus salt and melted butter — served as the major shock absorber in the crate. Our fingers worked frantically as the show's producer kept calling Mrs. Boehm to sit down on camera to have the lighting and her voice checked and to go over a list of questions which would be asked by Dave Garroway during the interview. In our haste, I accidentally broke open one of the oversized plastic bags of popcorn. Out popped the entire contents, all over the studio floor in joyful bursts, as though released from a high-powered gun. The cast and crew looked at us with disbelief, but several of them helped rectify the mess, using brooms, mops, and anything handy. As the program went on the air, we thought we had cleaned it all up. But the uncontainable popcorn had not all been recaptured. Every time an errant piece of popcorn crackled beneath somebody's foot, the sound engineer made an agonized face. By the end of the show, his head was buried in his arms in frustration. The telephone calls into the studio demanding to know what the weird noise was did not help the ladies' overall popularity with that particular station.

+-+

Walter Hoving kept marking "No" on my proposals to lend Tiffany baubles for society fashion shows. He had valid reasons. The jewels are tossed around carelessly; the clasps are often broken; pieces are dropped and chipped; the insurance is too expensive; the jewels aren't visible on the runway anyway; and they're out of the store when they could be on the premises being seen and purchased by serious customers. In spite of all his protests, I kept urging our participation. Finally, he allowed me to accessorize a designers' show at Bonwit's. No dress or fur being shown cost under $1,000. The background was worthy of our jewels.

Chandra and I checked out nothing but big, splashy pieces.

With each new piece we marked the item in the case books and added it to our special lists for the Service Manager, Mr. Syring, the insurance company, our own checklists and the memoranda checks. Then the tortuously attached tiny tickets had to be removed from each piece. The jewelry had to be washed sparkling clean and checked by the Diamond Office. The process was long and complicated, but we finally arrived at the show, confident of success.

The models paraded so quickly, we did not have time to open half the clasps, much less secure them with the safety catches. Many of the models went out without wearing any of our jewelry. Chandra and I worked at a feverish pace, trying to keep up with the change of clothes. It was impossible. All the Tiffany security clasps were complicated and required that the wearer be absolutely still. Voices rose to a hysterical pitch in the dressing room. The models were impatient, the fashion coordinator surly. We put clips on bags, used earrings as clips by mistake. Everyone involved with that show was glad to see it come to an end, and to get rid of us, the jewels and the guards. At midnight, Chandra called me at home. "The jewelry," she said in her usual low, emotionless voice, "is not all back in the Service Manager's safe!"

"What do you mean?" I barked.

"Just that I have done another count, because I took home all of the receipts with me tonight. I was uneasy. We had taken too many batches out at separate times. The number of pieces we put into Mr. Syring's safe and the number out on memo do not jibe."

"For Lord's sake, what is missing?" My heart was at the bottom of the bed, down in my toes.

"An all-diamond clip, for $12,500 — you know, the one that looks like an heraldic emblem."

I knew the exact piece. It had obviously been stolen. We had lost a costly piece. We would be fired, our department disbanded. This was the end of my publicity career. It was sloppy, irresponsible work on my part. We would never find it — it was probably already in the hands of a fence. Nevertheless, we would have to look.

"Chandra, meet me at Bonwit's trade entrance at nine-thirty tomorrow. Tell no one about this. We'll try to get into the store with the employees before the store opens. Then we'll check the dresses in the stock room."

The next morning we successfully smuggled ourselves into the employees' entrance, past the guards. They were so used to seeing us in that store, they probably thought we worked there anyway. Getting into the stock room of the better dresses was more of a problem. It was forbidden territory. There were hundreds of thousands of dollars' worth of gowns in there. We snuck in and ran quickly through the clothes that were still grouped together from yesterday afternoon's show. No clip. We examined each dress and shook it to see if the jewel might fall out.

Then we ran down to the bag department and checked all the handbags, since we had attached some jewels to them. Our last stop was the better hat department. No sign of a clip still on a hat. We glumly began to turn back to Tiffany's, knowing we would have to report the loss immediately and face the music. On our way out, we passed by the $10 and $15 hat bar on the first floor. St. Anthony had heard me. There, sitting unpretentiously on a $15 black velvet beret, twinkled $12,500 worth of diamonds, masquerading as a rhinestone clip. The sales girls had not caught it yet. They had not yet checked through their morning stock. It stood out like the Nantucket lighthouse beam. I spread my tent coat in front of the hat bar, Chandra went behind me, and, hidden by the folds of my coat, her fingers dextrously undid the safety catch and removed the clip. We rushed back into Tiffany's and stuffed it into the box of other jewels in Mr. Syring's safe, without anyone's noticing it. We were saved — by prayer (said I) or by luck (said Chandra). I realized the great responsibility we did have in taking out this expensive merchandise. We had become blasé about its value and about what could happen to it. There was no other course to take than to tighten up our working procedures and our own efficiency. We also thereafter said "no" automatically to any requests for accessorizing for fashion shows.

My friend Wiley Buchanan, the Chief of Protocol for President Eisenhower, called me one day from the State Department. How would we like some distinguished Arab customers to come in and look around? I naturally replied we would be more than pleased to see them, and we made arrangements to receive His Majesty King Mohammed V from Morocco and his party on a specified morning. The morning arrived, the large party came to New York from Washington and were caught up in activities at the UN. Wiley telephoned to say he was sorry, but the trip to Tiffany's was off. There simply was no time.

I worked late that night, captioning photographs. At six-fifteen, one of the night watchmen at the trade entrance called me up. "Miss Baldrige, for heaven's sakes, come down here quickly. There are a lot of guys around here in sheets making a lot of noise and getting very excited." I, of course, knew at once the identity of the men in sheets. I dashed down on the service car, the only elevator running at this hour, and greeted His Majesty, His Majesty's son, and five other Moroccans in their long garments with scuff slippers. They had one State Department official with them who spoke no French, plus both American and Moroccan security officials who did not speak each other's language. They had somehow become separated from the rest of the bilingual State Department staff, but the King had insisted on seeing Tiffany's anyway. The State Department officer was consternated and most unhappy. He wanted to get them back to the Waldorf. They were already an hour late.

I chattered away in French and escorted His Majesty up the rather dilapidated back elevator, which was hardly the royal way. I switched on the lights on the Silver Floor; this was the only floor he really wanted to see.

The King explained he wanted to make some purchases out of his own money, but that he wanted to stay away from jewelry. He had just asked Congress for a large sum for his country. He winked at me, feeling I would be sympathetic: "When one asks for a loan, it is better not to be found buying diamonds, is it not?" I agreed with him, so we turned to lesser items. I saw his eyes light up when we reached the vermeil. He called his male secretary, who opened a big notebook and made notes in what was to me a completely unintelligible script. He wanted a complete service of vermeil service plates, with his royal coat-of-arms engraved in the center, candelabra to go down the center of the banquet table, place settings of flatware in vermeil, compotes, salts and peppers and so on. My pencil flew quickly as the order grew juicier and juicier. The King's taste was impeccable — he chose centerpieces in the Georgian gadroon-edged motif. They were my favorite, too, and I told him so. This failed to impress him. He selected everything that was the least ornate, a tribute to his taste. Surely, his all-gold table would be the most splendid one in the entire Arab world. I could visualize a crew of twenty from the *Ladies' Home Journal* dashing over to photograph it.

As he rushed away from the store, his robes billowing in the winds, he invited me to come visit him in Rabat. This was a part of my education from which I was unfortunately never allowed to profit. At one point during the visit, his small black eyes had surveyed me up and down as I towered over him. He had said, "Heureusement vous parlez français, Mademoiselle." French is a very useful language to know in New York City when dealing with either Moroccan kings or hairdressers.

The rumors had been adrift for many months. When the first telephone call from Hollywood finally came, announcing that the film *Breakfast at Tiffany's* would soon go into production, I was elated and optimistic over what it could do for Tiffany's image.

Finally, after months of planning, we came to terms about our role in the making of the film, and in the autumn, with the precision of a major operation by the Joint Chiefs of Staff at the Pentagon, the movie company descended upon us. The group included young director Blake Edwards and his uncountable camera and technical crew, Audrey Hepburn, George Peppard, hairdressers, stylists, cosmeticians, wardrobe mistresses, and Miss Hepburn's small but yapping dog.

Charles L. Tiffany would have been astounded to know that his private diamond room (a small enclosure on the first floor where gem salesmen show large pieces to customers who wish to shop inconspicuously) was transformed into a glamorous movie star's dressing room, littered with hairpieces, cosmetic jars and photographs of her infant son.

The crew worked in Tiffany's from Saturday evening to Monday morning, and shot on location in other parts of New York during the week. They used the store the following weekend as well. I got to know them well, because the house in which Holly Golightly and her friend supposedly lived was a block and

"No, Madam, Tiffany's Does Not Serve Breakfast" · 141

a half from my own apartment. Each morning, in going to and from work, I found the crew working in front of that house. At five-thirty on Saturday, closing time, they brought their monstrous lights and cameras into Tiffany's and constructed towering scaffolds all over the first floor. The aisle space soon became a writhing mass of snakelike cables and wires. They worked all night Saturday, and on through Sunday until Monday's opening hour. One short scene required many hours of work. Mr. Hoving insisted that our own salespeople play themselves on the first floor, for security reasons, if for nothing else. The producer swallowed several times at this dictum, because he knew what this would do to his budget. He capitulated, of course. It meant that every Tiffany salesperson kept after work during shooting hours had to be paid double time by the film company, plus their regular extra's fee. The film company also had to induct the Tiffany sales force into the actor's union, and pay their dues. All of this because the camera was to sweep once or twice over the entire first floor as Audrey Hepburn and George Peppard walked in to buy something. The entire scene took just over three minutes. A Hollywood actor was allowed to play the part of the salesman who waited on them. We had to change the script of the store scene, because it did not conform to Tiffany standards. Ellsworth Hyde, the Controller, once again reached for the aspirin bottle: the insurance costs shot up after closing time with all the regular stock out on the floor, instead of in the big vaults. The movie company had to bear all of the expense of the extra insurance, which was a lordly sum, even by Hollywood's standards.

Gene Moore had to change his Fifth Avenue windows seven times in order to please the lighting crew out in front. In the opening scene of the movie, Audrey alights from a taxi and walks alone up Fifth Avenue in her long, black sheath dress with gaudy rhinestone bib collar, and with a rhinestone tiara in her hair. She is carrying a paper bag with a cup of coffee and a donut; she stops and looks longingly at Tiffany's windows. It is supposed to be dawn, with deserted streets. The scene was shot at dawn, too, with all of us helping the police halt traffic at the intersections when the actual takes were made. The streets of New York are never deserted. Miss Hepburn did the walking scene over and over and over again in her sleeveless dress, carrying a raincoat over her arm, her arms covered by a mass of goosepimples from the chill. The lighting of the jewels in the window to catch the proper reflections in those early hours made innumerable problems for the technicians. Gene Moore realized that his own lighting problems for the windows were infinitesimal in comparison.

The entire store was in a perpetual state of excitement over the filming for two weeks. Miss Hepburn and Mr. Peppard graciously signed autographs to all of the children, nieces and godsons of the staff, and the Hollywood crew ran up a terrific total on the cash register in presents to bring back to their wives. When the Publicity Department of the film studio went into action to publicize the film, I realized what a neophyte I was in the business. They took my breath away with their elaborate plans and tie-ins. The movie and the television reruns have continued to be seen by millions all over the world, and every month tourists come into the store and ask where the restaurant is.

When those wonderful, unpredictable Tiffany days came to an end for me, it turned out to be not the end after all. In the White House I was to be in constant communication with the store over the ordering of the Presidential State Gifts. Then

"No, Madam, Tiffany's Does Not Serve Breakfast" · 143

Tiffany's turned up in Chicago in 1966, after I moved there, with a small, elegant branch on Michigan Avenue.

I had, after all, made my world-of-big-business debut with the firm, a big step in one's life. Tiffany's staff had seemed to me at first to be peopled with slow-moving turtles. Later, I could only appreciate their methods and the results. To watch silver designer Oscar Riedener was to watch patience, as he pondered and tested for one entire week the shape of a knife blade on a new silver flatware pattern before making his decision. To watch Arthur Gough was to watch patience as he sat in the calligraphy department, spending three months buried like a medieval monk in his tower; however, instead of illuminating the Bible, he was working on a few letters of his new alphabet of script, which would be immediately copied and used by the country's leading stationers, engravers and printers. To watch the head of the engraving department, Bill Demarest, was to watch patience as he presided over each order with the same meticulous paternal pride, whether it was the engraving of two initials on a baby spoon ordered by Mary Smith, or the Pope's coat of arms on a letter box ordered by the President of the United States. If I could not adopt this patience and striving for perfection, at least I could admire it profoundly.

As in each of my jobs, the contacts made and the experience stored away at 727 Fifth Avenue formed an invaluable repository from which to draw throughout the rest of my business life. For one thing, I learned the fashion game at Tiffany's, beginning with the confused maze of the Seventh Avenue garment district. There the ornately furnished, crystal-chandeliered dress salons are reached from dirty sidewalks congested beyond belief. This was the land of tired men pushing two-thousand-dollar mink coat garment racks through narrow streets past $3.98 cotton housedress racks, in the din of affected magazine editors' voices, excited conversations in Hebrew, and heavy accents from many countries. I learned how to "shop the market," where to go and how to go in assembling the right fashion look for a publicity photograph that should look six months ahead of itself, fashion-wise. Knowing the leading designers personally was to be another constant help throughout my business life.

From the shelter magazine editors, the interior designers of New York and their shopping sources, and from the city's museums, art galleries, boutiques and antique shops, I learned the importance of style and taste in home furnishings — and why self-education is the key to developing the eye. There is no greater formulator of a woman's taste than New York City. Money, opulence and show are everywhere; that elusive, undefinable quality of good taste is not. From the fashions on the streets and from the decor in homes tucked away in ordinary holes of the city's beehive, it is obvious that good taste is not a question of riches. It is a question of proper selection — and proper combinations of selections — whether one shops at Bergdorf Goodman and Henri Bendel or at the dime store.

This is the real joy — for a woman — of living in New York. It is a training ground. Any person who haunts the stores, galleries and shops, and who spends her weekends surveying her environment, cannot help but be impressed by the beautiful; nor can she help but reject the ugly. There are the furniture galleries of the great French kings to peruse at the Metropolitan Museum and the honeycomb of art galleries pushing everything from Rubens to Andy Warhol's Campbell Soup cans; the latest designer room settings on Bloomingdale's furniture floor; the geometric paintings at the Guggenheim and well-designed objects for the home at the Museum of Modern Art; the fashion windows at Lord & Taylor and the contemporary accessories at Bonniers and Georg Jensen; the auction galleries at

"No, Madam, Tiffany's Does Not Serve Breakfast" · 145

Parke-Bernet and the tapestried salons of French & Co.; the antique porcelains and furniture on Madison Avenue and on 57th Street; the crystal at Baccarat and the linens at Leron; the artificial flowers at Helen Cole and the eclectic exhibits at Hallmark. There are important taste-shapers of this country residing at every turn of the corner on Manhattan's East Side, whether it be a wacky art nouveau fabric or the latest fad in belts at a way-out boutique. Even the salamis and cheeses hanging from the ceilings of the Italian delicatessens in this part of the world seem to be displayed with more verve than anywhere else.

One can only respect the terrifying intensity of the fashion magazine editors, working on location with the city's top photographers and models for their editorial pages. To watch them in action is to learn not only the beauty of the medium of the camera lens, but to learn patience, too. To them, the minute detail is monumental in importance, whether it be the position of a tiny bow on the shoe, the shaping of a false lash at the corner of one eye, or the shade of a glove only half-peeking from a faraway coat pocket. These people are the taste-shapers of tomorrow, guiding our advertisements, our store buyers, our way of life. They take pictures that sometimes seem bizarre and absurd. These are in fact a preview of "tomorrow," a concept with which they are continually obsessed. These photographs are the pioneers of the line, form and color that will come to pass in our marketplace. It is a heady, crazy world, never stereotyped or dull, and always blessed with touches of that greatest of all saving graces: the art of not taking oneself too seriously.

New York is a tough city for the working girl. She is under constant high-intensity pressure — whether it is a question of her emotions or her daily physical fight to survive. It is hardly a romantic atmosphere, concerned with boy meets girl. It is rather a preoccupation with excelling in one's job and paying one's bills. The competition to look well, wear the latest fashions, affect the latest coiffure and be "glowing" or "glittering" with the latest cosmetic look is far too compelling to be able to budget into the average salary. Therefore, compromises have to be made, and each one is agonizing. The "in" girl must look a certain way, have her apartment decorated a certain way, and entertain with a stamp of individuality and flair. On top of this, she is buffeted in the subway, elbowed at the lunch counter, and constantly challenged for her job at the office by a younger, prettier face.

The New York "in" girl has to be familiar with all the big city small talk, which can consist of anything from the extra-marital affairs of advertising agency presidents to the financial status of well-known dress designers; and from the orgies of underground movie makers to the cost of having Billy Baldwin do your Long Island beach house. The fact that one has never been to a Long Island beach nor witnessed an underground movie is immaterial. One must be au courant. Artificial? Yes. A lot of phoniness? Yes. But there are always laughs and creative stimulation, and a delicious masochistic thirst of "tomorrow." If today is this crazy and hectic, what will tomorrow bring?

New York is a unique steaming cauldron. There isn't a girl who doesn't emerge from it slightly scalded, but always the wiser for it.

It even made a businesswoman out of me.

PART IV

Office Address:
1600 Pennsylvania Avenue

IV

My feelings as the limousine drove through the southwest gate of the White House on Inauguration Day of 1961 were an equal combination of anticipation and fear. To me, the White House had always been an imposing edifice. I had known it since early childhood, when as a Congressman's child, I had accompanied my brothers to Easter Egg-roll parties on the grounds. We were always served orange juice and cookies in the East Room after our athletic efforts on the lawns. I was the perfect little lady in those days, proud of my white gloves, and horribly embarrassed at the gaucheries of my brothers, Mac and Bob, who ran races with each other to see who could down the most orange juice. In later years I had gone through the house on public tours, but it awed me, as the home of the leader of our country should.

On a bitter cold, crisp day, as the sun seemed to hit the newly painted whiteness of the mansion with a thousand shafts of light, I was beginning a new life — one that was to be part and parcel of this structure. We circled up toward the South Portico, and it hurt our eyes to look at the house gleaming against a bright blue sky and a deep blanket of fresh snow. Mrs. Kennedy's maid, Provy (short for Providencia), the President's valet, George, and I had to miss the swearing-in ceremonies in front of the Capitol. We had work to do, to ready the house for its new occupants and for their tight schedule of Inaugural activities. At twelve noon on Inauguration Day, the house officially passes from the hands of its previous occcupants to the new regime. At exactly 12:01, the two White House limousines brought us through the gates.

J. B. West, the Chief Usher, was the first to greet Provy, George and me, as we stepped from the cars, laden with boxes, Mrs. Kennedy's ballgown and evening coat, and file folders. The baggage followed in cars behind us. J. B. and I by now had become old friends. We had suffered together through the incident of the lending of the White House vermeil collection to Tiffany's over three years ago. We had been on the telephone constantly for one month, going over details of the move, and J. B. had clandestinely received and stored much of the Kennedys' personal luggage during the previous week.

J. B. was symbolic of the warmth of the house. He was to become my constant companion in the blood, sweat and tears of that life. His title is archaic and ridiculous. "Chief Usher" sounds like the lead man of the bellboy suits at the Paramount Theater. In actual point of fact, he practically runs the White House, and the President and First Lady along with it.

After he had shown us to the Kennedys' private quarters, I squared away Provy, George and their suitcases. Provy asked her first question, the same question she was to ask in every city in every country of the world, "Miss Baldrige, where is the iron and ironing board?" I will always associate Provy with ironing — in fact, I am sure that through the years she sighed with dismay at the backs of my skirts and dresses, so un-ironed was I through the entire administration.

As soon as I could I rushed over to the East Wing to my Social Office. I had toured it with Mary Jane McCaffree, Mrs.

(*right*) The author in the drive of the White House. (*below*) The author shows President Kennedy's office to a visitor

(*left*) President Kennedy, a military aide and the author, walking from the South Portico of the White House to a children's concert. (*below*) On the steps of the White House after addressing the women delegates to 'The American Women in Radio and Television' convention

Eisenhower's Social Secretary, but it looked very different now. All of their pictures, all of their bibelots and mementoes were gone, and what was left was a starkly painted set of offices. They were not to look stark for long. In one week they were to resemble the inside of Macy's shipping room the week before Christmas.

Crafty, well-trained secretary that I was, I rushed through all the offices of the East Wing, trying all of the electric typewriters. We *had* to have the best. I stole one from the Military Aide's office, another from the Air Force Aide's office, and still a third from a downstairs office that was to be occupied by Arthur Schlesinger. What these men didn't know wouldn't hurt them. After all, they were enjoying an historic occasion on Capitol Hill. I replaced their machines with our older models, with the help of a young Signal Corpsman I found wandering aimlessly in the corridor. He was strong, and there were heavy typewriters to lift, so I gave my first order of the day. A month later, my ruse was discovered, as the typewriter maintenance men came around to check on all the equipment and found none of the machine numbers checking with the locations.

The shower-bath in the private bathroom belonging to my office fascinated me. I outfitted it with the most exotic of bath soaps, but subsequently was to find I could never take a shower without fourteen interruptions requiring my rushing to the telephone, bath-towel-wrapped and dripping water all over the carpet. I learned my lesson and took all baths at home in my own apartment. We subsequently used our office shower for watering the plants — I knew the taxpayers would want to know it was being put to some use.

The two large windows of my office looked out over the East Garden and directly over a terrace to the East Room of the Mansion. I have been "view lucky" in my jobs. In Paris I had the Palais Chaillot to gaze upon from my window, in Rome the spacious rose gardens and boxwood-lined alleys of the Villa Taverna, and in CIA days the reflecting pool in front of the Lincoln Memorial. Only Tiffany's had been a letdown. For one half of my tenure there, my view had been a former packing closet off the service elevator, a place which discouraged any thought of poetry.

By six o'clock both the President and Mrs. Kennedy had come into the house from the parade reviewing stand. They were exhausted and chilled with the cold. Underneath the flush of excitement, their eyes were tired, and one could tell they looked around at their new house apologetically — as though they should be reacting like wide-eyed schoolchildren undergoing such a fantastic experience. Silent, they went upstairs to change and to have a hot drink.

The guests were pouring in behind them. I had had to arrange my first White House party in two hours' time. As usual, I had no idea how many people were coming. All of the family, relatives, out-of-town friends, political big-wigs, parade marshals, and the big guns behind the whole week of Inaugural festivities came in to gape at the house. The press was not admitted. Everyone could relax, say what they wanted to, and no one would be peering down at the buffet, itemizing the food in detail to thrill the American public the next day in print.

I stood in the State Dining Room watching the footmen glide effortlessly over the thick carpet, carrying their trays, replenishing the cold buffet and the platter of small hot hors d'oeuvres. The head butler, Charles Ficklin, had them trained with military precision. If this was to be our staff, my task would be easy.

This was the second party I had organized for the day.

The preceding one was a very early buffet lunch at the Mayflower Hotel, before the swearing-in, which Ambassador Kennedy said he would pay for. I was to invite only the family on both sides.

When Ambassador Kennedy saw that I had rented a sizable room at the hotel, and that the buffet table resembled a squash court in size, he sternly called me over.

The buffet looked exquisite, the Mayflower had outdone themselves with decorating the platters in honor of their distinguished guests, and I had expected him to praise me.

"Who are all these people?" he asked in an extremely irritated tone.

"Your family, Mr. Ambassador."

"They are *not*," he replied. "Just who are all these freeloaders? I want to know exactly why you asked them."

He was furious. So was I, at this point. I was too tired from all the Inaugural preparations to be reticent. "They are either your family, your wife's Fitzgerald cousins, your children's in-law's families, or the Bouvier-Auchincloss relatives."

He went up to four or five and asked them outright who they were. They were, of course, bona fide family. There were so many Kennedy-Fitzgerald cousins, so many step-cousins and step-children on the Bouvier-Auchincloss side, they added up to a political rally in themselves.

He came back to me, his eyes twinkling. "This is going to cost me a lot of money, Tish. But you're right. They *are* all family. And it's the last time we get 'em all together, too, if I have anything to say about it. And it is a nice party. You're all right."

I fell in love with Ambassador Kennedy on the spot. He was quick-tempered, outspoken, and had a sense of humor. I decided I just was not going to be afraid of him, and I never was.

That first year, he was to help me and raise my morale when it most needed it. He was to call me from Palm Beach when I had been blamed for yet another social disaster in the press. His voice came over the wire:

"Tish, they giving you a hard time up there?"

"Yes, Mr. Ambassador."

"Well, tell 'em all to go to hell. They think the world revolves around them up there in Washington. I have news for you, it doesn't. The rest of the country is very different from Washington, D. C. You just buck up and tell 'em all to go to hell."

He had no idea what a telephone call like that did for a crushed, miserable lump of a Social Secretary. He also endeared himself to every member of my staff by bringing us on the family plane, *The Caroline*, or by sending us, special flavors of a rich ice cream. On his rare visits to the White House, he would come over to the East Wing, sit down on the sofa in my office, ask how our problems were coming along, and dispense a gallon of ice cream with spoons and paper cups to all my staff. We adored "Papa Joe."

The "settling-in" at the White House was hard for everyone, including the old-time regulars on the staff — the Secret Service, the White House Police, the Navy stewards in the White House Mess, the gardeners, the telephone operators, the footmen, and the administrative staff that remains from one administration to another. The old pros were the ones who saved all of us rank young newcomers. They gently trained us, and taught us the necessaries of our jobs and responsibilities. Ensconced in my Social Office was a handful of highly skilled, trained, loyal staff that should have been pulling in high executive salaries. They weren't. They were grossly underpaid, overworked, underpublicized. They had been the backstay of the First Lady's wing for years.

Mrs. Kennedy herself, still trying to regain her strength from the birth of her son, John, two months before, had to take it easy. A gigantic task of setting priorities awaited her. My task was to see that those priorities were carried out, but I also had an enormous list of my own priorities, in organizing my own staff. The mail load was unfathomable, seemingly unanswerable. Democratic headquarters simply dumped all the piles of unanswered mail that was not addressed directly to the President right in our laps. We had mail addressed to "Senator and Mrs. Kennedy," "Mr. and Mrs. Kennedy," to the children, to the children's nurse, and to the children's dog. Reading the addresses on that first batch of mail should have prepared us for subsequent letters, which would arrive addressed to Caroline's hamster or canary, "Robin."

There was no chance to stop and reflect, bewildered, on my job or its responsibilities. With five lines ringing into my office at once, one had to act — and if one did not know what to do, one bluffed. And if one made a mistake in one's bluffing, it ended up in the front section of the *Washington Post* and the *Evening Star*, with either an AP or a UPI mark on it, so that one had the comfort of knowing one's indiscretion would always be published from coast to coast.

Everything happens *very* fast when you work for the Kennedys. Every once in a while the realization of the abrupt change in my own life would strike me in those first few days of the New Frontier. For years and years, Jacqueline Bouvier had been "Jackie" to me. Now, as of Inauguration Day, she was "Mrs. Kennedy," and Jack had become — forever — "Mr. President." The dignity of the positions they both held commanded this respect.

On January 1, 1963, I was supposed to have been in Milano,

nicely set up in an office handling public relations accounts. I had notified Mr. Hoving at Tiffany's the preceding spring that the call to Europe was too strong to resist anymore. It would be a challenging, exciting new stage in my life to enter the business world in what for Italy was a brand new profession — public relations. I had learned the trade at Tiffany's. I knew Italian. The combination should succeed on fertile ground.

I had spent my summer vacation in Big Sur that year, atop Partington Ridge, writing away on a novel in Louisa Jenkins' lovely contemporary home. The glass-walled house overlooked the Pacific Ocean in a world far removed from civilization. Then that telephone call came. The telephone was in the master bedroom, a long walk from my chaise longue on the terrace. I heard an insistent ringing as I sat with a portable typewriter in my lap, meditating on the carefully swirled gravel of the Japanese garden beside me. The only noises on Partington Ridge are the sounds of bees in the bougainvillea, the occasional passage of a jeep bringing supplies up the mountain, or the trickling of the water fountains in the gardens. The ring of a telephone is a very discordant, unwelcome sound.

It was Jackie Kennedy, calling from Hyannisport. Her husband had won the Democratic nomination for President a week before. She told me she thought "Jack will make it" in November. And if he did — wouldn't I come to the White House with her as Social Secretary?

I told her I was all set for Milano, had already taken on some business accounts and arranged for office space. She replied that I couldn't let her down.

And I couldn't. And I didn't. One does not refuse such a call. It was chance, or sheer luck, or Divine Providence. Whatever it was, my decision had to be in the affirmative, and I called her back the next day.

She announced my appointment in a press release issued in Washington in November, shortly after the election. The press began to hound me, and the week before Thanksgiving, I found myself down in Washington to give an illustrated lecture at the Sulgrave Club on Schlumberger jewels and, just incidentally, to hold my first Kennedy Administration press conference.

I had always gotten along very well with the press. Some of the so-called "Washington newshens" had been friends of mine for years — like Betty Beale of the *Washington Star*, Dorothy McCardle and Maxine Cheshire of the *Washington Post* and Bess Furman of the *New York Times*. I went before the klieg lights in the Women's National Democratic Club in Washington with the innocence of the proverbial lamb, quite enjoying all the fuss and prestige of my new position.

If I had only known then what I knew one day later!

Television cameras whirred, radio microphones seemed to grow like dandelions in the air in front of me. There were so many lights on me, I couldn't see the whites of anybody's eyes. My own must have been scarlet red. I wore a brown suit, a Dior copy, and a newly purchased leopard hat, which I thought was the last word, but which one male reporter later described as a "floppy animal-skin kind of sun-hat."

My first mistake, when asked what I really thought of Jacqueline Kennedy, was answering in a flip way, "She is a woman who has everything, including the next President of the United States."

I heard a wild eruption of laughter. Nancy Dickerson (Hanschman in those days) patted my hand and said, "Great, Tish, great!" However, I was to discover later that no one in the administration, including Mrs. Kennedy, deemed that proper and appropriate to say.

I was teased about being a lifelong Republican, the daughter of a Republican Congressman, the sister of an active Republican politician in Connecticut. Instead of cutting all this teasing off with a statement that my job was not a political appointment in any sense of the word, and that one's politics were a personal matter, I talked all over the lot, apologizing, explaining how I had been a Kennedy supporter for a long time, and that I had voted a Democratic ticket this election. Someone countered with, "Yes, but you even worked for John Lindsay in this campaign," referring to my long friendship with the Republican Silk Stocking District Congressman, now the Mayor of New York, for whom I had always campaigned.

I decided to hold my own here, and proudly admitted that yes, I had indeed supported him and always would. I could hear the groans of the Democrats from the clubroom right down to Capitol Hill.

Then, in answering a question about all the clubwomen who would be trying to meet Mrs. Kennedy, I referred to them deprecatingly as "those great vast hordes of females." There was an immediate titter and outright laughter. I saw the pencils fly faster. I corrected myself, "I mean those large groups of very interesting ladies." All through my White House days I would hear repercussions from club groups about that crack.

I was also on the hot seat about Mrs. Eisenhower's not having invited Mrs. Kennedy to the White House. I had been grateful for the hospitable lunch and entire afternoon spent in the East Wing with Mary Jane McCaffree, her very capable secretary. I respected Mrs. Eisenhower very much. The press was trying to cause friction between the two First Ladies, and I knew it. I could not lie and say Mrs. Eisenhower had invited Mrs. Kennedy. I simply stated the invitation had not been forthcoming — some of the press said I reported it with a snicker.

The final straw was my statement on Mrs. Kennedy's plans to make the White House "a showcase for great American artists and creative talent." I talked about the performing artists Mrs. Kennedy wished to invite to perform there, but some of the press headlined their stories that Mrs. Kennedy was going to pile modern art shows into the Mansion. I had obviously not explained myself clearly, it was my fault, not the correspondents'. These stories upset the Fine Arts Commission, who later denied in print that permission for such a sacrilege to the historic house would be granted. The press leaped into the fray with great glee, and I was awakened in my Boston hotel room in the middle of the night by a Washington reporter with the following question, "How do you feel about having caused a war between Mrs. Kennedy and the Fine Arts Commission?"

When Mrs. Kennedy intimated that I would not be called upon to handle any more press conferences, I could not tell who was happier about the decision — she or I.

Mary Jane McCaffree laughed off the stories of friction between Mrs. Eisenhower and Mrs. Kennedy which supposedly I had perpetrated. "Tish, relax. I know you didn't imply this. Just relax. This is going to happen to you all the time in this job. You might as well get used to it or you'll grow ulcers."

I went and cried once more on the shoulder of a lovely lady in her eighties, Mrs. James Helm, who had been Social Secretary to Mrs. Woodrow Wilson and Mrs. Roosevelt. "You have much to learn, my child. When I was in the job, we didn't have the press coverage there is now. We remained as anonymous as we wished to, and we were left alone. But just remember, you will make lots of mistakes, and you must learn only not to suffer because of them."

I was to remember that comforting piece of advice forever. In fact, ever since that day, a saying of the famous Spanish philosopher Gracian has hung in my office: "Let it be a mistake to confide your errors even to a friend, for were it possible, you should not disclose them to yourself; but since this is impossible, make use here of that other principle of life, which is: *learn how to forget.*"

Our first official White House party got me into the hottest of water with the President. In fact, one can only say it was boiling. I planned the party with J. B. West in the same manner I had planned all the big Embassy cocktail parties, logistically speaking. There was an easy disposition of food tables and tables for mixing the drinks all over the first floor, so that service would be fast and efficient. Society reporters the next day reported with ecstasy that the whole thing had been too precedent-shattering for words. The party was in honor of all the Presidential appointees and their wives. It was held on a Sunday evening, which was earth-shaking to the ladies of the press. Then they were allowed to mingle with the guests and be served drinks, as though they were just guests, too. This in itself was tradition-breaking. Ashtrays were in abundance everywhere (never permitted at official functions in former administrations). The food was "splendid and imaginative," not just the traditional cakes, cookies and sandwiches. One reporter waxed eloquent on the delicious fresh shrimp, raw vegetables with a spicy dip, and the hot cheese hors d'oeuvres. I almost sent her a doggy bag of leftovers from our official luncheon the next day, because I think the poor girl was hungry.

The main item of excitement, however, were the "bars" in the reception rooms. Hard liquor had never been served in the Eisenhower Administration — when it was an official party and when the press was present.

The President called me into his office the next day. I was expecting to be patted on the back and praised for what had been an obviously successful, warm, cozy party. I must have looked like a puppy dog walking into his office, wriggling all over with happiness and anticipation.

"Tish," he said in cold anger, "why didn't you tell me there had never been hard liquor at a party like this before?"

"What do you mean, Mr. President?"

He replied that there had already been three delegations from the W.C.T.U. and other organizations trying to see him, and he had been called and told off by every Congressman from the Baptist Belt.

"But — but," I sputtered, not quite knowing what to say.

"And — to make matters even nicer," he said, turning around from the windows he had been looking through into the garden, trying to calm down his voice, "it was on a Sunday. We had to break all precedents, and do it on a Sunday. Just look at these headlines." The pile of evening newspapers were marked with headlines such as, "Liquor on Sunday at the White House Draws Criticism" and "Never On Sunday at JFK's House says Baptist Congressman."

I suddenly realized that, of course, a hornet's nest had been opened, and I was the cause of it. He went on to explain that he should have been notified of the whole tradition of the White House, and then have been left with the decision on how to handle the matter. I had no right to make that decision myself, without consulting him.

He was mad — and rightfully so. I went back to the East Wing to lick my wounds and take an anti-ulcer pill. He picked up the telephone that same afternoon to call me. He said he had been "a little rough" that morning, that I must understand that he had a lot of things on his mind, and that he didn't mean to be short with me.

He was that kind of a man, JFK.

And a year later, he stopped me in the hall and said, "Do you know what happened a year ago today?"

"No, Mr. President."

He recalled it was the anniversary of our first White House

official party — when we had bars and served liquor. He then said that the decision to continue with that policy "was the best thing we ever did for entertaining in the history of the White House!" My starting it, he added, gave them the courage to go on giving guests a good time.

He laughed and went on his way.

So we did continue to serve liquor, but the "bars" were never seen again. Drinks were mixed in the butler's pantry and passed on trays.

The temperance groups continued to complain, but the battle was won — by a glorious majority. How can one give a cocktail party without cocktails, anyway?

Many will agree that the staff with whom one works in any job makes or breaks it. The regulars at the White House spoil one for any other job — the Police, the Secret Service, the Ushers, telephone operators, etc. My own immediate staff was divided into four sections: Pam Turnure and her press responsibilities; Sandy Fox and the calligraphy-protocol-social records department; Hortense Burton, who rode herd as "Mother Hortense" on our Correspondence Pool; and Stan Clark, the head of our Social Files, a busy squirrel, hopelessly buried in the tree trunk of the Executive Office Building. In all, about forty people worked for me in the "First Lady's Secretariat." Everyone's favorite on our staff was a Negro gentleman, Fred Jefferson. However, I subsequently learned this was not an original feeling. Fred was the hero of the Social Office in *every* administration.

In my outer office sat two super-smart secretaries, Anne Lincoln and Barbara Keehn. They stood the gaff between the public and Mrs. Kennedy and screened hundreds of the more important incoming and outgoing letters each week. They also took endless pages of my dictation in answer to VIP or problem mail, of which we seemed to have ever-increasing quantities.

When Anne later became the Housekeeper, Betty Hogue, another crack stenographer, moved into our office.

Pam's secretary was French-born Pierrette Spiegler. We had a great deal of mail from France, because of Mrs. Kennedy's Gallic origins. Under my guidance, Pierrette would compose warm answers in French for my signature. Occasionally we incurred the anger of the French Desk at the State Department because of small errors or indiscretions. (How were we to know we were writing to the daughter of one of France's leading Communists?) If we sent this mail to be answered through official channels, it would not have been answered for months on end, due to overworked, understaffed translation facilities at the State Department. It was important for our French public relations to acknowledge this mail on Mrs. Kennedy's behalf at once.

As time went on, I had to become hardened to the inevitable flaps caused by our errors. "Don't worry," I said once to Pierrette, as we were swaying in the backwash of State Department wrath, "as long as we're not responsible for the start of World War III, we're all right."

Our mistakes involved not only the French mail. One night, my staff was working until 11 P.M. to try to move a mountain of mail from the Correspondence Pool. One of the girls wrote a form letter answer in reply to an invitation from a Catholic priest to the Kennedys to attend his one-man art show. The priest wrote, saying that since the President and Mrs. Kennedy were so interested in art, they should be interested in seeing his work. It was a presumptuous letter, and the yawning typist wrote him back one of our stock form letters:

DEAR FATHER————:
The President and Mrs. Kennedy thank you for informing them of the birth of your son, and they send you and the baby every good wish for a long, healthy, happy life.

The priest hit the roof, and bombasted me on the telephone, thinking I had done it to humiliate him. He was totally lacking in any sense of humor, and I wanted to tell him so. Instead I had to apologize abjectly for fifteen minutes to calm him down.

The duties of a Social Secretary change from administration to administration, to fit the needs of each Presidential family. In the Kennedy Administration, the responsibilities centered around the entertainment in the Executive Mansion and the social life of the Presidential family, as well as the handling of the First Lady's and children's mail, the scheduling of her appointments, the attending to priorities of her official activities, and the overall public relations policies governing her speeches, appearances, official written statements, and honorary chairmanships. Some of the decisions required no checking with anyone, except the Secret Service, which had to be kept informed of every step Mrs. Kennedy took, in action or in name. Others required the full knowledge and consent of Mrs. Kennedy, Pierre Salinger, the Attorney General's office and the President himself. I had learned in my CIA days that subversive groups often hide under the most innocent of names, and Mrs. Kennedy must be protected from their clutches.

In a job like mine, just deciding that it was all right to make a certain decision without anyone's further approval was a big decision in itself.

The only thing I refused to agitate over was the Kennedy mail to which we could send form answers: the thank-you for an inexpensive gift or for a fan letter; the polite turn-down of a woman's invitation to her daughter's high school graduation in Seattle; and the gentle refusal to tell a college girl how many rollers Mrs. Kennedy puts in her hair at night, if indeed any. My Correspondence Pool and "Mother Hortense" dispatched those with great alacrity, often forging my name in the signature block. Occasionally, I would receive clippings showing a front page reproduction of a letter supposedly signed by me, but which I had never seen. It was big news in most people's lives to receive a letter from the White House. I continuously pleaded with all the Sarah Bernhardtian theatrics I could muster that these letters, however brief, must leave the White House without an error or an erasure — or, heaven forbid, a misspelling or improper punctuation. This was one originating address in the United States from which stenographic errors could not be allowed.

The numbers of people who wished to communicate with the Presidential family never ceased to amaze me. We were fully aware of how the mail was running on the President's side on major issues, because a great volume of mail was addressed to Mrs. Kennedy as "an intelligent wife, a woman who understands the problems of the day, and one who can gain her husband's ear." In other words, thousands of people felt that by writing Mrs. Kennedy, they could swing more weight with the President than by writing him directly.

The "serious mail" on international and local issues we passed automatically over to the President's side for answer. We were, of course, charged with the responsibility for mail addressed directly to Mrs. Kennedy. The infant shoe industry got after us, because baby John was photographed continuously barefoot. "How are we going to sell baby shoes to Americans when their own President's son never wears a pair?" lamented one poor manufacturer. We were constantly lobbied by the millinery industry to force Mrs. Kennedy to wear more hats, and to force her to force her husband to wear hats. A rhinestone jewelry manufacturer wrote that his industry was in a terrible slump, and would Mrs. Kennedy please single-handedly pull them out of it? All she had to do was forget about diamonds and wear rhinestones instead. I felt the pressure of all this so much myself, I always wore a hat in public and long, gloppy rhinestone earrings with evening gowns, but I certainly could not oblige the infant shoe industry.

It was impossible to ignore the shouts of laughter from the Correspondence Pool across the hall from time to time. I would, of course, go over to investigate, and would inevitably be handed a letter addressed to Mrs. Kennedy from a child, or a letter addressed to Caroline or John from a child. There were some classics. Perusing this mail made one realize that there were thousands of little souls praying to God that the pony Macaroni was not suffering from the snowstorm that just passed through Washington; hoping that the dogs in the White House were not allowed to marry the cats in the White House; and asking Caroline if being the President's daughter gave her diplomatic immunity from beets and carrots. All the small fry drew pictures for the children, of their own pets, of their mommies and daddies, and of their saintly or beastly teachers. One child sent in a drawing: "This is my daddy," showing a child sticking a bleeding dagger into a grown man's back. In thanking that child for the drawing, I wanted to instruct the Correspondence Pool to throw in as a last sentence, "And I hope you ask your mommie to take you to a child psychiatrist." Of course, I didn't.

Mrs. Kennedy was written to by what seemed like every teen-aged girl and every young wife in America. They poured out their marital woes, their skin problems to her; asked her advice on makeup, baby care, toilet training, and wardrobe planning. Fortunately, we could answer each of these, "Mrs. Kennedy is not at liberty to comment on personal matters of this nature . . ." If a child wrote in professing an interest in Gov-

The author checking the tables in the State Dining Room before guests arrive

President and Mrs Kennedy at a State Dinner, standing in the State Dining Room with all the social aides

(*above*) The author signalling Mrs Kennedy in the State Dining Room while she talks with members of the Bolshoi Ballet.
(*left*) The author introducing dancers who had performed at a State Dinner to President and Mrs Kennedy

ernment as a career or asking a serious question, we always tried to answer with some small nugget that would inspire that child to keep on in such patriotic aspirations. What really heartened us were the numbers of mothers who wrote in to thank Mrs. Kennedy for her good grooming, which had greatly affected their daughters, or for her simplicity in dress, and for her "queenly posture" — which caused thousands of slumped-over, curved-spine teen-agers to stand up and start walking with a little grace.

The criticisms that poured in had to be ignored — except when it looked as though America was going into a mass revolt. Little John's long Beatle haircut was one of these. The time was several years pre-Beatle, and America was not ready for long hair as yet. Mrs. Kennedy ignored my pleas, so finally I sent over to the President a batch of extremely articulate letters. A week later, I noticed John was shorn of his Little Lord Fauntleroy haircut. It was a great way to endear myself to Mrs. Kennedy.

Some of the letters were "real hookers," and Hortense Burton had a bird-dog nose in spotting them. These would come to my desk immediately. I would ask for the advice of one of the Presidential Assistants in replying — and at times I would forward the letter to Bobby Kennedy's office or another Cabinet member's staff, to let them "take the rap," and get the onus of the reply off the White House's back. This was an important part of my job — to know when something needed asbestos-glove handling. We were confronted with many such problems — "Mothers Strike For Peace" was one hooker. When they stormed the gates of the White House, seven hundred strong, no one in my office was allowed to meet them and receive their petition to Mrs. Kennedy. They really let us have it after that. Nina Khrushchev had invited them in to tea, and they had been welcomed in the grand manner in Moscow by the Government. They never let us forget this action in their subsequent protest meetings and publicity campaigns. Drew Pearson, and much of the other press, criticized us for not receiving them.

I also got the Kennedy Administration involved in a juicy fight with the D.A.R. We had already incurred their wrath by refusing to give a reception for their annual spring congress in Washington. There were thousands of them, and we did not have the room for them, nor the time for such a party on our spring calendar. Their backs went up, and I received enough nasty letters to fill my own letter box for a lifetime. Then the UNICEF (United Nations International Children's Emergency Fund) began their annual Christmas card campaign, and the D.A.R. came out and urged that no one buy their Christmas cards (their only major fund-raising support for the year). The D.A.R. charged the sale of these non-religious cards was part of a communist plan to destroy all religious beliefs and customs.

My hair literally stood on end at this accusation. After all, this was taking food and milk from pathetic little children around the world. I called Kenny O'Donnell, who gave me an OK, and I ordered ten boxes of UNICEF Christmas cards from "A Child's World" collection for Mrs. Kennedy's personal use. This action was released to the press, the public reacted at once, and UNICEF sold out on all the designs we had chosen in two days. In fact, they had never sold so many Christmas cards before.

I stayed out of the President's way for several days. He had enough enemies without my bringing the wrath of the entire D.A.R. down upon his shoulders. This was one of the burdens with which he had to live — the actions of his staff affecting the course of events without his knowledge.

Office Address: 1600 Pennsylvania Avenue · 169

Our first affirmative story on the distaff side of the new administration concerned my old Tiffany friend, "vermeil." The beautiful collection of antique vermeil which Margaret Thompson Biddle had willed to the White House was put on display throughout the public rooms by Mrs. Kennedy. Thus, the big touring crowds going through the Mansion every morning could enjoy it, too. The candelabra, tureens, bowls and compotes were placed on tables, mantelpieces and hall consoles. Photographs of the exquisite pieces blossomed in the women's pages of the country's newspapers. The star performer was, of course, the tureen with the artichoke finial, which I had taken five years previously to Professor Dauterman of the Metropolitan Museum. He had discovered it to be one of the most important pieces of French silver extant — one of the state presents given by Louis XV to the Prussian Ambassador to take to Frederick the Great. I was delighted that the press office had to use my old Tiffany releases to explain what vermeil was, as well as the history of the pieces, all of which I had dug up during Mrs. Eisenhower's regime. Once again, we had the pronunciation problem. The White House Police, on their tours, who now pointed with pride to the lovely objects around the reception rooms, wanted instinctively to pronounce it "ver-meel."

Our first unfavorable story in the new administration raged around my own head, unfortunately. Pierre Salinger was questioned at one of his morning press briefings about the report that had just come out of London that the Kennedys had tried to steal the famous chef of the French Ambassador to London. Everyone chuckled, but the press scented a delicious stew in this boiling pot, and they immediately blew it up into front page headlines around the world. Bui Van Han, the fifty-year-old Vietnamese chef to Ambassador Chauvel in London, had taken it upon himself to announce to the world that the White House had tried to hire him away from the Chauvels, at a "large increase" in salary. And a certain Miss Letitia Baldrige had done it all, even to the point of a transatlantic call in the middle of the night, to wheedle him, in French, to come over to us.

Bui announced he had taken the day off to consider our tantalizing offer, but finally decided in favor of La Belle France. He announced he had even wired us he did not want to come. Ambassador and Madame Chauvel, in a fit of pique, backed him up, announced to reporters they were "surprised, even a little shocked." "It's nice to know," said Mme. Chauvel, "that Mr. Kennedy thinks so highly of our cook. He has been with us a long time and is very happy."

The President and Pierre hauled me in to give a full report of what really happened. I started at the beginning. Mrs. Auchincloss, Mrs. Kennedy's mother, was asked by her Vietnamese manicurist in December before the Inauguration if the new regime wouldn't like to have a fantastically talented chef, who was a good friend of hers. Mrs. Auchincloss, knowing that the food situation was going to be one of the first major problems to tackle on the female side, pressed for details. It seemed that Ambassador Chauvel was soon to retire, and Bui Van Han desperately wanted to come to the United States. Mrs. Kennedy thought that the timing was perfect and asked me to follow up. I asked our Embassy in London to check on the security aspects of this man and his moral character. I did not communicate with him at any time, because we were far too busy with other priorities after Inauguration Day.

Word then came back from Bui that he wanted our answer. What had happened to his chances for the job as White House Chef? I realized he had been dangling with false hopes for a couple of months, so I wrote him for the first time, a short letter in French, telling him I was sorry — but there was no interest. We were all set for the time being.

Whether it was loss of face or disappointment or whatever triggered his reaction, the chef and "L'Affaire Bui" became the darling of the journalists for several days. Newspapers had enormous fun with headlines such as "Cooknapping Threatens to Make Serious International Crisis," and "JFK Ends Up in International Soup."

Cartoons flowered in the press, showing tugs of war between the President and Président de Gaulle, each pulling the poor chef apart. Radio and TV commentators from abroad sermonized to their audiences, "Steal a man's wife? Maybe. But a man's chef? NEVER! That is a very dirty game."

My family thought the whole thing was very funny. I didn't. The press simply would not believe my denials, and the Kennedys continued to be made the butt of a big joke. As the smoke was just beginning to evaporate, I found myself seated at a table in the Mayflower Hotel, attending a dinner given by the National Press Women's Club in honor of the new members of Congress. Those particular magazines had been very sarcastic about the whole event, and I considered their stories heavily weighted in Bui Van Han's favor. At a certain moment, in the middle of the limp shrimp cocktail course, I felt the hot red blood surging in my cheeks, and I addressed all of them. "Do you, as American citizens, choose to believe the mutterings of a Vietnamese chef in England over my words, me, an American working for the President and First Lady?"

It must have sounded as though I were accusing them of tearing the flag out of Betsy Ross's lap and shredding and stamping on it.

They were slightly aghast at my outburst and subsequent sermon; then they all started to laugh at once. I burned even harder inside, and felt like upsetting the table on all of them. The shrimp cocktail was terrible anyway.

One of the *Time* staffers reached out and patted my hand.

"You've only been in this White House business a short time. You won't stay out of the hospital long if you take yourself this seriously. Now, no one else takes the chef war seriously. Stop blowing up the story and your own importance out of proportion. There just wasn't any other big news around at the time the story broke. You've got a lot to learn."

It was like cold water splashed on my hot face.

I tried to remember his words at many other moments in my White House career.

Our culinary problems were shortly solved when, through Ambassador Joseph Kennedy, we latched onto a French chef recommended by the Caravelle Restaurant in New York. I interviewed the robust gentleman for a couple of hours, then sent him up to meet Mrs. Kennedy. She approved of his selection, and before the month was out, René Verdon, with his starched white aprons, tall chef's hats, and gray and white checked cotton pants, had moved into our kitchen. He brought as an assistant — really as a pastry chef — a round-faced compatriot, Ferdinand Louvat, who could make baskets of spun sugar that looked as though the angels had been at work in the pantry.

René was the very model of a perfect French chef. He loved to eat, and he had great success with women. His accent was properly un-understandable. Dark-eyed and Gallic-tempered, he looked with apprehension at his staff of Filipino assistants and decided to try to make them learn French. They looked at him, and decided they'd stick to their dialect. What evolved was an international language of cuisine that was to be understood only by the crew themselves. I quite envied them their secret esperanto. During the first few weeks when René was settling in, I heard him mutter rather pathetically, "Ce n'est pas possible, ce n'est pas possible." But it always turned out to be *possible,* as he adjusted to the impossible routine of a single kitchen which serves small family gatherings, ladies' luncheons, children's parties, and State Dinners for 140 people, all on the same day.

++

Mrs. Kennedy was determined from the first to personalize the White House parties. Administrations had come and gone on Pennsylvania Avenue, but many old entertaining traditions had survived — through habit, and not through merit. The fact that guests attending former White House parties felt the atmosphere stiff and glacial was not to be criticized. I remember my own parents' descriptions of the dinners that had left them excited, happy, but nervous and ill-at-ease at the same time. It all seemed to go with the history of the house and the awesome function it fulfilled.

The Kennedys felt, however, that the addition of warmth to the whole entertaining concert did not exclude dignity and a sense of awe at being a guest in the President's home. There was no one more respectful of history and tradition than the President, but there was also no one more ready to change customs that had no historic value.

So we sallied forth without trepidation to amend certain traditions. In the former regimes, guests would arrive at an official party by the Southwest entrance and check their wraps. Then they would mount the long stairway from the ground floor to the first floor and go into the East Room in cold silence, escorted by the Social Aides. One former habitué of the White House described it as being "immersed in frigid marble all the way." The Marine Band was not permitted to strike up a note until the President and First Lady had come into the ballroom to start the receiving line and lead the guests in to dinner. As the guests strolled by, the red-coated musicians would sit silently in their folding chairs in the marble foyer of the first floor, looking like so many mournful bellhops on a coffee break.

No cocktails were served, either. One just stood in the East Room, tittering nervously with whomever one could reach. No drinking or smoking was allowed. Many of the guests, fully aware of this situation in advance, would be forced by nerves or habit to imbibe their alcoholic beverages in advance — and they often overdid it.

In the new administration, happy, peppy music by the Marine Band flooded the house the minute the guests began to arrive. The music was contagious. Everyone walked with a spring in his step, from footmen to dowagers. The handsome Social Aides, young military officers stationed around Washington who helped us with the large parties, would escort each lady into the East Room, followed by her escort, and then a footman would offer both alcoholic and non-alcoholic drinks on a tray to each guest. The half hour spent awaiting the Presidential party passed in relaxed informality, indeed conviviality. The Social Aides were trained to make sure all loners in the group found someone to talk to. They were ordered to heed the Social Secretary's nod, but there were many moments of agony written on their faces when one of the senior Presidential Military Aides would countermand one of my orders. My favorite young Marine captain came up to me one afternoon when a general had issued instructions counter to mine, and said, "But Miss Baldrige, think of the predicament. You're a girl — and hell, I mean, excuse me, Ma'am, the General is my commanding officer here."

A conversation with the First Lady fixed that situation and the poor Social Aides found themselves under Presidential orders to follow the Social Secretary's "war plan" for parties, not the

Military Aides'. (I was also to understand, of course, that my command did not affect military matters!)

At large White House parties, when the Kennedys were ready to descend the grand staircase from the private quarters, the footmen would gather up all the glasses in the East Room on trays again and the Marine Band would call the party to attention with a ruffle of drums, followed by the President's own song, "Hail to the Chief." President and Mrs. Kennedy would walk into the East Room with their honored guests, preceded by the military color guard, who then posted their flags behind the receiving line. This ceremony never failed to move all of us, no matter how many times the staff witnessed it. The martial music, the vivid Presidential flags carried with absolute precision, narrowly clearing the massive sparkling chandeliers, the sight of our handsome young leaders, walking poised and erect, together with their foreign guests, made us all feel terribly proud.

Mrs. Kennedy changed the look in the State Dining Room very quickly. The green walls gave way to two tones of antique white, which highlighted the magnificent carved moldings, and which contrasted beautifully with the bronze and golden chandelier wall sconces and gold upholstered chairs. All the floral table decorations were lowered. Before, they had been overpoweringly magnificent, too distracting, impossible to talk around or across. In their place came delicate small bouquets in vermeil containers, which Mrs. Paul Mellon's gardener taught our White House gardener how to arrange. Exquisitely simple, imitable by any housewife, they were reminiscent of the old, lovely Flemish flower still lifes.

The lighting in the dining room was changed — the overhead chandelier no longer blazed a harsh white light that put wrinkles on the ladies' skins. Instead there was candlelight everywhere, even on the side wall sconces, and the room glimmered with pastel colors and the occasional brilliant mosaics of light cast by jewels.

We had larger dinner parties — abandoning the one rather stodgy U-shaped table and utilizing instead round tables for eight or ten in both the State Dining Room and the Blue Room. The use of little round tables in an informal way was considered revolutionary, but it was frankly responsible for the success of dinner table conversations. The old guard was horrified — one of the more outspoken press ladies silenced her by saying, "Wait until you are invited yourself, my dear lady, then maybe you won't be so critical!"

Instead of the traditional white damask banquet cloths, we used pale yellow round tablecloths to the floor in the State Dining Room to match the gold and white color scheme, and pale blue linen cloths in the Blue Room. Even the ugly dark ballroom chairs saw their demise — graceful little gold wood chairs replaced them, with gold silk seat pads to match and blue seat pads for the Blue Room. A *House & Garden* editor and I figured out that if a young housewife were to follow Mrs. Kennedy's table setting theme at a State Dinner, she could emulate the entire theme at very low cost — by making her own lemon yellow cotton tablecloth and napkins; by placing daisies, yellow carnations and tiny kumquats in an inexpensive little golden container in the center; and by combining the simplest crystal with gold and white china. The place cards written in flowing script and topped with the Presidential seal in gold would be missing from her table setting, but she could always make gold and white place cards of her own — and write white menu cards for each place. Taste means making an extra effort; it means stressing simplicity, and using the eye. There are no dollar signs attached.

Everyone violently disliked using the traditional U-shaped table, but occasionally the Kennedys had to, particularly at State luncheons when the guest list did not exceed eighty. In the Eisenhower regime the President and First Lady sat side by side, and no guests sat opposite them. The Kennedys used both sides of the U, and sat in the middle opposite each other, so that each one of them could be flanked by two honored guests, instead of just one. Sandy Fox and I labored over these seating problems, and would occasionally become enmeshed in absolutely hopeless dilemmas. Then we would decide which person could take the offense most lightly. We would seat that person beneath his official rank, and I would go up to him before the meal began to explain that we had ranked him in a new special place, accompanying it with a rather snobbish aside, "It's part of White House protocol, you know."

The innovations on the social scene continued with a vengeance. Betty Beale, Washington's social scribe, paid the supreme compliment in the *Star*, while looking back over Jacqueline Kennedy's first year: "At *every* type of party, the arrangements have been varied and improved."

But we did not enchant everyone. At the first White Tie Reception for members of Congress and their wives, the receiving line was abandoned, at my urging. The Kennedys decided they'd try it, and they merely walked through all of the reception rooms, smiling and waving at everyone, pausing here and there to chat, and keeping up a promenade so that everyone there saw them several times during the evening. In former times, the Presidential couple had to stand in a receiving line through the whole list of 2,000 guests. Many guests never even got to the punch bowl, and most people spent most of the two hours in an endless snaking line, right out onto the driveway, like the worst of wedding reception crushes.

Carolyn Hagner Shaw, the doyenne of the Washington social register, "The Green Book," tut-tutted all over Washington at this informality. The Congressmen, however, were enchanted. Mrs. Clement Miller fainted in the crush, and when she came to, her husband said, "She's always pregnant, don't worry." Mrs. Miller added weakly that if she had been forced to stand in a receiving line for two and a half hours, she would have had the baby on the spot, instead of just fainting. I congratulated her on her historic selection of fainting spots.

The next year the President himself pulled a fast one on all of us. "The Congressional Reception will be black tie this year, Tish," he called to say. "But, Mr. President, we can't — I mean, it's a steadfast tradition, they won't like it. I mean, we're in trouble . . ." He did not let me finish. "Tish, I have this piece of news for you. The Congressional Reception this year will be black tie. Did you get that?"

"Yes, Mr. President, I certainly did get that one."

He went on, "I have enough proof from enough of my good friends on the Hill that there is no present I could give them they would appreciate more than that. They have to rent the monkey suits every time this party comes along. It's ridiculous."

Carolyn Hagner Shaw was aghast. She wrote a lengthy article reprimanding the Kennedy regime — "this is all going too far." She also decried the banishment of the receiving line once again.

I'm sure, however, when the smoke died down, the only ones who were really affected by the Kennedy informality were the white-tie-and-tails rental establishments.

On July 11 of the first summer of the Kennedy Administration, a State Dinner was offered the President of Pakistan, General Ayub Khan, that not only broke all tradition, but also the hard-working pencils of the press. It proved to be such a gigantic undertaking, one of the Military Aides remarked afterward that this party took the planning of a full-scale military engagement.

Mrs. Kennedy chose Mount Vernon as the site for the party because the Director of the historic shrine, C. Cecil Wall, had offered to cooperate with the White House on any program the First Lady might wish to initiate. If he had but known what this little project would entail, he would probably have pulled up the Veto flag — and not the Welcome flag — on the Mount Vernon lawns.

We began our first organizational steps in attempted secrecy, much like the famous bride who tries to keep her wedding dress design from leaking in advance to the press. Like all other such attempts at the White House, it didn't work. We made a clandestine rendezvous with Mr. Wall for a 2 P.M. meeting. Handsome Captain Tazewell Shepard, the President's Naval Aide, dashing General Godfrey McHugh, the Air Force Aide, Chief Usher J. B. West, Pam Turnure, my secretary Anne Lincoln and I sailed down the Potomac on the *Patrick J.* to test out the voyage. Mrs. Kennedy met us at Mount Vernon by car from Glen Ora. Director Wall and Mrs. Francis F. Beirne, the gracious Regent of the Mount Vernon Ladies Association, received us in the former's office, and off we started, to tour the site, posing as any ordinary group of tourists. Within two minutes, the press and cameramen were upon us, and we were forced to converse in whispers the rest of the afternoon. As a press lady would surge forward, ears straining to catch a crumb of news from the table, we would immediately begin talking to her about something of historic interest nearby. Luckily, the details gleaned for the next day's newspapers were sketchy at best.

The decision having been made to go ahead with the party, all I had to do was to draw up the battle plan, implement it, rehearse it, and pray every day in all seriousness that it would not rain. The *Farmer's Almanac* said we were in good shape. I figured God, as well as the *Farmer's Almanac*, should be on our side.

J. B. West and I took more practice runs down the Potomac — including a trip on a PT boat, which also would have to be utilized the night of the party, along with the three conventional Navy yachts pressed into service. One hundred fifty guests would have to be transported from the Naval Weapons Plant in downtown Washington to the Mount Vernon pier. I'm glad we tried out the PT boat, too. It was cold and coiffure-ruining. We would have to supply each lady guest on that boat with a sweater and a scarf. In fact, we would have to put the younger women on that craft — it was by far the most fun, anyway.

Our dress rehearsal two nights before the party was a disaster as far as the military leaders were concerned. They insisted we run it all through the next night as well. A contingent of Marines in dress uniform and at parade attention lined both sides of the winding road leading from the Mount Vernon dock up to the house. As we pretended to be the Presidential party being slowly driven up the narrow road in White House limousines, I heard a slight crunching sound. It turned out to be the sound of a car running over the Marines' boots. There was not a complaint or a sigh out of one of them. Upon my registering horror at the crime we had just perpetrated, their commandant reassured me that the Marines were not injured in the slightest. Besides, he said, his men were tough. In the interest of cracked bones and toes, as well as my own peace of mind, I had the Colonel withdraw the Marines on one side of the road and redeploy them elsewhere, thus giving the cars plenty of room to miss the men.

Office Address: 1600 Pennsylvania Avenue · 181

I practically set off my own fireworks with joy when the green wooden bandstand was finally completed on the opposite side of the lawns from the outdoor marquee over the dining area. The timing had been too close. The National Symphony Orchestra musicians, who were to perform the after-dinner concert there, came to me and cheerfully announced they couldn't play under those conditions — they knew no music was being projected into the air at all. Every sound was muffled in a cul-de-sac of giant trees overhead. Therefore, three hours before the guests were to arrive, J. B. West and I informed the carpenters the entire prestige of the United States of America rested squarely on their shoulders. They began furiously constructing an acoustical shell backdrop — a mere trifle at this point.

Chef René needed a tranquilizer by then, too. The menu had been kept simple — as René said, "This food will travel well." Such an expression usually refers to wines, but in this case it was appropriate to the food too. The menu finally agreed upon by Mrs. Kennedy was Avocado and Crabmeat Mimosa; Poulet Chasseur; Couronne de Riz Clamart; and Framboises à la Crème Chantilly with Petits Fours Secs. (It somehow sounded a lot fancier than stuffed avocado, chicken casserole with a rice ring, raspberries with cream and cookies.) Château Haut-Brion Blanc (1958) (from Douglas Dillon's vineyard in France) and Moït et Chandon Imperial Brut (1955) would be the wines. René's problem revolved around cooking and preparing all the food in the White House kitchens and then transporting it by "hot and cold trucks," as we dubbed the vehicles that rolled into the Mount Vernon driveway. There was no electricity at Mount Vernon, so the Army had to move in three generators to light the marquee, the concert area, and René's hot and cold transportable kitchens.

The existing toilet facilities were too far away from the party area, so we borrowed the portable Red Cross "Eight Holers," and I just kept hoping none of the ladies in their glamorous finery would be compelled to use them. Even my favorite French room spray did not help those functional interiors.

The marquee built near the house on one side of the lawn was a lovely one, green on top, buttercup yellow inside. The floor was constructed of wood covered by a green grass carpet, to keep guests' feet from becoming damp, as well as to protect the rich turf of the lawn from high heels. We asked my old New York cohort, Gene Moore, Tiffany's window designer, to decorate the 30′ x 50′ tent. He graciously donated his services, with boss Walter Hoving's concurrence. He turned the inside of the marquee into a wonderland of hanging green garlands, wound with yellow ribbons, flowers and illuminated hurricane lamps. The round tables for eight were covered with pale yellow circular linen cloths to the floor. The little black wrought iron garden chairs, with pale blue seat pads, were borrowed from Mrs. Paul Mellon. Her gardener arranged the yellow and blue table centerpieces — explosions of daisies, yellow carnations, blue delphinium and bachelor buttons. The china was white with gold rims — each table was a harmonious pastel still life of yellows and blues, with candles in the hurricane lamps adding a golden glow to the tables.

We had a tremendous job just communicating all of the details of this evening to our guests. The invitations ended up looking like a store's Christmas catalogue, with one insert after another. Each envelope contained:

1. The traditional gold seal embossed invitation to dinner
2. A card asking for immediate response to the Social Secretary
3. An insert card reading "Dinner and concert in honor of His Excellency, the President of Pakistan, to be held on

Office Address: 1600 Pennsylvania Avenue · 183

the lawn of Mount Vernon. Depart by boat at 6:10 P.M. from Pier No. 1, Naval Weapons Plant (see map). Guests will be returned at midnight to the same landing. In case of inclement weather, please call the White House operator at or after 4 P.M. on July 11. Short evening dress, black tie."

4. Map of Naval Weapons Plant and Pier No. 1
5. Admission card for car at Naval Weapons Plant
6. Admission card for guest to board vessel.

As the hour of the party drew near, I had just a few details to check. The Army had carefully sprayed the area that noon for bugs, but at 4 P.M. I began slapping my legs and ankles from mosquito bites. I put out an S.O.S. for the sprayers, and they returned just before the guests arrived. I heard angry mutterings in French from René that they were spraying his food, too, and everyone would die of poisoning. Luckily, it was only artistic exaggeration. The portable toilets were rolled into place, and they looked so hideous, we spent almost an hour having them wheeled back behind bushes and trees, to be carefully camouflaged. Someone reported poison ivy all over the new area we selected, but Mr. Wall assured me such a thing would not be permitted to thrive on the estate of the Father of our Country. The military buses rolled in like an *Anschluss* all afternoon, and everyone changed into his dress uniform or Colonial American Revolutionary troop costumes by hiding in Martha Washington's beautifully landscaped shrubbery. The Army rolled in a portable kitchen to feed all the military, and I found myself quietly ordering full colonels to remove every single Army vehicle in sight — one simply could not see the house for all the trucks and buses. My staff — on order — prayed every hour on the hour for clear weather. The Weather Bureau was making us no promises. The Almighty, however, heard us. If He had not, we would have been forced to hold a very undistinguished picnic indoors at the White House, without any after-dinner concert.

The evening went off without a hitch. The boats came slowly down the Potomac, laden with guests in a merry mood for an unusual outing.

A trio of musicians played on each craft, drinks and hors d'oeuvres were served, and as each boat drew alongside Mount Vernon in the middle of the Potomac, the engines stopped, the crew and guests stood at attention, and the "Star-Spangled Banner" was played over the boat's loudspeaker system. This is a naval tradition observed since President Washington's death.

As each boat docked, the passengers were greeted with a military salute from a group of Marines on the pier, then were transferred up to the house in a parade of White House cars, which by now did *not* run over the highly polished Marine boots lining one edge of the road. The men executed a rippling salute with their guns in magnificent precision as each car passed.

The guests were shown through George Washington's beautiful house and offered mint juleps in silver cups on the colonnaded veranda — the exact same hospitality offered his guests by George Washington.

Then, with all the guests assembled, President and Mrs. Kennedy led President Ayub Khan and his daughter out onto the plaza again, on the driveway side of the house. Fifty-four Marines lined the drive holding the flags of the states and territories of the United States. A military drill was held featuring the Army's Colonial Fife and Drum Corps, dressed in red coats, powdered wigs and tri-cornered hats of Revolutionary days. They executed the same drill their forefathers did in 1776. They are part of the 1st Battle Group, 3rd Infantry, and are affectionately known as "The President's Own" — as indeed they have been, since General George Washington's day.

At the end of their Colonial drill, they fired their muskets — with blanks, of course — exactly as we rehearsed it. President Ayub Khan had been forewarned of the musket charge, so that he and his bodyguards would not jump to uncomfortable conclusions. What we had *not* rehearsed was the position of the press corps, who were watching and filming — at least sixty strong — on the receiving end of the musket fire. The troops aimed and fired right at the press, much to the astonishment and discomfort of their human targets. A cameraman in the stunned group then raised his handkerchief aloft to wave in surrender. Both Chiefs of State and the guests broke out into uncontrolled laughter. I overheard a reporter from a New York paper tell President Kennedy later, "That's no way to solve your press problems, Mr. President. Total annihilation won't do it."

At eight-thirty, the military pageant was over, and the Kennedys led their guests in to dinner. The night sky was covered with a glittering veil of fireflies. Inside the marquee, candles turned the crystal goblets of wine into pools of red rubies, and the Air Force "Strolling Strings" serenaded their guests with harmonious bowing that sounded better than any gypsy group I had heard. Below us, on the river, the boats going slowly by made necklaces of light streaking the black water.

Presiding over her guests was a beautiful First Lady, radiantly sun-tanned, in a white organza and lace evening gown, sashed at the waist in chartreuse green silk. President Ayub Khan's daughter, dressed in a sumptuous silk sari, sat on President Kennedy's right.

After dinner, we walked over to our seats in the outdoor concert hall, the passageway lit by an aisle of burning citronella tapers. The seventy-four-piece National Symphony Orchestra played with gusto a program of American classics by Morton Gould, and George Gershwin, under the historic old trees. The shell did its part. I could tell the musicians were now acoustically happy.

It was a magic night, an unforgettable State Dinner. I kept wondering if all our work and planning, or if the sacred spell of this historic shrine had at least gotten through to the imperturbable Pakistani. Could they possibly realize how greatly they had been honored?

And I also knew that in my own entertaining in my little apartment, I would never again refer to anything as "a complicated party."

＋＋

Of course, as Clare Luce says, no good deed goes unpunished. Certain of the anti-administration Mount Vernon ladies were aghast that we had "defiled the sacred ground" with a dinner party. If it had been a Republican President who had first done it, I am sure they would have applauded his creative genius.

But the Congress began to howl after the lavish press reports finally hit home. The ones who screamed their criticisms loudest were, of course, the ones who would never have been invited. They complained about the extravagant costs of the party, "the lavish spending of the new administration to the detriment of the poor taxpayer's pocket . . ." An investigation was demanded, and we had to make a detailed report to the Government Accounting Office. Fortunately, our major expenses, such as the orchestra, the decorations, and the marquee were all donated — and the cost of the simple three-course meal did not even approach the normal cost of a White House State Dinner. This kind of petty bickering and sniping at everything imaginative we were attempting to do *always* roused our aggregate ire. Luckily, the walls of my office were thick, the furniture was sturdy and kickable, and the mutually sympathetic memos sent back and forth between "JBK" and "LB" after such a contretemps, were psychologically therapeutic for both of us.

Our next outdoor party of magnitude was the Military Reception, held in May of the next year on the Southwest Lawn of the White House. Over two thousand of the top brass and wives of the Defense Department and the four military services were invited. Once again the Colonial Fife and Drum Corps in Continental Army dress red uniforms stood ready to perform. Bands of the four military services were to play separately on a bandstand draped in red, white and blue bunting; and gay red and white striped tents dotted the lawns, shading the various serving areas for the food and punch. It was a beautiful day, and the Weather Bureau assured us we were in for another lovely May evening.

The party was from six to eight. The military being the military, most of the guests were parked and ready to enter the Southwest gate on foot by five-thirty.

At five-forty-five, with all the party food ready on the tables, I surveyed the scene with joyful serenity. In five minutes we would let the guests walk up the lawns, and the Kennedys would descend to receive them.

A sailor from the Naval Aide's office ran up to me, panting, and handed me a note. The message was concise, merely that a major squall was reported a few minutes away from us, with sixty-mile-an-hour winds.

I notified the Usher's office, called for all hands in the East Wing to come to our aid, and Charles the head butler rallied the staff in the pantry and kitchen. In two minutes, the scene on the lawn turned into a comedy worthy only of silent film slapstick days. We started carrying — on the double — trays, punch bowls, platters, glasses, ice tubs, everything that had required five hours to set up properly outdoors. The President heard the commotion in his office, walked out through the Rose Garden and asked what had happened. I gave him the news in hardly a cool, collected manner. "It's good practice for you, Tish," he said. He laughed, went inside his office and called those of his special assistants and secretaries who were still in their offices to come help us.

Well, we did it. In ten minutes flat, we moved a party for 2,200 people indoors, into a house with no flowers, no ashtrays set out, and no tablecloths on the dining room tables. The Mansion was not to have been entered during the party. It was not prepared for the onslaught. Chef René held his head and moaned as he saw his artistically decorated hors d'oeuvres sliding on their platters from a beautiful design into what looked like a bowlful of spaghetti. The butler groaned when he saw Presidential Assistant fingerprints all over the big silver punch bowls. The food was thrown down on any available tabletop. The scene looked more like a military rout than a planned party. The military bands were dismissed and sent disconsolately home in their buses, while the Continental Army drill took place in the rain, with a few onlookers pathetically pressed to the windowpanes from the floor above.

The luck of the Irish would not always hold out for us. Neither would the Social Secretary's suggestion of an ulcer, which grew more incipient by the minute.

⁎

The warm atmosphere of the White House in the Kennedy days can never be over-emphasized. By rights it should have been formal and austere. It was, after all, the home of the President and the office location of the center of power of our country.

Office Address: 1600 Pennsylvania Avenue · 189

There is one reason and one reason only for a relaxed, intimate quality to a house — and that is its occupants.

There were two occupants in particular, called Caroline and John, who made this house come alive in a beguiling fashion. No matter how stern or unbending a foreign official and his wife might be, as I was escorting them through the Mansion, I loved to watch their faces change from sternness to enthusiasm, from seriousness to laughter, at the sight of one roller skate peeking timidly out from under an historic damask drapery — or a tricycle dumped momentarily against the marble pedestal holding Abraham Lincoln's bronze bust. Every morning, like the merriest of tinkling chandeliers, the house resounded with the laughter of the children and their friends. No matter how hard pressed my staff was, it was always a welcome interruption when the nurse, Maud Shaw, would call apologetically to ask, "Is there by any chance an extra teddy bear around? Caroline has to go to a birthday party this afternoon, and we forgot about a present."

Looking out from our East Wing over the South Lawns, the vestiges of children's play dotted the landscape everywhere — swings, a jungle gym, a tree house and toys of all descriptions. We would stop our work to watch Caroline taking a ride on her pony, Macaroni, or Mrs. Kennedy driving the children around the snow in an old-fashioned horse-drawn sleigh. Caroline's bedroom was a confection of pink and white, with a canopied bed — exactly like the dream of a bed I had cherished all through my own childhood. Her dolls, toy animals, pet hamsters and favorite friend "Robin," the canary, held forth here. Pierre Salinger spent many exuberant and totally amusing press conferences coping with the escape of the hamsters, and with the constant activity of the Kennedy dog world. Pushinka — an offspring of the first Russian space dog — was sent by Premier

Khrushchev to the children, and no Hollywood celebrity, with the exception perhaps of Elizabeth Taylor, had her marital and maternal activities spread across the newspapers as much as that fluffy white dog. "Charlie," the terrier, however, always won the first love prize in Caroline's ever-growing dog family.

We watched John grow from a pink-cheeked picture baby (who seemed to spend most of his time being aired in his pram outside on the Truman balcony) into a handsome, curious little boy, who looked like a Bouvier but acted like a Kennedy. There were so many exciting things around for little boys in that house — flags, marching men, splendid uniforms, helicopters in the Naval Aide's office to play with and escape with, and real live helicopters sputtering down intermittently in front of the tree house on the South grounds, like giant, angry grasshoppers.

One could not say that helping organize the children's parties was "work." I remember Caroline's fourth birthday party best of all, probably because I remember so vividly President Kennedy's own enjoyment of the festivities when he came over to play with the children toward the end of the afternoon. We rented miniature round tables and chairs, and transformed the family dining room into a fairyland of colored balloons, party favors and big crepe paper "surprise pies" as the centerpiece of each table. Little John had his own first birthday cake that day, too, and succeeded in dunking his entire face right into the sea of gooey white frosting. Quite unsteady on his legs, he managed to keep time with his little arms to the cymbals and drums of those fascinating red-coated Marine bandsmen, looking like a junior Stokowski leading the entire ensemble. Mrs. Kennedy's talent for playing with children is immeasurable — I quite envied her "keeping her cool" through one childish crisis after another, making sure that there were no wallflowers, that tears were quickly forgotten, and that every child had a good time. The work of the East Wing was delightfully interrupted by the screams of excited children having a tricycle race in the lower hall. The movie theater ran continuous cartoons that I found far more tantalizing than did the children — there were too many other distractions for them. The pièce de résistance for the afternoon was, of course, the specially invited guest from the Baltimore Zoo, Suzie, who was appropriately enough also going on four years old. Suzie was a clinging monkey, perfect for children-hugging, but she still wore diapers. Shortly before the party began, her handler brought her right into my office, unannounced. This was the only familiar place he knew to come to in the building. I was talking at the time to a staid Ambassador from another country, preparing advance plans for the visit of his Chief of State to Washington. The fact that the Ambassador was seated by my desk on such a serious mission did not in the least deter Suzie's keeper, who without any conversation whatsoever, laid her down on my green sofa, tickled her tummy like a fond mother, and deftly changed her diaper. The Ambassador went on talking without changing his expression, but after the man and monkey had departed, he asked, "Miss Baldrige, is this — er — a normal part of your office routine?"

One day I happened to be in the West Wing to see Kenny O'Donnell, when I saw trooping out of the President's office a group of Indian men and women in full ceremonial dress. They were the leading representatives of the National Congress of American Indians and had just unburdened to the President their grievances about conditions on the reservations. I immediately thought of Caroline's play group holding forth on the top floor of the Mansion. The Indians were delighted at the prospect of meeting Mrs. Kennedy and the children. They pat-tered behind me in their soft beaded moccasins, alas, not, however, in single file. We all crowded with great difficulty into the private family elevator, tribal feather headdresses sticking in the eyes of the startled footman attempting to operate the elevator. We met Mrs. Kennedy in the upstairs hall, then tip-toed into the solarium where nursery school teacher Alice Grimes had her four-year-old charges entranced with her story-telling. Suddenly we were all in the room — chieftains resplendent in headdresses, beaded pouches, soft leather suits; squaws bedecked with beaded headbands, each decorated with a tall feather, and each clanking with silver jewelry and colored beads around their necks and wrists. They were a very splendid sight indeed. We waited for the childish cries of delight and awe that were certain to greet them. There were plenty of cries all right, but not of delight. Several children turned white from fear, others burst right out into sobs of terror.

Of course, these were little Eastern children who had never seen real Indians — only on television, where they are constantly killing, scalping and running around with tomahawks. They were not prepared for these Indians — in fact, they were just plain frightened, as though their little fort were undergoing a massacre siege.

The Indians were marvelous. This had obviously happened to them before. They did not move for a couple of minutes, just stood there and smiled. Gradually, young tears gave way to curiosity. Within five minutes, the children were climbing all over them, pulling at their headdresses, pigtails, and jewelry. Then a childish chant rose, "War dance, war dance!" The number one chief explained very apologetically, "But we have no drums — we can only do a war dance to our drums."

Caroline and her cousin Ivan Steers personally fixed that dilemma. They presented them with a couple of totally shattered toy drums. The Indians laughed, and then "Donald Deer Nose" began to tap the hypnotic beat on both little drums. The entire band went into the tribal dance, performing it in single file, then closing into a circle. We all watched in total fascination — and I kept wondering if Stonewall Jackson's portrait had fallen off the wall downstairs in surprise at these savage shenanigans going on right in the President's house!

I had wormed my way into a bit of popularity with the play group by operating the Sicilian puppet theater for the children from time to time. It had been presented to Caroline by Italian Ambassador Sergio Fenoaltea. However, every time I saw the play group after the Indian incident, they kept asking when there would be a return engagement. I finally decided I had better come up with something pretty glamorous again to hold their love — like a bunch of Eskimos in fur parkas, some hula dancers from Hawaii, or maybe even some belly dancers straight from Cairo.

✦✦

From the beginning of the administration, there had been an accent on youth in our activities. I sent a form letter to all Congressmen, Cabinet officials, and leading members of government in Washington, asking for the names and ages of their children living in the city. A front page story the next day was headlined, "Children May Invade White House." The Pentagon, fortunately, did not take alarm at such a threat to Presidential security.

We seemed to be entertaining young people constantly — while in former administrations about the only time hordes of children made the White House scene was during the traditional Easter Monday Egg-Roll on the South Grounds. We gave numerous parties for underprivileged or handicapped children of the District of Columbia, parties for the Embassy and Government officials' children, for staff children, foreign students, and talented young people. These were executed on a minimum financial budget and a maximum blood-sweat-and-tears budget.

We began a very successful series of outdoor concerts on the White House lawn, given for a young audience by young performers. The Kennedys wanted to encourage the performing arts in every way possible — and by giving young amateurs a chance to be heard in this famous location, students of music and dance all over the country were inspired to continue working hard in their own artistic fields.

The first of these was a concert given by the Greater Boston Youth Symphony and the Breckinridge Boys' Choir from Breckinridge, Texas. It was supposed to be a beautiful April spring day. Instead, it was 49°, with sharp, biting winds. We quickly changed the drink order for the guests from iced lemonade to hot chocolate. The White House officials' children acted as hosts and hostesses, helping seat the children, passing them programs, hot chocolate, and cookies. The weather didn't matter — the musicians and singers on the stage were so excited seeing Mrs. Kennedy and Caroline, Lynda Bird and Luci Johnson in the front row. They remained totally unaware of the frigid temperatures. The audience was inspired by President Kennedy's words of welcome and encouragement to follow the paths of music. He apologized for not being able to stay through the concert, but promised to leave the door of his office open, so he could hear everything. The children kept looking back, and sure enough, the French doors of the Presidential office were kept open throughout, as they were for every children's concert thereafter.

The following August, the Transylvania Music Camp performed an excellent symphonic program before a heartbreaking audience of crippled children, most of them on crutches or in wheel chairs. I had my friends in the White House Garage — all Army sergeants — blow up three hundred balloons for us in their "spare time." We decorated the ugly old Army tent (erected over the spectators' seating area) and the bandstand with balloons. In the intense afternoon heat, and helped along by the abrasive action of the tent's guide ropes rubbing against them, the balloons popped with terrifying volume all during the entire performance. The noise and ensuing giggles from the audience did not affect the young musicians' concentration, fortunately, and music eventually won out over the noise of what seemed like machine gun fire.

I learned a valuable lesson about using balloons on hot days, but I had also learned another lesson from the first concert that I put to good advantage this time. The amount of food required for young people is not to be understood by a French Chef. René had prepared a buffet luncheon for the Boston Youth Symphony musicians and the Breckinridge boy singers before our first concert in April. He made the same amount of food he would for adults. Consequently, we ran out of food halfway through the serving line, and the kitchen was sent scurrying for substitutes. This time, J. B. West and I decided the only solution was to double the actual number of guests to be fed when giving orders to René. It worked to perfection. We had too many plates, but the right amount of spaghetti with meat balls, sandwiches, salad, milk and chocolate frosted cake. When President Kennedy walked into the dining room in the middle of the lunch, an eleven-year-old boy stuck out his hand to shake the President's. The only trouble was that the boy had been devouring an exceptionally gooey piece of chocolate cake, and it looked as though half the frosting was still in his hand. This, of course, was transferred to the President's hand. He smiled mischievously, licked his palm in front of the delighted children, and said, "Mmmm. Good. I'll have to have a piece of that, too."

The Central Kentucky Youth Symphony Orchestra performed in a program with the exuberant young Berea College Country Folk Dancers before an audience of 1,200 cheering children. Dr. Joseph Maddy's famous Interlochen Music Camp National High School Symphony Orchestra and their ballet corps performed before an enchanted audience of handicapped and orphaned children. The Interlochen children played in their camp uniforms, looking like an army of scrubbed angels Fra Angelico would have loved to paint. When President Kennedy walked across the grass to greet them, they burst forth in a perfect rendition of "Hail to the Chief," the President's own song. This, of course, had to initiate another flood of tears on my part, but it was heartening to notice that even some of the Social Aides were flicking tears away from the corners of their eyes.

Organizing these concerts put a terrible load on my staff. It was one of the few times, however, when we could say that here was a good deed that did go unpunished. The only problems the young musicians had were the acquisition of funds for their transportation to Washington and the calming of their nerves at performance time. Inevitably, some large corporation in their home state picked up the tab for their chartered buses or train fare to Washington. We assumed the responsibility for the nerve-calming. Our Social Office, in the meantime, had to clear and print the musical program; make press arrangements; work with the carpenters and sound engineers on the acoustical shell and loudspeaker system; arrange with the appropriate District of Columbia office for the selection of the children for the audience and the bussing of them to the White House; have the portable toilets and first aid facilities set up; invite and brief junior hosts and hostesses; arrange for the housing and feeding of the visiting musicians and chaperones (usually around 100 people) most inexpensively at Army barracks just outside Washington; order escort buses for them and take them sightseeing around Washington, including a private tour of the National Gallery of Art; give them a special tour of the White House and a hot buffet lunch in the State Dining Room; and arrange for the photographing of all of them and the distribution of White House souvenirs to take back home.

With Tony Bliss of the New York Metropolitan Opera, we arranged for the young professionals of the Metropolitan Opera Studio to perform Mozart's delightful *Cosi Fan Tutte* in the East Room on our portable stage. The performance was cut to ninety minutes in length. We invited the children of the diplomatic corps, as well as children of Cabinet officers for a four o'clock performance. Afterward, the children and colorfully costumed cast mingled in the State Dining Room for sandwiches, cake, cookies, milk and fruit punch. The Johnson girls — as always — proved to be charming teen-aged hostesses. The Marine Band played in their usual front hallway spot — but their program ran mostly to such heavies as "Farmer in the Dell," "London Bridge" and "Jingle Bells." Caroline and a couple of her friends performed a sing-along on these songs, much to the delight of the foreign guests. One of them asked the President's daughter:

"What do *you* do around here?"

"I walk my daddy to the office every morning."

"Then what do you do?"

"I walk back again."

(Caroline had already learned how to handle herself in an interview.)

In the midst of the scintillating conversational parlays of the younger set, the President came in to join Mrs. Kennedy. He was well aware of what five or ten minutes out of his life meant to other people.

The Ambassadorial parents of these children, of course, were as delighted as their offspring over the Kennedy hospitality. Evidently detailed reports of every minute of the proceedings were filed back to their home Foreign Offices, as though the meeting concerned top-level political developments.

The President missed one of the more spectacular party moments. One of the exotically costumed members of the cast stood too close to a wall sconce containing burning candles. His towering oriental potentate turban was further graced by a waving feather plume. Said plume was soon ablaze, and very quickly the satin turban was too. A thorough dousing from a nearby milk pitcher quickly put out the flames, but the smell of burnt fabric and plume permeated the whole room. One of the other singers looked at him in envy. "I wish it had been me." I asked her why. "So I could say *I* caught on fire at the White House!" That spunky girl surely must have a whole book of press clippings by now.

Children were very much a part of our lives. Every day we seemed to be involved with them. It was that kind of a house. Upstairs in the family quarters, the first part of every official visitor's program was to meet the Kennedy children. One day I led thirty-four exquisite little porcelain oriental dolls, all looking alike and dressed alike, on a special tour of the house. They were the members of the Korean Orphans' Choir, presently touring America to raise funds for their institution. Their manners were perfection, and the sweet almond-shaped faces charmed everyone we passed. As good fortune would have it, we bumped into Caroline and her nursery school classmates, on their way out to the South Grounds to play. The Korean children needed no one to introduce them to the blue-eyed, ash-blond little girl. They recognized Caroline immediately. Without saying a word, they grouped themselves into two symmetrical rows, and burst into song right in the hallway. Caroline's play group stood quietly and respectfully, listening. When they finished off with "John Brown's Body" and "God Bless America," the footmen who were listening smiled over at me. They knew perfectly well by now that the Social Secretary would be grabbing for her handkerchief again. The nursery school tots applauded vigorously.

We sent the orphans away laden with presents and shy smiles. The boys had President Kennedy's PT boat tie clasps, the girls little link bracelets with the PT boat charm. Each child had an enormous lollipop in his hand — and, of course, the precious memory of having sung for Caroline Kennedy.

I think everyone in the country knew how much President Kennedy loved children. No matter how formal the occasion, the small fry were singled out from the group. One morning my two red-headed nieces, Alice and Jean Baldrige, were with me in the ground floor corridor when the buzzer rang that gave the signal the President was coming through. The Secret Service always cleared the corridor of extraneous people at this time, so I hid in Dr. Janet Travell's office with the girls, where they could peek through the door crack and glimpse their Chief of State striding by.

Out of the elevator he came, obviously late, his daughter Caroline by the hand, in animated conversation with Prime Minister Karamanlis of Greece, the Greek Ambassador and two of their aides. He suddenly stopped.

"I see some red hair through that door, Caroline, go see who that is." Caroline swung open the door, the President looked in and found the Baldridge girls. He also found me, looking very sheepish.

"Tish," he said gravely, "aren't you ashamed of hiding behind doors, a girl of your age? Who are these young ladies?"

I introduced them. He shook their hands and ceremoniously introduced them to Caroline. The President and the Greeks then waited while Caroline opened her new umbrella and explained the animal embroidered on the pocket of her raincoat. It was a serious fashion discussion, and finally, with a Presidential pat on Alice's and Jean's heads, the men moved off to the office.

"There," I said proudly, "you met him. What did you think of it?"

Alice responded exactly as her Auntie Tish would have done — a flood of tears. It runs in the family.

One of my most sentimental memories of the President concerns the day that favorite White House tour greeter Homer Gruenther and I took a large group of spastic children on a private tour of the mansion. Their wheel chairs could never have gotten through the masses of people during the regular visiting hours.

We showed them the house and, although none of them could talk, they took everything in. Their eyes glistened with excitement at every detail. The White House Police, Homer and I took turns explaining things. The President, we knew, would be upstairs having lunch, prior to rushing to the State Department Auditorium for a televised press conference. We led the wheel chair brigade into his Rose Garden, where we would not be disturbing him.

The garden was filled with fragrant blossoms and the sun shining on the vivid colors against a lush green carpet made it look like a gloriously trimmed, shiny Christmas tree.

A man suddenly strode out through a French door onto the terrace. It was the President. He was running late on his schedule, and had seen us from his office. He crossed the lawn to us, insisted on being introduced to each child, and either picked up each limp, paralyzed hand to shake it, or touched the child on the cheek. He had a different conversation with each child. What amazed Homer, the policemen and me was that he could comprehend what the spastic children said to him. Their speech had been so affected by their affliction, I could not understand one word. He knelt down by the side of a young boy and held a long conversation with him. Then he dashed back into his office, returned with an old PT boat skipper's hat he had used in the war, and plopped it down on the boy's head.

The child's face radiated a joy totally impossible to describe. I will never forget the look in his eyes.

"His father was in PT boats, too," the President said to me by way of explanation. "His father is dead."

He said good-bye to all the children and stepped into the waiting limousine. Pierre Salinger was pacing impatiently by the car — they were late for the press conference.

And the President had missed his lunch.

✦

To many stolid citizens of this country, "culture" is a smelly word. In fact, it even has a faint scent of communism to it. The Kennedys, in their enthusiastic embrace of the arts in the new administration, were to be accused of losing a lot of votes for the Democratic Party. "The intellectuals are a very small minority," said a florid politician at a fund-raising party one night, "and we intend to keep 'em that way. Your President thinks he can play footsie-wootsie with those long hairs, and come out of it ahead. He damned well can't!"

The picture of JFK playing footsie-wootsie with the long hairs has always amused me. He was the only man I know who could be completely conversant with another person's lingo, way of life and ambitions, and yet remain utterly aloof from that person's touch. He could be totally unfamiliar with an artistic concept, yet appreciate the merit of that concept with all the enthusiasm of an impressed critic.

I guess he simply understood the *quality* of *greatness*.

The Kennedy thrust into the arts was direct and powerful. The results were immediately felt. Dore Schary summed up the general feeling in saying, "When Kennedy endorses ballet, painting and the theater, the average man is bound to change his mind about such things as being effete."

Our dinner party lists began to sparkle with names like Stravinsky, Carl Sandburg, Aaron Copeland, Sir Ralph Richardson, Stokowski, Elia Kazan, Gian Carlo Menotti, Leonard Bernstein, Andrew Wyeth, Robert Frost. The after-dinner entertainments in the East Room became legendary.

It was all made possible because we put up a stage — and a stage was absolutely necessary. The trouble with suggesting such a thing, however, was that I fell heir to a responsibility no one else would undertake — stage-managing. J. B. West, who is the miracle maker of 1600 Pennsylvania Avenue, waved his magic wand, and with amazing speed we had our first portable, storable stage. A simple series of lofty panels, stretching across the end of the East Room and down two sides of the walls, covered in a rich red velours, were mounted on top of a wooden platform about 18 inches high. Once the stage was up, a rather glaring and unsolved problem presented itself — lighting. The big velvet panels seemed ponderous in the light of the East Room chandeliers. The human figure on stage was completely lost in the dark shadows.

I called Georgetown University, because I knew they had a good drama department. In no time at all, the head of that department committed his boys from the Mask and Bauble theatrical group to order the proper stage lights for us from a rental company for each performance, and to work the lights for us. They were delighted to have the experience. It was a pretty high-powered theater, after all.

The Georgetown boys saved our lives. Our first crew, who worked with us for a year and a half before they graduated, included a very attractive, efficient young man called Tony Hope. It wasn't until his last night working for us that I discovered he was Bob Hope's son. The Mask and Bauble boys gave me one of my most treasured mementoes when I left Washington — a sterling silver box, with their insignia, and an engraved message "To Tish" upon it.

I was to become embroiled in a dispute with one of the electrical labor unions the following year. One of the officials called me and told me in no uncertain terms we were breaking union rules by not having union labor working those stage lights. My protests were to no avail. I argued that these were private parties in the President's own living room with no one being paid any salaries, with no admission tickets sold, no money changing hands. He grew more obstinate, ruder and ruder. As for me, I lost my Irish temper with such effectiveness, Secretary of Labor Willard Wirtz had to personally intervene with the union to smooth things over. President Kennedy called me after that one, gave me a verbal dressing down for irritating the union, and then laughed. "You know, Frances Perkins made a darned good Secretary of Labor. That's one job I'll *never* give you, Tish."

Our first major tryout of the new stage came when the Kennedys approved my suggestion to invite the American Shakespeare Festival Theatre from Stratford, Connecticut. Our guest of honor at that State Dinner was His Excellency, The President of the Supreme Council for the Armed Forces of the Republic of Sudan, El Ferik Ibrahim Abboud, who happily had attended university in England and was a Shakespeare buff. I called Lawrence Langner, the Chairman of the American Shakespeare Theatre, with a timid plea of an invitation, knowing how terribly difficult and expensive it would be for his organization to move all its actors, costumes and props to Washington for a one-night stand on an improvised stage.

That was the last time I was ever timid about inviting people to perform at the White House. Before we had a chance to study our Elizabethan plays again, the Shakespeareans were upon us.

Their director, Jack Landau, submitted several suggestions for program content to the Kennedys. They chose the Prologue from *Henry V*, and scenes from *Macbeth, As You Like It, Troilus and Cressida* and *The Tempest*.

We put the stage troupe up overnight in a hotel, fed them during rehearsal and after the performance in the State Dining Room, and learned the hard way that our basement makeshift dressing rooms were inadequate. We were to learn new lessons with each type of performer — actors, singers, dancers and musicians. Gradually we would iron out the logistical support kinks. We would soon have enough full-length mirrors for costume checks, enough hangers and enough chairs for performers to flop in, enough ironing boards and irons, and makeup mirrors with good, strong light.

Somehow the Shakespearean performance miraculously jelled at the last minute. The rehearsal had been a shambles in the best theatrical tradition. The press was kept waiting and began beating on the doors to gain entrance. They wanted to get their stories, take their pictures and TV newsreels and be off — they had deadlines to make. During the actual performance, I fed cues to the actors and electricians, patted each one on the back as he finished a role, and prayed continuously that the actors would find the exit off stage. I also held a flashlight in that one small exit wing to help the actors find it. All during rehearsal they had exited dramatically off into the wings, running smack into the walls of the room, causing great mirth but little theatrical effect.

The actual performance was a smashing success, with applause swelling the walls of the East Room for a full fifteen minutes.

I cannot forget a haunting conversation that had taken place before the performance between the President and Director Jack Landau. They were alternately laughing and worrying about the propriety of the bloody scene from *Macbeth*. They wondered aloud if President Abboud was sensitive to assassinations and gore on the stage, coming as he did from the new, unsettled part of the world.

The horrible irony of that conversation is that President Abboud was not assassinated. John F. Kennedy was, however, two years later, and in 1967 in Boston, Jack Landau was found murdered in his room.

••

We varied the White House artists, just as we varied their programs to fit the visitors. Roberta Peters and Jerome Hines appropriately sang songs in Spanish for President and Señora de Prado of Peru; and the story of "Billy the Kid," as performed by Lucia Chase's great American Ballet Theatre, was printed *en français* in the program for our guest of honor, President Felix Houphouet-Boigny of the Ivory Coast. The African President was fascinated with the legend of the romantic outlaw, and I heard one of the dinner guests say, "It's too bad today's American crooks aren't as attractive as the last century's."

I learned another stage-managering lesson with this ballet — namely, that we had to put a linoleum flooring on our stage to permit the dancers to perform properly. We managed to get it laid about fifteen minutes before the ballet began. It would have been boring to have had everything settled long before.

When the Kennedys entertained Governor Luis Muñoz-Marín of Puerto Rico and his wife in November of 1961, history was made once again. Pablo Casals played his cello for the first time in the United States since he began his self-imposed exile. It was as though it were his American debut all over again, and the audience was weighted with music connoisseurs and great musicians. Casals played with Mieczyslaw Horszowski (piano) and Alexander Schneider (violin), and the three superb musicians together made music that the walls of the East Room had never before been privileged to hear. Guest Alice Longworth, Teddy Roosevelt's daughter and the dowager duchess of Washington, sat in the audience reminiscing. She must have felt intense nostalgia, because in 1904, she had been in this very room listening to a young man named Pablo Casals, who was playing solo for her father.

But I had a memory no one else in that room had, except for George Washington and Martha Washington, both hanging on the walls in gilt frames. The day before the dinner, Casals and his group rehearsed for three hours. Two Signal Corpsmen sat at their recording instruments, and I sat alone on one of the ballroom chairs, as the audience. It was three hours of exquisite, almost excruciating purity of sound. The discipline of the three men, their love of the notes, the mutual joy of each other's part in the overall composition was exciting, exhilarating, and calming all at once. The faces of the young sergeants were transfixed by the sound coming over their earphones. I had seen them many times before during taping sessions — their expressions placid, even vapid, with an occasional flicker of a facial muscle from chewing gum — but usually portraying sheer boredom. This afternoon, from 2 to 5 P.M., they were as I was, totally, emotionally involved in the fingers of three men.

When the Shah of Iran and his beautiful young Farah Diba came on a State Visit the following April, we chose a ballet of contemporary, youthful zip — Jerome Robbins' "Ballets: U.S.A."

The East Room resonated with the hot rhythm and dissonance of Robert Prince's music, as the lithe young dancers danced to "N. Y. Export, Op. Jazz." Their costumes were sweatshirts and black leotards, which totally confused Caroline at dress rehearsal. She kept asking when they would change into their costumes. The male dancers had many high lifts in the choreography, which Jerry Robbins had to keep changing — or the boys would have lifted the girls right into the low-hanging chandeliers. We were not equipped, insurance-wise, for skulls fractured from encounters with the White House light fixtures.

The Iranian State Visit made our favorite quipster internationally famous. He was Dave Powers, our Boston leprechaun, White House greeter and great friend of the President's. He simply met the monarch at the door and said, "You're my kind of Shah."

The visit of His Imperial Majesty Shahanshah and the Empress of Iran had caused a great deal of excitement also in the private quarters of the White House, as rumors reached Washington long before "The Arrival" that the elegant Farah was bringing a wardrobe of such splendor as had not been seen in the twentieth century. She was also bringing every available gem from the royal vaults, which means a lot of rocks in anyone's vernacular. She obviously hoped to fare well in comparison with the American President's wife, famous for her chic and her beauty. I heard the President teasing his wife about having to borrow the best from all the nation's leading jewelers in order to stack up to Iranian royalty. We all began teasing her — and it became quite a game guessing how JBK would dress for the State Dinner.

The Empress arrived that night, flashing a million golden lights like the enchanted queen that she was. Her full-skirted Dior ballgown was made of encrusted gold paillettes woven into sheer gold fabric. Other jewel-colored paillettes gleamed as she moved in the light. Crowning her elaborately upswept dark hair was an immense diamond tiara, studded with emeralds the size of robins' eggs. The same design of diamonds and emeralds made up her necklace and bracelet. She was tall and slim, and carried the weight of the gems with every bit of majesty required. A diagonal ribboned order was caught at one side by another explosion of gems.

Mrs. Kennedy played it just right. She wore a pale pink and white dress of shiny, stiff silk, very *jeune fille*. She wore a simple pair of diamond earrings and one diamond spray embedded in her brioche hairdo. The effect was one of total simplicity and understatement. She looked far younger than the Queen, who was actually several years Mrs. Kennedy's junior. She was a stark contrast — and as far as all of us were concerned, from ushers to footmen, from secret servicemen to Marine bandsmen, from State Protocol officers to pantry boys who peeked through the dining room doors, this round was definitely won by Jacqueline Kennedy.

I had heard about the fantastic success of an unknown young American, Grace Bumbry, at the Bayreuth Music Festival in Germany in 1961. She was invited by the Kennedys the following February to sing after their white tie dinner in honor of the Vice President, Speaker of the House, and Chief Justice. She arrived on a plane from Europe to sing for us, and flew back the next day for another concert over there. She sang in Italian, German, French and English — and sent lusty cheers pouring through the reception rooms because of her rich, velvety voice. She was stunning and poised; she was gifted; she was a Negro; and this was her American debut. History was made once again that night as critics wrote their Bravos with flourishes. It was also an inspiration for other unknown young Negro artists.

That spring saw two very exciting dinners — the Nobel Prize Winners Dinner on April 29, and the dinner for French Minister André Malraux on May 11.

LIFE, in its coverage of the dinner for all living recipients of the Nobel Prize in the Western Hemisphere, headlined it as "Cognoscenti Come to Call." The President remarked in his toast at dinner, "I think this is the most extraordinary collection of talent, of human knowledge, ever gathered at the White House, with the possible exception of when Thomas Jefferson dined alone." The guest list was simply the most distinguished names in science, government, and the arts. Two widows represented their husbands. Mary Hemingway graciously released unpublished portions of Ernest Hemingway's latest work, hitherto kept in a bank vault, to be read to the guests after dinner by Fredric March. Mrs. George Marshall almost burst into tears when I telephoned her in her southern retreat to invite her to the dinner. "But I never go anywhere anymore," she said. "My health won't permit it."

"You have to come to this," I replied. "The General would want you to. We'll send a plane for you. The Army and our country owe your husband's memory that much."

She came — and said her life had now been lived to its fullest. I watched the change of expressions on her face as Fredric March read parts of her husband's address, in which he had proposed "The Marshall Plan," which was one of the great moves of statesmanship in the history of the world. It had special meaning to me, too, as it had meant my first job.

The Air Force Strolling Strings, as usual, came into the dining room at dessert time that night, and then led the diners out of the room. They stationed themselves lining the scarlet carpet in the long hall, like a group of disciplined pipers, beckoning guests to their seats in the East Room. The party mood was too much for chemist Linus Pauling. The fact that he had spent that entire day picketing the White House for "Ban the Bomb" measures did not deter him in the least from enjoying our hospitality. He began to swing his wife over the polished marble floor in a lively waltz.

I sputtered and muttered, to no avail. No one was listening to me. They all started dancing in the hall, and for a while, it looked as though our terribly high-powered intellectual dinner had metamorphosed into a waltzathon. Fortunately, after thirty minutes, we were able to break it up.

I had taken Fredric March (he and his wife, Florence Eldridge, were dinner guests) upstairs to compose himself before his performance. His task was to read to the audience excerpts of the works of Nobel Prize winners Hemingway, Marshall and Sinclair Lewis. I showed him into the Lincoln Room and said, "I'll be back for you in twenty-five minutes. Here, lie down on the bed — there's a coverlet."

He motioned to the enormous, intricately carved rosewood bed, so typical of the fine Victorian houses of the time. "You mean, I'm to lie down on *that*, Lincoln's bed?"

"Of course. It's the best room in the house."

There was moisture in his eyes. He told me how he had

played before many distinguished audiences in his life, and in palaces before many kings and queens. But never had anything touched him so much or meant so much as this night to him. Resting in Lincoln's bed, he said, was the crowning part of it.

Our guest list for the André Malraux dinner was such a celebrity roster, I kept wishing I had brought an autograph book and swallowed enough pride to use it. There was one super-special name that shone like a klieg light in the midst of the Thornton Wilders, the Paddy Chayefskys, the Archibald Mac-Leishes, the Hervé Alphands, the George Balanchines and the like — that of Mr. and Mrs. Charles Lindberg. I have been raised on hero worship of the legend of that man. When I was advised he would automatically refuse our invitation — as he had every White House invitation since his historic flight — I decided to try the Bell telephone system. It was only by pulling strings at the FBI that I obtained his telephone number. Three telephone calls to him and his wife finally did it. Because of their love for France, but particularly as a compliment to the young Kennedys, they came. No two people I have ever met so totally lived up to and beyond their legend.

Pierre Salinger's good friend, violinist Isaac Stern, played in the East Room that night, accompanied by Leonard Rose on the cello and Eugene Istomin on the piano.

The President had always had a little problem with classical music. He had been caught in the East Room on several occasions clapping at the wrong time and not being sure when the concert was finally over. Even following a program, the number of different movements within one composition confused him — as it does many people. We therefore worked out a code system for the Stern concert. As the last piece was almost finished, I was to open the central door of the East Room from the outside about two inches — enough for him to glimpse the prominent Baldrige nose structure in the crack. It worked beautifully that night and for all future concerts. When the President noticed the door slightly ajar, that meant the last piece was in progress. He would await the applause; then, clapping heartily, he would take Mrs. Kennedy by the arm, and escort the honored guests to the stage, to congratulate the musicians. Both Kennedys thought I was brilliantly sophisticated in music to be able to do this. What they did not know was that I knew less than they did about the serious music. I simply made one of the Social Aides stay by me. He happened to be an accomplished musician who was familiar with all major classical compositions.

The arrival of Grand Duchess Charlotte of Luxembourg and her son, Prince Jean, hereditary Grand Duke, occasioned an evening of utter charm and off-beat entertainment. The late Basil Rathbone and "The Consort Players" put on an all-Elizabethan evening, reading poetry, playing the instruments and singing the songs of the times. At Mrs. Kennedy's request, Mr. Rathbone quoted by heart one of the President's favorite passages — Shakespeare's "St. Crispin Day" speech, spoken on the eve of the Battle of Agincourt by Henry V. Our houseguests that evening were a man to whom John F. Kennedy felt tremendous political gratitude, Mayor Richard J. Daley of Chicago, and his wife. I could not understand why a Chicago politician could wield so much power and influence. When I moved to Chicago, the doubt no longer remained.

There were many memories evoked when Angie Duke's staff in the State Office of Protocol and my staff started preparations for young King Hassan II of Morocco's State Dinner on March 27, 1963. When I had last seen the monarch, about five years previously, he had been an undistinguished-looking young man in Moroccan dress, padding wordlessly and meekly along in the court retinue of his father, the late King Mohammed V. The occasion was the monarch's famous visit to Tiffany's to buy vermeil. I wondered if Hassan was using his father's purchases in his palace today.

The Kennedys decided the King would want something light and youthful — so for after-dinner entertainment, we invited Sally Ann Howes and the New York City Center cast of *Brigadoon* to the White House. Lyricist Alan Jay Lerner, a good friend of the Kennedys, came along to supervise, as did Sally Ann's then husband, producer Dick Adler. Choreographer Agnes de Mille put her dancers through a grueling rehearsal on our limited stage, and the result was a polished, zestful performance of excerpts from the musical fairy tale. The story of *Brigadoon* was related in French to King Hassan before the show began.

Caroline had attended the dress rehearsal, sitting breathlessly the entire time, mesmerized by the music, the Scottish costumes, and the dancing — particularly the sword dance, done by the men in kilts. One of the girls, Gemez de Luppe, told me during the coffee break she was pregnant. "Just think, I'll be able to tell my daughter-to-be next September that before she was born, she danced in the White House!"

The President stopped by the rehearsal, as he often did, and expressed concern that we were using taped music, played on a recorder, and not the Marine Band. I explained that because of space limitations and an overflow of guests, we could not station the Marines in the center hall, as usual. We simply had to use the tape.

"But what if the tape breaks?" he asked with a worried frown.

I could feel the imperiousness and triumph in my own voice. Of course, I had a brilliant answer ready for him.

"It's easy, Mr. President. We're prepared for everything. Look, don't you see two recorders over there?"

He nodded in assent.

"Well, if the tape should break on one machine — highly unlikely — the sound is simply turned up on the other one, which is playing simultaneously."

"Smart girl," he smiled, and walked away, with yet another small problem removed from his consciousness.

That night a rotating trooper light was installed by the Georgetown boys at the back of the room to give a very strong center spotlight. They had not used it at rehearsal. Toward the end of the first half of *Brigadoon*, they turned it on. Voilà — the electrical circuits could not take it. Every fuse in our part of the mansion blew, plunging the East Room into total darkness. No lights, no music, no nothing. The Secret Servicemen sprang to all exits, guns drawn, fearing the worst.

The audience was shocked into silence, but I heard the President from the first row, saying in embarrassment, "Your Majesty, it's part of the show, you know."

It was the longest minute and a half I ever spent in my life. I half prayed in English, half swore in Italian, for those fuses to be fixed. Then the lights went on again, and the tape began to revolve. The dancers on stage had frozen in their stances, without a word, when the electricity failed. They began again exactly in step; they had not missed one beat. It was an incredible tribute to the dancers and to Agnes de Mille's training. It was also a tribute to the sanity of the Social Office that we all lived through it.

After each of these State Dinners, I would receive a memo from Mrs. Kennedy, brought over the next morning on a silver tray by one of the footmen, giving her thoughts on the party, and suggestions for improvement. She was a perfectionist of a hostess — who knew what was moving well or slowly at every step of the way. She would include a quip each time about annoying circumstances over which we had no control. It always made us laugh — and feel better. She, fortunately, had a fatalistic acceptance of errors, and *no* party, big or small, formal or informal, well-planned or last minute, is without errors.

Whenever there was a tribute to the Social Office in the press, it was always a delicious treat. The *New York Times* in a Sunday magazine article on the Kennedy Administration stated:

> Miss Baldrige is perhaps the most indispensable member of Mrs. Kennedy's cultural cabinet. She is in touch with the key people in the theater world and in her job of sifting numerous offers and suggestions of groups clamoring to perform at The White House, she has the help of a network that seems almost as comprehensive as the C.I.A.

The White House parties not involved with State Visits were always simpler to run; this did not, however, put them in the category of a last-minute simple buffet supper. Protocol, military fanfare and the prestigious furbelows that accompany the President and First Lady are as important to the mystique of the White House as the food, service, table decorations and illustrious guests.

One party that will always stand out in my mind centered upon what was and always will be a matter of great emotion, — our heroes. After eight years of living abroad and some fifty-eight trips to foreign countries, there is nothing that makes "God Bless America" course faster through my veins than a glimpse of a real live war hero. To have two hours worth of 240 living war heroes at once was enough to make me red-eyed and puffy-faced for an entire day. The occasion was the Military Reception honoring all living recipients of the Congressional Medal of Honor, held on the South Grounds on May 2, 1963. The logistics of getting all the medal recipients to Washington, with their wives, was a major headache for the Military Aides.

P

Once they were bussed into the White House grounds, it was my headache. I sent the following memo over to the President, which Evelyn Lincoln, his secretary, sent back with a simple "This is O.K.":

SCENARIO ON MILITARY RECEPTION
SOUTH LAWN, THE WHITE HOUSE — MAY 2, 1963

Guests arrive via East Gate — proceed to South Lawn.
  Punch served from 5:45 on.
  Marine Band plays from 5:45 on.
Congressional Medal of Honor winners are transported in buses from International Inn through Southwest Gate. They enter President's Rose Garden by 5:55.
  Color Guard, commanded by Capt. MacLendon Morris, consisting of seven service flags, moves into position on steps of Rose Garden by 5:55.
VIP's are ushered to terrace outside President's office.
President comes out of office flanked by Presidential Aides.
  Marine Band plays ruffles and flourishes, very short "Hail to the Chief" as President moves into position on the steps.
President talks for a few minutes, then steps down for receiving line to quickly move through. (Photographer to get record shot of each handshake.) Medal of Honor winners move right from receiving line out onto South Lawn to join other guests.
At approximately 6:40, President should be able to move into formation behind color guard on side path off his office terrace. Other VIP's will form behind him or beside him.
On ruffles and flourishes and "Hail to the Chief," the President will follow color guard up driveway to South Door. Stop in front of awning while Color Guard posts its positions flanking the awning posts.
"Star Spangled Banner" played (short version). President and VIP's remain at attention in place, and through the next part of the program: The Drum and Fife Corps.
When national anthem finished, the Drum and Fife Corps in Colonial uniforms move up from South part of lawn. Social Aides move

Office Address: 1600 Pennsylvania Avenue · 217

guests back in the center, to form wide aisle. The soldiers perform in exact center of this aisle. They move off out of sight within 9 minutes.

Marine Band strikes up again, and President and VIP's now move onto South Lawn to greet guests.

(The curving driveway will be kept clear of people and vehicles at all times)

Fifteen minutes later (it is now approximately 7:05 P.M.), the Air Force Bagpipers band appears over the grassy knoll on the East part of the lawn. They march up on a slant toward the South Door, to the driveway. They then follow the curve of the driveway down and out to the Southwest Gate. Total time of bagpipes: 9 minutes.

Marine Band commences again.

When President leaves, the colors leave their post.

Regardless of their ages, the men wearing the medals attached to the blue ribbons around their necks, seemed to stand taller and to look in better shape than any group of men I had ever witnessed. Ninety-one-year-old Major General Charles E. Kilbourne sat in a wheel chair and told me about his experiences in the Philippines; and eighty-nine-year-old Brigadier General Charles D. Roberts reminisced with clarity about the Spanish American War. There were Korean and Viet Nam War winners, but the largest groups were the World War II and then the World War I winners. It was a perfect spring day, and the red and white striped marquees that dotted the green lawns sparkled crisply in the late afternoon sun. The President made a touching speech to the men and their wives in the Rose Garden, and all of the top military brass and the Cabinet were there to greet the heroes. The bands played, reunions were held all over the lawn, and my tears weren't the only ones shed on this auspicious day. The flying aces all still looked like Steve Canyon from the comic strip, in spite of their age. I wish I could have imported carloads of draft card burners into the party to have one look at what a real American man looks like.

※

To the average newspaper reader or television newscast watcher, a State Visit to Washington is full of stirring band music, waving flags, twenty-one-gun salutes, and effortless entertaining. It is all very glamorous and uncomplicated, if one goes by press reports. There are cozy trips to Williamsburg or Mount Vernon to steep the guests in American history, two days of "the usuals" in New York City, and for the lady, a tour of Washington's National Gallery and an inevitable trip to a children's hospital or orphanage.

Behind every State Visit are days and days of agonized planning between the State Department, the Washington Embassy of that country, and the White House. All of the armed services, too, are deeply involved, as they perform military salutes, dress parades and escorts every day of the visit. State's Office of Protocol is responsible for the overall logistics of the entire foreign party, and by the time the escort officers have returned to Washington and kissed their foreign guests good-bye — with whom they have lived for two weeks and escorted to perhaps five American cities — a million premature gray hairs have grown on official heads, several hundred tranquilizers have been consumed, and hundreds of untellable stories that Drew Pearson would love to get his hands on have been filed away in official minds.

I always enjoyed working with Angie Duke, his wife Robin, and his Protocol staff from State. The Dukes made a fabulous team. Together we had a lot of unauthorized laughs and tried to keep cool — because the most important part of the entire schedule for the visiting couple is that involving the Kennedys. The First Lady's participation was every bit as important as her husband's, and Mrs. Kennedy was forced to give her all, in spite of her fragile health in those days. Split-second timing was our biggest headache. The visiting couple would be ready to leave Blair House and cross the street in a limousine for the State Dinner, while Mrs. Kennedy's hair was still being worked upon — unspeakable flap in the Ushers' Office as we tried on the through telephone line to Blair House to stall off their departure. The President would have an emergency call in the Oval Room, just as everyone was ready to descend the grand staircase (for the ceremonial entrance, the ruffles and flourishes and "Hail to the Chief"). Everything would be in readiness, the guests hushed and excited in the East Room, the Marine Band silent and waiting for the dramatic signal, and nothing, absolutely nothing would happen. We had to wait for the President to get off the telephone.

The Social Secretary is in charge of the logistics of the evening and the smooth functioning of the Social Aides (who act as escorts for the woman guests and help with the receiving line and general movements of the guests to and from the various rooms). But she also has to brief her bosses on the ritual of the evening, which differs with each party. The President was always impatient and chafed under ceremonial protocol. At the beginning of the administration, he would charge off by himself, eager to get the action going, and find the flag-bearers, his wife, honored guests and Military Aides far behind. At his first large official stag luncheon, he got off the elevator on the first floor with his guest of honor and ignored my motions to turn to the left. He charged straight ahead with his guest by the arm, opened a door, and startled eight footmen, the butler and the chef, all working in the pantry on the drink trays and hors d'oeuvres platters. His recovery was beautiful.

"And this, Mr. President," he said lightly to his guest, "is one of the historic rooms of the Mansion, too. Now I'll show you some others."

After that incident, he promised to follow my signals, and did. I was always trying to get him into the right spot, the right line at the right time. Mrs. Kennedy and the guests would follow him. One day, when I passed him in the ground floor corridor, he introduced me to his visitor as "Miss Push and Pull" and called me that often ever after.

I sent a memo to the Kennedys before every dinner as a last-minute briefing. A typical one is the following:

April 28, 1962

MEMO FOR THE PRESIDENT AND MRS. KENNEDY
Drill for Nobel Prize Dinner April 29, 1962 8 P.M. Black Tie

1. At 7:45 P.M. the four 1961 Nobel winners and wives will go to the Oval Room for drinks with you. Plus the Johnsons and the Norwegian Ambassador, Paul Koht and wife. Plus the Swedish Amb's wife, Mme. Jarring and her escort, the Swedish Counselor Lewenhaupt. (Swedish Amb is in Seattle)

2. At the proper moment, the Color Guard will fetch you (when most of the guests are in the East Room and the receiving line is ready to go). Photograph taken at bottom of stairs. Honors as usual on red carpet, facing the East Room. Only *the two* of you will receive guests — since any more in line will slow things up interminably.

3. The Marine Band will play before and during dinner. The Strolling Strings will play in far end of corridor when you are saying goodnight to your guests.

4. The microphone will be brought to the President by Charles for his toast — so that the Blue Room can hear it on loudspeakers.

5. Coffee and liqueurs have to be served at table.

6. When President arises, everyone comes into the carpeted part of the hall, the Green or Red rooms. Champagne will be passed on trays in these areas — and noses can be powdered now.

Office Address: 1600 Pennsylvania Avenue · 221

The men Nobel winners (49 of them), who have been tipped off beforehand on this procedure, will join the President immediately upon rising from table in the front uncarpeted part of the hall, where we will quickly line them up for a group photograph. Then they can grab a quick glass of champagne themselves.

7. When everyone seems to be back from the powder rooms, we will get them into the East Room for Fredric March's reading.

8. We hope you both will pose with Mr. March at the end of his reading for our White House photogs and the one pooler. We haven't gotten very successful "congratulations" shots lately — mostly your backs.

9. Mr. President, we are giving you Mrs. George Marshall, Mrs. Hemingway as your dinner partners, plus some Nobel prize types. Mrs. Kennedy gets Norwegian Amb., Fredric March, Col. Glenn.

Another important part of the State Visit, whether it be the foreign guests coming to Washington, or the Kennedys going to a foreign country, is the exchange of gifts. In previous administrations, a traditional Steuben glass bowl or a sterling Paul Revere bowl was the usual item. The Eisenhowers threw tradition aside when they gave Princess Elizabeth and Prince Philip Edward Marshall Boehm's lifelike sculpture of "The Polo Player" in ceramic bisque. It was particularly appropriate, because Prince Philip was such an aficionado of the sport, and it could have been his own portrait on the horse.

Mrs. Kennedy spent a great deal of time discussing the State Gifts with her husband. Together, they came up with some of the most unusual items imaginable — historic letters involving a famous American with the country of the foreign guests; an Irish flag for Premier Sean Lemass of Ireland (it had been carried by an Irish Civil War Brigade in the Civil War in a famous battle); historic etchings and paintings that were appropriate in subject to the foreign country. We gave my old alma mater, Tiffany's, back-breaking tasks for their engraving department — during the Kennedys' visit to France, for example, they brought the Mayor of Paris a large vermeil box, with the map of Paris engraved upon it, as well as the original plan of L'Enfant, the famous French city planner, for Washington, D. C. All of the silver and vermeil items for Ireland were engraved in Gaelic, which the Tiffany engravers announced took them exactly three times as long to execute. For the Holy Father, a magnificent red velvet-lined letter box was made of vermeil, with the Pontifical and Presidential seals engraved on the lid. The ladies would receive vermeil dressing table sets, engraved, or a vermeil rose in a vase. After a trip to the Smithsonian, Mrs. Kennedy had an inspired idea involving paper weights. New York jeweler David Webb executed a series of them, using American minerals and stones, each held in a design of gold. For example, Grand Duchess Charlotte received a New Mexican azurite and malachite piece, wrapped in 18-kt.-gold blades of grass, and studded with tiny gold flowers, which had centers of turquoises. President and Señora de Betancourt took back to Venezuela with them a Montana green copper ore piece, tied with 18-kt.-gold rope, and King Hassan II of Morocco received a beautiful hunk of citrine quartz, set in gold.

Every member of the visitors' family received a memento, whether it was a teddy bear for the grandchild, or a silver engraved compact for the daughter left at home. Autographed photographs of the Kennedys were distributed en masse on our trips abroad, as well as the President's familiar PT boat tie clips or pins for the ladies. The American Ambassador and his wife, every motorcycle escort policeman, member of the foreign security detail, the Mayor and ranking officials of every town visited, the butler, footmen, maids and gardeners of every house where the Kennedys resided, were given some memento. The President would sometimes present his books, autographed;

Mrs. Kennedy would carry deluxe editions of the White House guidebooks and the National Gallery of Art collections to autograph and give away. The compilation of these gifts and mementoes, the gift-wrapping of them, and the eventual distribution of them through proper channels, fell on the shoulders of my staff. The President's office coped with the PT boat clasps and his photographs. We coped with everything else, and if I became an expert on anything in my White House days, it was the system of tipping the household staff in twelve foreign countries.

※

There is probably no job in the world that has more infinite variety to its routine than that of Social Secretary to the White House.

When my family would call and ask what I had done that particular day, often my mother would interrupt me with, "Don't go on. I'm too tired thinking about it." I never thought about it myself. There was no time.

I would try to begin each morning at eight forty-five with urgent dictation to Barbara Keehn or Betty Hogue. A few minutes would pass, and then began the inevitable interruptions. No task was ever completed in one session. I would have to dash into a waiting White House car to go to the Mayflower Hotel to represent Mrs. Kennedy at the Congressional Wives' Prayer Breakfast, writing in the back seat of the car. There were always little chores to work in like drafting a statement to be published under Mrs. Kennedy's name on the importance of the U. S. Food for Peace Program. Back to the White House to greet the Heart Fund Twins, beguiling little girls dressed in white organdy dresses trimmed with red hearts. The press records Mrs. Kennedy posing with them and giving them little gold bracelets with gold heart charms as mementoes of their White House visit. My office had ordered these bracelets so long ago, we had lost them, and the ceremony was rather reminiscent of the best man under pressure to find the wedding ring. Setting up this simple meeting between the Heart Fund people in New York and Mrs. Kennedy had cost about eight hours worth of ground work for my staff. After it was over I whisked off through the house to take on a private tour the gracious and interested ballerina Margo Fonteyn, who was accompanied by her bored, petulant co-star, Nureyev. We finally left him sitting in one of the reception rooms and went on by ourselves. Dame Margo pretended not to notice my soft aside, "Perhaps he would feel more impressed with Leningrad Palace."

Then out to the North Portico to address a large group of "American Women in Radio and Television" to carry them Mrs. Kennedy's warmest personal greetings. I enjoyed this. Many of them were old friends from all over the country, and there was truth to my comments that we appreciated — and needed — their support.

An informal lunchtime huddle with Angie Duke concerned the upcoming visit of Indian President Radhakrishnan. Then a seance on the South Grounds with J. B. West on the placement of the stage for the Opera Society of Washington's performance of *The Magic Flute* for the Indian President. Then a dash back into the office to receive the "Candy Queen" and the representatives of the National Confectioners Association. This was a welcome annual visit, accompanied by boxes of goodies for the Kennedy children and for my staff. A telephone call from Ambassador Duke's office at State brought on the big laughs again as they informed us that the *Magic Flute* costumes of the Washington Opera Society would simply have to go — they

Office Address: 1600 Pennsylvania Avenue • 225

were caricatures of Indian dress, including the Sikh turbans, and would offend Radhakrishnan.

I returned an urgent call from Pierre Salinger, and then regretted having done so. Would I please leave in one hour for Philadelphia to pinch-hit for him before the American Symphony League Convention banquet? He had to rush to New York for an emergency television appearance. "And what is the subject of your talk, Pierre? It might help for me to know that."

"The Kennedys' assistance to our national cultural effort," he replied. "Easy, Tish. I'll send my speech over to you and you can read it." If only I could have seen those diabolical eyes on the other end of the telephone, as he sat puffing his big fat cigar. Of course, there was no speech, but he was not going to let me know that little piece of information until I was on my way to the station.

Pierre left for National Airport, and I for Philadelphia, with a yellow legal pad, a small bag and an unpressed evening dress in a plastic cover. I had all of one short train ride to compose an entire speech of thirty minutes' duration, to be delivered before several hundred sophisticated people.

If one were not numb so much of the time working under that kind of pressure, one would not survive such trauma. Fortunately, a kind of euphoria sets in — not the drug-induced kind, nor the starvation-induced kind of the Far Eastern monks. Ours was simply a White House-Mania.

The benefits of this difficult job were as widespread as the pressures. There is a joy and a privilege to such duties as greeting Mrs. Truman and Mrs. Eisenhower when they came back for visits, or taking Anna Roosevelt Halsted and family through the House on a sentimental tour. There is the pride of relationship that came over all of us as we sat in the V.I.P. Gallery watching our President give his State of the Union Message before the joint session of the Congress of the United States. There is an overwhelming sense of history in helping organize the ceremony, transmitted to Europe via Telstar for the first time, when Sir Winston Churchill was made an Honorary Citizen of the United States. It is also permissible to be very wet-eyed in the Rose Garden as President Kennedy jokes with and pins a medal on Astronaut John Glenn with a few words of congratulations. There is the hidden amusement of watching the Maypole dance of Connecticut politics as Mrs. Kennedy christens the S. S. *Lafayette* submarine in Groton, Connecticut. And there are the frivolous emoluments, too, which could never be discounted. How would I have been escorted by Cary Grant for a long, glamorous evening in New York, if I had not been Social Secretary, or how would I have been invited on fourteen private yachting trips in one year? Unfortunately, one's position in the White House means accepting Cary Grant, but regretting the fourteen boating invitations. It's nice to know one *could* have been there — with the stellar jet sets of the Mediterranean and the Aegean.

Another plus was getting to know "the public." Nothing surprises, shocks or amazes me anymore. I rather miss some of my contacts with them now — like the long distance call from a very important Garden Club President with a very distinguished name. "Miss Baldrige," she said, "I *must* know what the flowers were for the centerpiece for yesterday's State Luncheon for Princess Beatrix of Holland. It is imperative that I know at once."

"Well, now let's see," I replied, rummaging through my "BEATRIX LUNCH" file, which was still sitting on the corner of my desk. She was obviously desperate for this piece of information. I could not withhold it as being important to national security. "Here it is. There were yellow and white marguerite daisies, white gypsophila, and lilies of the valley."

"Gorgeous," she sighed.
"And mixed freesia, yellow and pink tulips . . ."
"Unbelievable," she gasped.
"And blue bachelor buttons . . ."
"I can't bear it," she said.

I was pinching my wrist to keep the laughter from openly breaking forth.

"And leucocrinum. That's all."

"Oh, Miss Baldrige, I can't bear it. How utterly, utterly lovely!"

And with that, Mrs. America concluded her conversation with me, and I knew that one more citizen, through her personal contact with the White House that morning, was in a state of ecstasy — which would undoubtedly last through the length of her Garden Club meeting.

⋈

My secretaries would hand me a piece of mail destined to lighten the heart when the pressure in our office got tough. One of these was Ambassador and Mrs. William Tapley Bennett's little daughter's letter to her grandmother. It was a child's-eye view of a White House tour; and we were fortunate to have something like this to read almost every day.

September 1962

DEAR GRANDMAMMA,
I hope you are well.

Yesterday or the day before yesterday we visited the White House. We entered through a side door and waited for Mrs. Kennedy's secretary, Miss Baldrige to appear in the room because she was to show us around. When she came this is what happened.

We saw the China Display Room as Daddy calls it and there

were plates that even Washington had kept. I liked it alought.

We went into various rooms downstairs, one of which had an old rug. It was so old it was already beginning to come apart.

Soon we went upstairs. First we visited a ballroom where they held concerts too. Then there was a library, and a dinning-room. We came to a sort of hall. There were ropes on the sides but as we had Miss Baldrige we were able to slip under the ropes. We past an office and saw a magnificent elevator. We came to a room that workmen were tearing down. Miss Baldrige explained why, but I didn't quite catch the explanation.

Soon we went into a lovely room with a simply gorgeos view. after a while we went downstairs. Miss Baldrige also showed us the guardhouse. There was also a sort of playhouse for Carolyn Kennedy and also outside it quite a few swings and slides and things like that.

We were told we couldn't go to the swimming-pool because our shoes had dirt and other germs and nobody except enemies really would want President Kennedy to catch a disease. Then we went to the council-room. I sat into President Kennedy.

Later we looked into a waiting room which had lots of people waiting to speak to the President. He didn't come out when we were there much to our sorrow.

Much love to Granddaddy and to you.

Much love,
VICTORIA

What may have been the greatest gift Ambassador Kennedy ever gave to his son was the commissioning of artist Bernard Lamotte to do a 97-foot mural around the swimming pool. The President used the heated pool for his back problems every single day. Sometimes he would spend as long as an hour swimming, exercising his muscles, chatting with Dave Powers and other cronies, and gaining his only relaxation from the pressures of the job. The walls of the pool house looked like a penitentiary laundry room until Bernard Lamotte and his brushes got at them.

Office Address: 1600 Pennsylvania Avenue · 229

The peppy little Frenchman, famous for his murals at Le Pavillon, La Côte Basque and other expensive restaurants in New York, submitted sketches to the Kennedys of scenes of the marina at St. Croix in the Virgin Islands. He even included the President's little sailboat, "Victura," docked in with the other sailboats; on another boat the name "Kennedy" was spelled in signal flags.

Bernard worked all day long for many weeks, clad in blue denims, a long blue French workman's shirt, a blue Breton fisherman's cap, and a white handkerchief tied around his neck like the railroad engineer of yore. His elegant wife, Lilyane, visited him from their suite at the Mayflower, keeping his supply of vin rouge, salami, and imported French cheeses and bread well stocked. Bernard liked good food, and when he knocked off for lunch, he would sit down unobtrusively in the garden, or in the florists' headquarters to cut his cheese and meat with a special little French knife he always carried with him. Everyone in the White House came to adore his eccentric outfit, his Gallic gestures, and his delightful French wit. He became such friends with René Verdon that we shared glorious lunches together right in the big kitchen with the conversation flowing *en français*. Our wine was the very best from the Kennedy's stock, and we kept these culinary feats a secret from everyone, for fear we would be discovered. Bernard also was *un grand ami* of our head gardener, who made room in the big refrigerators (housing all the flowers for the house) for Bernard's cold cuts and cheeses.

One day J. B. West and I received several reports that the main reception rooms had a funny odor. We combated it with room spray, but still the odor persisted. It was not something dead or rotting — but it was definitely unpleasing. Finally, someone suggested the East Room was reeking of smelly cheese and liverwurst. We traced it to the flower arrangements.

I immediately went down to the pool where Bernard, on a raised platform, was daubing away at the St. Croix sunset horizon. There was nothing to do but accuse de Gaulle of having sent him to sabotage our White House entertaining. After a good chuckle over such a possibility, we retired to the kitchen to consume a few Quenelles de Brochet that René was concocting for a stag luncheon. We rationalized our behavior as being the official White House tasters for the security of our leader. In actuality, we were more like a secret gourmet confraternity.

This is one of the things I miss out in Chicago, needless to say. My roast beef sandwich at the Walgreen counter in the Merchandise Mart just isn't the same.

++

President and Mrs. Kennedy were to achieve perhaps the greatest successes in their administration while representing America on State Visits abroad. The first one was to Canada, in May of 1961. Some of the Presidential Assistants, the Secret Service and I flew to Ottawa two weeks ahead to make the arrangements for the Kennedys' separate schedules. Some of us were to stay in the residence of Governor General and Madame Vanier, called "Government House"; the rest of the staff was to be housed in hotels. My own room, in the British tradition, was referred to as the "lady-in-waiting's room." The Canadians kept saying over and over to us that the Kennedys should not be upset by the lack of demonstrative welcome on the part of their countrymen. "We just do not show our emotions," they said, "and we don't want your President and First Lady to think that because no one cheers, we are not happy to see them."

I cautioned both President and Mrs. Kennedy that they were to receive a non-Latin type of welcome, and related stories of how upset the British monarchs had been at the traditionally cool Canadian reception. When the day of the visit arrived, and as the motorcade bearing the Kennedys started through crowded streets, the noise of shouting, clapping, screaming, joyous people almost deafened us. One strong chant came through above the others: "Jac — kie," "Jac — kie."

The Canadian welcome was a total upset — the Ottawans acted like Italians at a soccer game, and the Kennedy charm was proved once again to be totally, immeasurably effective.

The Secret Service had a good look at the real Miss Baldrige each night in Ottawa. They were stationed in the corridor outside the Kennedys' bedrooms. In order to reach my bathroom, I had to plod past the Kennedys' rooms. This was the Secret Service's first glimpse of my beautiful brown hairnet and extravagantly cold-creamed face. By the time we were to make the next trip to Paris, they summoned the courage to tell me they could not take it. In Canada, they just swallowed hard and accepted it, along with their other duties.

Mrs. Kennedy was supposed to appear on French network television, and a special studio was rigged up in Government House. At the last minute, her health did not permit it, and the only French-speaking substitutes on the team were called in to pinch-hit. Pierre Salinger, born in Canada, Godfrey McHugh, born in Belgium, and Letitia Baldrige, born in Miami Beach, carried on bravely in the French idiom for one-half hour of TV time. We had had exactly twenty minutes' warning, but the show had to go on.

Our stay in Canada could not have been more delightful. A beautiful State Dinner was held in Government House — what a joy to be a guest, oblivious of logistics, protocol and kitchen crises. Mrs. Kennedy's schedule, in particular, was appealing

— going through the National Gallery of Art to see the best of Canadian painters' work, and viewing the inimitable "musical ride" of the Royal Canadian Mounted Police. I had written in my diary at the age of nine, after seeing the Mounted Police perform in the Ak-Sar-Ben Coliseum in Omaha, that there was only one sure thing in my entire life: I would marry a Royal Canadian Mountie. Unfortunately, none were available on this trip.

↦↤

The Kennedys' visit to France, described in a preceding chapter, was immediately followed by the historic Kennedy-Khrushchev encounter in Vienna in June of 1961.

Our departure from Paris was not without incident. I was to fly to Vienna on the back-up jet, along with the press, on the tail of the President's plane. Provy and George were supposed to be in one of the lead cars of the motorcade, so that they would be among the first to board the President's jet. I was relaxing with some press friends, waiting for our plane to be loaded, when I noticed a station wagon coming out of nowhere, containing George, Provy and all the Kennedys' hand luggage. The doors of the President's jet had already swung shut. The big engines had started. I had to make a decision fast. Grabbing a startled Provy and George by the arm, I ran with them across the tarmac as the jet began to taxi away in front of the large group of French officials and diplomatic corps.

The pilot, Colonel Swindell, saw me and reacted immediately. I'm sure there were not a few swear words being uttered in the cockpit as the engines were stopped. The ground crew wheeled a stairway up to the rear door on the run, and Provy and George boarded, with their boxes and suitcases thrown in behind them. They would be needed by the Kennedys en route to Vienna.

Provy even had the coat and hat Mrs. Kennedy was to wear for the welcoming ceremonies on the other end.

The press reported that "Miss Baldrige was very late — for unexplained reasons — and stopped the Presidential aircraft, right in front of the official departure committee." I received letters of complaint from all over the world because of these stories, stating I had no right to get up so late in the morning, to be so inefficient and indifferent. What the press did not know, and which would have made a much better story, was that I smuggled Olivier — the young assistant to famous hairdresser Alexandre — on board the back-up jet with me. When the press asked me who the handsome Parisian was, I replied, "Just a good old pal of mine." Some of the men wisecracked across the aisle that Tish had finally found herself a lover — and a young Frenchman at that. My only retaliation was to smile my most Mona Lisaesque smile.

The American and Soviet heads of state were the guests of President Schaerf of Austria. Our first night in the "City of Music" the Austrian Government gave a black-tie dinner (Khrushchev wore his regular suit, refusing even to wear a black tie), followed by a ballet performance, in the lavish Schönbrunn Palace. It was a special joy to the American staff to watch Khrushchev — a pudgy Kewpie doll, very out of place in the gilt-mirrored baroque surroundings — ogling the First Lady of the United States, who was exquisitely dressed and bejeweled. Beside him was his Nina, the plainest of dark dresses hanging apologetically on her square frame, looking school-marmish and self-conscious. We all immediately liked her. She was sweet and gracious whenever we talked to her. He was diffident and difficult, but then he was on the spot, being publicly compared to the glamorous young President in a city that frankly loathed anything Soviet. The only smiles that could be solicited from him all evening came from his conversations with Mrs. Kennedy, as they sat watching the ballet performance. Interpreters were, naturally, used all the time, but one could tell he enjoyed the extra time just to gaze at her.

During dinner, I sat at a table for ten, with an Austrian Foreign Office official as my escort. The other men at the table consisted of eight Russians from Khrushchev's party. I tried out my few words of Berlitz Russian on them, and then we had a convivial time, speaking in French together, the one language we shared. Our conversation remained on a non-political level, but they asked many questions about Caroline and John, and showed me dog-eared photos of their own children. At the end of dinner, I could not resist twitting them about my having been falsely arrested in the Soviet zone of Vienna in 1952 and held for a couple of hours. They did not appreciate the humor of my reminiscences. At the end of the evening, they greeted some Austrian officials passing by in perfect idiomatic English. "Why did you not speak English to me?" I asked, showing obvious irritation in my voice. Their answer was an enigmatic smile and a sort of "Move on, little girl" dismissal.

It was interesting to watch the Russian motorcades, bearing the hammer and sickle flags on the front of each car, being greeted with sullen silence by the Austrians in the streets. The Kennedys' motorcade instigated near-riots of joyous, screaming Viennese. The people ran through the streets with amazing agility, trying to keep up with the cars.

While the President lunched with the Russians at a conference meeting the second day of the visit, Frau Schaerf (the Austrian President's daughter and official hostess), entertained at a luncheon in the Palais Pallavacini for the ladies — having invited an exact balance of Austrian, Soviet and American guests. From the American side came Mrs. Kennedy, her mother-in-law, Eunice Shriver, the Ambassador's wife, Monica Wallner, and a Russian-born American woman who would act as the interpreter for our side.

I was exultant. At last, I would have two hours to myself. Finally, after many exhausting days of official-tripping, I could get *my* hair done. The need for this emergency maintenance service was apparent to everyone who looked at me. Olivier, my erstwhile lover, rushed me into Mrs. Kennedy's bathroom with the terse comment, "You look frankly impossible." He was lathering away on a mountain of frothy suds at the basin when there was a knock on the door. An embarrassed young Foreign Service officer put his head in the door, recoiled at the sight, then looked in the other direction as he spoke.

"Miss Baldrige — they — er — they need you at the luncheon. The American lady who was to interpret for Mrs. Kennedy was called away to the Soviet Embassy to assist the President. You are the substitute. You are due immediately at the Palais Pallavacini."

"But I can't possibly!" I argued, thinking about my head, looking down at my slip, and thinking how far away we were from the palace.

"All I know," he said, wincing as he looked at me, "is the telephone message I just received from the Protocol Office. It was, we might say, an order."

I could read his thoughts as he surveyed the mess in the master bathroom of the American Embassy.

"*Vite!*" I whispered to Olivier. "*Allons-y!*" He began to rinse my very thick head of hair with a full blast of water that splashed all over the bathroom floor. The fact that the full blast he happened to turn on was scalding hot mattered not to either of us. The prestige of the American Government was at stake. I threw on my dress, grabbed a hat and borrowed a pair of Mrs. Kennedy's clean white gloves from Provy. Olivier, armed with two Turkish towels, a comb and a determined expression, accompanied me on my dash downstairs into the car.

In the hysteria of my departure, I had also grabbed a pile of oversized hair-setting rollers, which I realized would serve no purpose whatsoever. A young Marine stood guard by the door. "Here!" I said to him, "take these and file with the top secret papers."

The look on the face of the proper Marine, as he stood with both hands full of hair rollers, would have won first prize in any candid camera contest.

We raced through the streets of Vienna in the Ambassador's own car, with the American flag flying over the front headlights. We had an escort in front of us consisting of two motorcycle police, their sirens blaring. Every time we had to reduce speed in the impossible noontime traffic, the crowds formed on the curbs, convinced it must be Jacqueline Kennedy going by. They must have turned over to the communist cause when they looked in to see a wild-looking girl, her hair wisping, flying and frizzing in every direction, with a young man sitting beside her, vigorously rubbing her head with a towel. When we arrived at the Palace, I pulled an Emme flowered hat, Garbo-style, down over my head, hiding the mess as best I could. Then I ran up two long flights of ancient stairs, three at a time, to join the luncheon party already in progress.

Still panting, with the dampness beginning to seep through my hat, I became the object of Mrs. Kennedy's gaze. She burst out laughing. "Olivier" she mouthed in my direction, and I knew I had been caught in the act. Every time Mme. Khrushchev looked in my direction, I could see her attempting in desperation to seek the answer to my appearance. Was it perhaps a new fad in the Western World?

I will never forget the conclusion of that small, high-powered meal. We were all chatting over coffee in the living room when a chant rose from the square, outside the palace. It was filled with people — the Secret Service later estimated the crowd at three thousand. "Jac-kie!" they cried, over and over again, in bursts of rhythmic cadence. In every country, the rhythm had been the same. But here, today, it became increasingly embarrassing that no one mentioned Nina Khrushchev's name. The Russian sat gazing sadly down at her feet, saying nothing. Conversation in the room was impossible, and I could see Frau Schaerf was beginning to be agitated.

Mrs. Kennedy handled the crisis with great diplomacy. She went to the open window to appease the impatient crowd, smiled and waved at them. The volume of noise became an ear-splitting symphony of cheering and applause. After about one minute, she took Mme. Khrushchev gently by the arm, and led her back to the window. She held up Mme. Khrushchev's hand for a second, and then the Russian began to wave on her own. The crowd loved it, crying this time, "Jac-kie! Nin-a!" It was almost as though they were obeying the American First Lady's request for courtesy to be shown to her fellow-guest.

We all attended Sunday Mass in St. Stephen's Cathedral, during which, as a special honor, the Vienna Boys' Choir performed. The pure, sweet voices of the little boys touched the soaring archways of the historic edifice with sounds so ethereal and unworldly, I noticed the faces of some of the tough-guy, non-church-going White House staffers, completely transfixed. It was a beautiful and touching mass, sung in Latin, with all the leading members of the Austrian Catholic hierarchy assisting at the altar. One could feel how much the history of this cathedral meant to the Viennese — and how proud this Catholic country was to have a President of the United States of their own faith, sharing in the sacrifice of the mass.

The Kennedys were alone in the front row, and I was right

behind them, right across the aisle. They kept turning around to sneak a glance at me. I began to worry. Their behavior was most unusual. Had I broken out in measles? Had I made another major gaffe?

Afterward, the President asked me to come to see him back at the Ambassador's Residence.

"Tish, did you know what you were doing at that mass?"

"It was a departure from the usual liturgy," I replied.

"But were you doing the right thing? I mean, kneeling, standing, genuflecting at the proper time?"

"I don't know, Mr. President." I had been totally unsure of my movements at that mass.

"You were the only Catholic I could see from our pew who should know what she was doing," he said. "Jackie and I didn't know what to do — we were in front — so we guided ourselves on what you were doing. I just hope it was correct."

I didn't have the heart to inform him that because of the boys' singing the procedure and liturgy absolutely stymied me. I was following two other people, both doing opposite things, and I picked whichever course of action seemed logical. Monkey see, monkey do . . . In the meantime, the rest of the congregation had to follow what the Kennedys were doing.

✦

Of course, everywhere we went, the official hosts would arrange something with horses, because of Mrs. Kennedy's love of things equestrian. We automatically blocked off a part of her program for "Horses," and in Vienna, it was most appropriate of all to do so. The famous Spanish Riding School is headquartered there in an eighteenth century palace. The crystal chandeliers from the ballroom still glisten over the riding ring, a very odd contrast to the soft turf below. A special performance was arranged for Mrs. Kennedy by the young men, dressed in the traditional nineteenth century Spanish Riding School uniforms. Their famous dancing white steeds, the Lippizaner breed, pirouetted with the grace and precision of a ballet troupe. I had seen these horses before on other trips to Vienna. Strangely enough, there is a vast disparity between attending such a performance on a tourist's tour and witnessing a private performance "for Mrs. Kennedy and Party."

✦

In December, our advance team flew to South America, setting up the stops in Puerto Rico, then Caracas, Venezuela, and Bogotá, Colombia. In San Juan a few of the fortunate ones were invited to stay in Governor Muñoz-Marín's palace, "La Fortaleza." The windows of my room in the ancient whitewalled monastery looked out over sub-tropical gardens, fountains, and busy city streets. The Governor and his wife gave a very relaxed, attractive dinner party for the Kennedys, at which we saw Pablo Casals and his wife again.

I was enchanted with my room in the Governor's Palace. It was furnished with the dark rough-hewn wood and black ironwork of seventeenth and eighteenth century Spain — against whitewashed walls. Hanging very high from the top of the lofty ceiling was an elaborate chandelier. I could not find the light switch to extinguish it at 3 A.M., when I was finally going to grab three hours of much-needed sleep. I had just finished briefing papers for Mrs. Kennedy, and we all had to move out again at 6 A.M. for Venezuela. I searched and searched, and finally called the Secret Service on duty in the hall below, near the Kennedys' rooms. One of them came up, muttering about dumb, helpless blonds.

He couldn't find the switch either. He was also a blond, I was happy to notice, but would not admit he was dumb or helpless.

It was now 4 A.M. The chandelier was much too high up to reach without a tall stepladder, and we could not wake up the Governor's personal staff to request one. They had all been working too hard taking care of the guests and serving the dinner. The Secret Serviceman announced that there were two courses of action. He could either shoot out each bulb with his revolver and risk starting a new war in the Latin Hemisphere, or I could pretend the lights were off and sleep with 300 watts of electric light shining in my eyes.

Two sleepless hours later — mostly spent cogitating this form of light-in-the-eyes torture practiced in the Far East, I was brought coffee and toast by a little maid, whose mission was to wake me up. She informed me that the light switch was next door — on the far wall of the big reception hall used for dancing. "But of course," I replied, thanking her, "how stupid of me."

In Venezuela, security arrangements were tighter than I had ever seen them before. The communists had been very busy before our arrival, making threats and stirring up trouble.

I stayed with the rest of the staff in a plush hotel in downtown Caracas, which seemed to be inhabited by the entire Italian jet set. Carloads of orchids began to arrive for Mrs. Kennedy. This flower seemed to grow like grass there, in many exotic varieties. I thought some dark-eyed lover had discovered me in the dark hotel halls, when I found a tremendous bouquet addressed to the Señorita Baldrige in my room. They were, of course, from the management. Much of the staff could loll by the swimming pool and drink in the sunshine and other things, but I had a drowning sensation trying to stay ahead of the mail and presents flowing into the Presidential home for the Kennedys. We all flew in helicopters to "La Morita," fifty miles southwest of Caracas, to watch land titles being presented to eighty-six families through the President's Alliance for Progress program. I wore a new beige coat and dress, with matching gloves, hat and bag, but the elegant monochromatic color scheme suddenly turned into black polka dots on dirty tan, my face included. Our group, as we stood waiting to board the next chopper near the landing pad, was completely covered with a fallout of sand mixed with heavy oil, from the earth displaced by the Kennedys' copter ahead. If only I had owned some oil stocks in this territory, I wouldn't have minded. My Bill Blass beige wardrobe was given that night to the hotel maid to use as polishing cloths.

The morning we were to leave Caracas for Bogotá, Pam Turnure and I reported in an Embassy car, driven by a Venezuelan, to President Betancourt's home, where the Kennedys were staying. In what seemed like one wild second, the call came from the Secret Service that we were all off schedule, late, and must leave at once. Everyone — Kennedys included — was hustled on the double into cars lined up in single file in the street. The motorcade included many helmeted policemen on motorcycles, Secret Service cars, and Caracas police cars.

There, of course, had to be one car missing — Pam's and mine. It contained all our luggage, items like Mrs. Kennedy's stationery, and briefcases full of non-classified papers. We begged the officers nearby for help in locating the missing car but were pushed into a car in the rear of the motorcade by an impatient Secret Serviceman who said it was just too bad — we would have to leave all our baggage behind.

I was furious. I knew our man had to be sitting somewhere in the neighborhood. Six blocks away, in the motorcade, we found him, sleeping in the car. I ordered our driver to stop, which he did suddenly. The Venezuelan Security car behind us barely missed crashing into us. I could hear them swearing in Spanish. Pam rolled down the window of our car, and I dashed around on the other side, into the back seat of the parked car, grabbing our bags and briefcases, and throwing them through the window to Pam.

We moved so fast, and confused the Venezuelan police behind us so thoroughly, I suddenly found myself with not one but two tommy guns stuck into my sides. The men holding the guns looked frightened; their fingers were unsteady. Nothing could describe the unsteadiness of my own rib cage at that point. I tried to calm them — but fortunately, there came quickly to my rescue two of our Secret Service from a car ahead, yelling at me very impolitely. It seems I had stopped the entire Presidential motorcade. The Venezuelan police behind us who did not know me thought Pam and I were international female conspirators bent on assassinating somebody or other.

The Secret Servicemen literally picked me up and pushed me by the rear end into the car where Pam waited. I will never be the object of a more vigorous bum's rush. The head of the White House detail on this trip came over to me as soon as the Presidential jet had lifted off the ground for Bogotá. The plane was now later than ever in its departure schedule.

"Tish, you did a very serious, quite unforgivable thing this morning."

"But we had to have our luggage for Colombia," I laughed. Pam and I had, in fact, thought the whole incident rather amusing, once we had survived our fright. It was really rather exciting, being mistaken for saboteurs.

"It's not laughable," he said softly. "You have done a grave thing, I repeat." His stern eyes bored holes right through my own shrinking eye-pupils. He then lectured me unmercifully, for one whole hour, saying no luggage, no worldly possessions, were worth stopping a Presidential motorcade. Not even for classified documents, which ours patently were not. I had endangered the security of the President of the United States by a rash act in a neighborhood where security conditions were extremely sensitive. It was a communist section of the city, and the orders had been to proceed through it fast. I was thoroughly chastised for my actions by the end of his sermon. Pam and I never laughed about the incident again.

Nor could anyone have foreseen that on November 23, 1963, one day after Dallas, I would feel compelled to send the Secret Service at the White House a telegram, stating that nothing would ever lessen my respect for their dependability — nor would I ever change my firm belief that they could not fail in their duty except when circumstances were completely beyond human control.

That South American trip in December of 1961 ended with a short stay in Bogotá, at the invitation of President Lleras Camargo. This stop was full of sentiment to me, because one of Clare Luce's young Foreign Service staff in Rome Embassy days had shot up the career ladder. He had become the United States Ambassador to Colombia, and was naturally in charge of the President's trip there. Fulton (Tony) Freeman and his talented wife Phyllis had made a quick success of their mission in Colombia.

Over a million Colombians lined the streets to greet the Kennedys, shouting and waving paper American flags. Mrs. Kennedy was once again the object of major adulation, with heavily accented cries of "Hi, Beautiful!" and "Heh, Miss America!" wherever her motorcade passed. By now she had completely conquered South America with her breathless little five-minute speech in Spanish, and by the pictures flashed across all newspaper pages of a beaming "Jackie" embracing children from orphanages, kindergartens and hospitals.

By the time the last mouthful of the last indigestible State Dinner had been consumed, and the last official statements were made by the heads of state, the White House team had had enough of official life abroad to last us a lifetime. We took off from Bogotá in our evening clothes from the presidential palace after midnight. But — as always — we returned to our White House desks to finish the day's work when we reached Washington, without having been to bed at all. Behind us were too-vivid memories of fighting crowds; existing without sleep and trying to maintain efficiency; rushing every second on impossible schedules; being constantly interrogated and interrupted in our labors by the press who were trying to fill out their stories; yawning through endless speeches; lugging equipment and materials with us — usually the wrong thing, of course; feeling sick from the heat; missing meals and eating all the wrong food when we did eat; and constantly struggling to keep both hair (a female problem only) and wardrobe looking decent under adverse circumstances. None of this shows in the stories filed on a President's visit to a foreign country.

✦✦

We will all remember the trip to Mexico in June of 1962, primarily because of the warmth of the Mexican hospitality. They showered all of us with presents, flowers and *abrazos*. The motorcade in from the airport was slowed to a halt several times in the middle of the city. Mexican emotions literally exploded at the sight of a young, bare-headed John F. Kennedy, and the curtain of confetti was so thick for several blocks that the drivers of the cars could not see beyond their headlights. The waves of tiny multicolored drops came down with the force of Lake Michigan rainstorms over Chicago.

There had been some earthquake scares in the city right before we arrived, and in our hotel rooms, the staff found lying on the beds a complete set of instructions in case of earthquake, entitled, "DON'T PANIC." The typography of the brochure was enough to inspire a quick exodus from the city. I cut out the heading and took it over to the Ambassador's Residence, to place on top of Mrs. Kennedy's briefing papers for the visit. She came rushing out of her room, looking rather worried, and asked if I had already sent on all the flowers to the orphanages and hospitals. I replied very proudly that I had already done the job.

"You sent every one of them, I mean, containers and all?"

I again answered in the affirmative.

"To how many institutions?"

"About thirty."

She sank in a chair and then related how someone had just informed her that one of the orchid bouquets had been sent to her in an 18-kt.-gold museum-quality container.

DON'T PANIC, said the printed piece of paper in my hands. In my haste to unwrap, card and dispose of the hundreds of floral tributes addressed to the Kennedys, I had not inspected the containers. They were usually ghastly looking, right out of a Florida roadside stand. I tried hard to console myself. Such a gold container could not possibly be worth more than a couple thousand dollars.

The next day at Sunday mass at the Basilica of Our Lady of Guadalupe, Mrs. Kennedy left roses blessed by the Archbishop Primate of Mexico at the shrine of the Virgin Mary, as is the custom for wives of leading officials. I stole a rose and crept up afterward to leave it for Our Lady with an extra word or two about flower bowls.

We got the gold container back — and someday I'm going to have to return to the Basilica and approach it on my bare knees, from a block away — over rough stones — as thousands of devout Mexicans do every week. Our Lady of Guadalupe got me out of a jam.

※

When Mrs. Kennedy traveled abroad without the President, it was not an exciting adventure into glory for me — it was more of a total nightmare.

If the President was along, the White House was along. This meant the press section, communications experts, proper secretarial backstopping, and services of all kinds from baggage handlers and medical corpsmen to mimeo-machine operators and drivers.

When Mrs. Kennedy went on a semi-official jaunt, only a small coterie of her own Secret Service went along. In the case of India and Pakistan, there also had to be one Press Aide and some Signal Corpsmen for radio communications.

The inevitable result was that I had to double as a little of anything and a lot of everything. As my parents would be dreaming of their little girl floating down to the Taj Mahal with Mrs. Kennedy on her Indian trip, in reality their little girl would be trapped in an un-airconditioned room in dusty New Delhi, swatting flies and wrapping sixty packages with Indian gift-wrap paper, which bears an amazing resemblance to our toilet paper, except that it is not available in pretty colors.

The first of these nightmares was a trip to Greece, following the Paris-Vienna State Visits. Mrs. Kennedy was invited by the Greek Prime Minister, Mr. Karamanlis, on a "private visit." This meant she only had to see the Royal Family once and be wined and dined by officials about four times. She took along with her her sister and brother-in-law, Prince and Princess Radziwill. John and Letizia Mowinckel came over from the

Paris Embassy, and some other friends spent a few days in the group.

I arrived in advance, as usual, and worked with the Secret Service on fixing up the lovely villa on the sea at Kavouri and the yacht graciously lent to Mrs. Kennedy by a wealthy Greek shipowner, Marcos Nomikos. The Greek police and our Secret Service managed to keep the press and sightseers away from her by land and by sea (including an attack on her yacht by camera-armed frogmen who appeared from the depths of the Aegean).

I had the dubious honor of running interference with the press every day — at a five o'clock press conference in the lobby of the Hotel Grande Bretagne in Athens. My duty was to release the latest hot news of Mrs. Kennedy's party as it proceeded on its merry yachting way through the Aegean Islands. I had to spend the rest of the day in my hotel room, coping with mail, writing thank-yous for Mrs. Kennedy, receiving delegations of Greeks — both official and nonofficial, while waiting for a two-way radio signal, which might mean a drop of news from the sea-voyagers. John Mowinckel would man the yacht's radio to give me anything of possible interest (usually nothing) to release to the poor starving press, who had been forbidden by the Greek Government to follow the party. At the conclusion of these painful two-way conversations, which were extremely difficult to comprehend and during which it was even more impossible to make oneself understood, John and I would lapse into Italian slang, so he could tell me some funny inside nuggets and raise my flagging morale. He was an old friend who knew what my Athenian life was like at that point.

When the party returned to Athens, a group of Italian journalists, who, unbeknownst to us, had been spying on the Nomikos yacht the entire time with telephoto lenses, came up to

John and me and congratulated us on our fluent Italian. They had eavesdropped with their ship's radio on every word we had uttered — in English or Italian.

I managed to work into my own schedule a few Melina Mercouri type evenings with friends at the local spots, as well as furthering my classical education with performances of *Electra* at the ancient Greek theaters of Herodes Atticus and Epidaurus. Otherwise, my basic knowledge of Greece was confined to the Hotel Grande Bretagne. If I learned nothing of the tourist pleasures of Greece, I at least became an expert on the stalling and bluffing of international journalists for half an hour every day. The Athens press referred to me as "The 6-Foot Commando from the White House," and I longed for the presence of Pam Turnure to take over her rightful duties. I would look up in the encyclopedia the islands at which the Nomikos yacht paused each day, and then come forth with some profound praise, paraphrased from Mrs. Kennedy's own lips, about the scenic wonders of each place. The journalists smiled and exclaimed with appreciation at my fabrications — especially the Greeks — but others were wiser. A *Paris Match* reporter paid me the compliment, "Miss Baldrige, you lie with great style, like a heroine in a Greek tragedy."

I felt that the Sacred Heart nuns who had educated me as a child in Omaha, Nebraska, would consider this a very laudatory remark about one of their products.

Coping with Greek food, wines and cooks for Mrs. Kennedy's "good-bye and thank-you" dinner at the Embassy, in honor of the Karamanlises, was not a simple matter. The Ambassador and his regular staff were away from Athens. The international language of cuisine broke down completely, and after many hours with the staff in the kitchen, I could not decide whether the *Gourmet Cook Book* needed re-writing, or whether I should consult a leading Athens psychiatrist. Tap Bennett, the American Chargé, put me on Mrs. Kennedy's commercial jet flight back to New York with a comforting promise that after all, I'd be back in Greece someday to enjoy it; he also left me a reminder of our President's Inaugural speech — "Ask not what your country can do for you . . ."

An interesting footnote to the Greek trip is that among the thousands of letters I plowed through in my Athens prison was a frantic plea for help for a poor rice farmer's daughter in southern Greece. The nine-year-old child had a serious heart defect, which required immediate surgery of a nature too delicate to be undertaken in Greece. The doctors said a trip to America was her only chance.

I asked the American Embassy to check — this letter had moved me deeply and did not sound like a phony. The Military Attaché had her examined by military specialists, and they sent us back an immediate report to the White House, corroborating the Greek report. I talked to Mrs. Kennedy, and a cable was sent to our Embassy in Athens. Within two weeks, the Greek child, accompanied by her father, was picked up by an Air Force cargo plane on its routine swing through the Near East to Germany and then to the United States. I met them at an air base outside Washington, my arms stuffed with toys for the little girl from Caroline and her mother. Neither the girl nor her father had any cold-weather clothes, and we had to outfit them from the inside out. We ensconced them in a delightful suite at Walter Reed Hospital, for which the President's father also paid.

The Greeks were wide-eyed with awe at the whole thing. Greek-speaking doctors and nurses came by to interpret when necessary. The Greek colony of Washington showered them with letters and gifts. The child underwent two weeks of tests and preparation for surgery, before undergoing a harrowing operation. Ambassador Kennedy picked up the entire tab for this mercy operation, which proved to be far more complex than we had realized.

Everyone was thrilled with her miraculous recovery. She and her father stayed in America several more weeks, while she recuperated and they were taken sight-seeing. She came to the White House to see Mrs. Kennedy and to be shown Caroline's room by the young lady herself. They returned to Greece laden with presents — and everyone thought it was the end of a perfect fairy tale. Since the whole project had been my idea since its conception, I was bathed in a glow of philanthropic euphoria — until I started receiving certain reports from Greece. The father had been closed in upon by his creditors, who believed some wild rumor that the rich Kennedys had presented him with a fortune as a parting gift. After all, the Kennedys could take care of the entire village. The local press began to berate the stinginess of the Kennedys and the Americans toward a poor Greek farmer and his daughter. It grew to such proportions, we had become dastardly villains. The village had expected to become an adjunct of Fort Knox, Kentucky, and again it all goes to prove that no good deed goes unpunished.

+-+

In the early part of 1962, I submitted to cholera, smallpox, yellow fever, typhus, typhoid and tetanus shots. There has to be a very compelling reason to induce me to submit to such torture — and there was.

In February, I flew to Rome as the first stop on a trip to advance Mrs. Kennedy's trip there in March, and thence to Pakistan and India. The Rome part of the trip was something I could do blindfolded, upside down. My contacts at the Embassy, from the Ambassador and Mrs. Frederick Reinhardt on down the line to the Embassy chauffeurs and messengers, were old friends of mine from Foreign Service days. Mrs. Kennedy was to stay as the guest of the Reinhardts at the Villa Taverna, the stamping ground of my Clare Luce time. Checking out the house with the Secret Service for Mrs. Kennedy's requirements brought me an almost unbearable nostalgia. The gateman Ferdinando, the gardener Nicola, and Wernon, the chauffeur, were still around. I had to make all the arrangements for Mrs. Kennedy's visit with the Holy Father, Pope John XXIII, through the good services of another dear old friend, the Most Reverend Archbishop Martin J. O'Connor. At that time he was Rector of the North American College, a large edifice on top of the Gianicolo, commanding a superb view of Rome, where thousands of young American seminarians have received advance academic training through the years.

The great long arm of the White House reaches everywhere. One night on the dark dance floor of the Cabala nightclub, I was notified of an emergency call. It was very unsettling to be locked in the warm embrace of a dark, handsome Italian, as only an Italian can embrace on the dance floor, and to be accosted by the maître d'hôtel, "Signorina, the White House is on the telephone."

It was Mrs. Kennedy. After teasing me about carrying on my official duties in such aphrodisiacal surroundings, she announced that for health reasons, she would have to change her entire India-Pakistan schedules, shortening both of them.

This meant I had a few more days' leeway of "La Vita Romana," and I was delighted — but at the same time, I knew this would throw the entire staffs of the Pakistan and Indian Government offices into a frenzy, not to mention our poor, harassed

American Embassy and Consular staffs. I had to get through on the Signal Corps radio at once to the men in those two countries who could relay the messages fast to our Ambassadors, who could then notify the host foreign governments. Everything, down to its last-minute detail, had already been arranged, and the schedule changes must be communicated to the proper sources before the delay leaked through the Washington press.

The Ambassador's office informed us we could not use our shortwave radio. Transmission privileges were not granted by the Italian Government to American officials, because our country would not let Italian officials transmit from the United States. They insisted on reciprocal privileges. I did everything but throw weeping fits in front of the Italian Foreign Office, asking how could they be so mean to a President's wife, and where was their sense of chivalry? Ambassador Egidio Ortona thought the regulations holding us back were ridiculous, but he ran into bureaucratic delays in his championing of our cause.

What did we do? The Signal Corpsman and I simply set up the transmitter in the basement of the U. S. Consulate, and began contacting our people in India and Pakistan anyway. We got our signals through to Lahore, Karachi, New Delhi, Jaipur and other places. We were, in fact, operating a clandestine transmitter, in the American Embassy, and unbeknownst to our Ambassador. We had to get through on the radio. Cable traffic was fraught with hopeless delays, and the telephone communications were similar to the success Alexander Graham Bell would have had if he had tried to call Karachi during the first week's use of his invention.

Between our juggling of code names and accidentally mispronouncing Indian and Pak names and places on the air, anyone eavesdropping and trying to follow our train of thought would have abandoned the task at once. We transmitted very quickly, at strange times, so that if the police were trying to zero in on us, they would never have had the time to trace us. In point of fact, we felt secure — everyone listening must have thought we were a couple of ham operators at play, united in a serious psychosis. After all this, official Italian permission to broadcast was granted, thanks to Egidio Ortona. The minute I reached Karachi, wide-eyed with tourist wonderment, the magic spell was shattered. It was a fascinating new world, an exotic fruit I had always longed to taste — but with my official duties, I could not even get close to the tree.

My schedule as "Advance Man" began with appointments at 7 A.M., and concluded with the last meeting at ten or eleven in the evening. We continued our meetings in airports, waiting to board planes, and when I had to break up the work sessions to powder my nose, I was looked upon as a flighty female. I finally told my American and Pakistani colleagues that, unlike them, I was not a camel.

At every stop, there was always a flood of memos being handed to me, questions and decisions to be made. These earth-shaking interrogations covered everything from what time Mrs. Kennedy likes her breakfast served to whether her maid would be carrying soap flakes for personal laundry with her . . . Would she hold a press conference? . . . How many hands per reception would she shake? . . . Will she wear a hat at all times during the day, so the other American ladies in the party can follow suit? . . . Long or short evening dress each night? . . . May the entire American colony be at the airport? Will she greet them personally? May an American school child present her with a bouquet at the airport? A Pakistani child? How long does she wish to hold the flowers? — and to whom will she hand them when she no longer wants them? . . . Will she respond to official toasts at meals, or rely on the Ambassador to answer for her? . . . Open-car motorcades or closed cars at all times? Can the American flag fly from the front of her car? . . . When will she exchange gifts? May the press record the ceremony? . . . Will she ever make a speech during the entire trip? . . . What kind of bottled water should be served her? What food can't she eat? . . . Will she walk around the pool once or twice at the Shalimar Gardens reception? . . . What kind of gifts will she bring to the children at the hospital? Can her gift of a movie projector for the school in Karachi be readjusted to Pakistan electrical current and voltage in time for the gift presentation? . . . Can we acquire some Mickey Mouse films to go with the projector? . . . Would she become alarmed if she were pelted with rose petals? . . . Will she allow herself to be photographed with some of the West Pakistan Rangers and their horses performing at the Torchlight Tattoo in her honor? . . . Would she enjoy a ride in the Governor of West Pakistan's pony cart around the grounds of his estate? . . . Will her short skirt permit her to mount Bashir's camel in Karachi for a short ride, or is that out of the question? (Bashir Ahmed was the camel driver befriended by Lyndon Johnson on a previous trip, who amazed everyone by accepting the Vice President's jocular invitation "to come visit him in the United States sometime.")

In between pacing out her schedule at Karachi and Lahore, a picnic at the historic ruins of Taxila, a visit to Rawalpindi, Peshawar and the Khyber Pass (where the tribal Maliks and the famed Khyber Rifles were to put on a special show for her), I found it impossible not to fall in love with the history and traditions of these Moslem people — the women dressed in their graceful baggy trousers and saris, and the men with their long shirttails hanging out almost to their knees. I witnessed the final prayers and celebrations marking the end of the annual forty-day fasting period. Their Moslem devotion was inspiring, their poverty depressing, their aping of British military tradition amusing, and their innate sense of humor revealing.

The day before I was to proceed to India, and the day Mrs. Kennedy would be leaving Washington for Rome, a bearer in the Minister-Counselor's house in Karachi woke me up in my room at 4 A.M. He informed me I was wanted on the radio transmitter from Delhi.

I knew it could be nothing but trouble, since I would shortly be there anyway. It was.

A USIS official at the Embassy informed me they had just opened the trunk, full of State Gifts for all of India, which I had gotten into their hands two months previously.

"Tish — all the leather picture frames —"

"Yes, Al." I knew too well what he was referring to, as we had custom ordered sixty dark blue leather frames through the State Department, bearing the gold Presidential seal at the top. There were five different sizes, from very large (for dignitaries like Prime Minister Nehru, the President of India, and Ambassador Ken Galbraith), to very small — for a lesser official at Fatehpur Sikri. It had been explained to us that a signed photograph is the gift the Indians hold in the highest esteem. It had taken me months of work to get the list of all the proper recipients with their long and complicated titles and protocol rankings from our Embassy in India. It had taken me weeks to get the sixty assorted photographic prints of both the President and Mrs. Kennedy, and the frames made to match in size. Then each picture had to be signed and dedicated with special messages by the Kennedys. It had taken my Social Office one entire week of wrapping each framed photo in a special box, encased in the Presidential white embossed gift paper, tied with the gold and white ribbons and the gold seal, not to mention a presentation card and envelope for each box hand-written in meticulous calligraphy by Sandy Fox's staff.

Consequently, when the voice from Delhi came crackling over the radio at that ungodly hour, with the simple statement, "Tish, those picture frames — they won't do," I wanted to commit a dramatic suicide on the spot. Hopefully, it would have been listed as martyrdom for my country.

"The frames are cowhide, Tish. We've just examined one. You know — the Sacred Cow and all that. Mrs. Kennedy can't give official Hindus leather presents. It's against their religion."

"All!" I screamed. "You've had that trunk for eight whole weeks! *Now* you tell me! And besides that, last October, five months ago, I dispatched a memo to you listing our State Gifts, describing the leather frames in detail."

"I know, I know," he said with all the proper tones of apology a man can muster. "We slipped up badly on this one. But what are we — I mean, you — going to do about it?"

I sat stunned for a minute, and then remembered Rome. Lovely, handcrafting, hard-working, be-silvered Rome. We woke up our Signal Corpsman there with the radio, and I gave explicit instructions to go to the silver frame shop near the Piazza di Spagna as soon as it opened. There was only one ray of sunshine in this flap — at least the Pakistani could be given their leather picture frames. If they had been made of pigskin, we would have been in the same predicament, but cowhide is acceptable there.

The Italians rose to the emergency with aplomb. The only thing they could not do for us was erase the "Made in Italy" letters on the backs of the frames. I happened to have all the Indian photograph measurements in my briefcase, so I read them over the radio in inches, the Italians translated them accurately into centimeters, and their silver factory custom-made

Office Address: 1600 Pennsylvania Avenue · 257

sixty sterling silver frames in three days — in time to load them onto Mrs. Kennedy's Air India plane flying from Rome to New Delhi. The bill for all the silver frames was no higher than the bill for the leather ones in America. The leather frames were shipped back to the State Department to be used for Presidential gifts to other countries. We were saved. I cannot, however, describe my emotions at having to undo all the work of my staff, to tear open the beautifully wrapped packages, then to refit the pictures in the new frames, and re-wrap the boxes all by myself, using the infamous Indian gift-wrap (already described earlier as puce toilet paper).

Mrs. Kennedy's arrival in New Delhi was a tumultuous success. Covered with flowered leis, she stood in the hot sun in her bright turquoise silk coat and hat, next to a frail, somber Nehru, with the ever-present rosebud pinned to his dark jacket. One could tell from the awe of the crowd that she looked like a mythological beauty from outer space. People had come from all over the country to see her, lining the dusty roads on bicycles, bullock-drawn carts, two-wheeled pony carts, motor scooters, Fiat taxis, and dilapidated trucks. Many of them had walked as far as fifty miles to see her. Mrs. Kennedy and her sister Lee Radziwill were to spend half their time in the charming little house of Gerry Gerold, the Pan American representative in Delhi, and half their time in Prime Minister Nehru's house. Jay Gildner, from the White House Press Office, accompanied Mrs. Kennedy (if he had known the nature of his task in advance, he probably would have arranged to have his appendix taken out the eve of his departure). Provy was along in the party, to cope with the gigantic Kennedy wardrobe (brilliantly designed in breathtaking Indian colors, and a great asset to her appearance everywhere). Mary Layton, from Kenneth's hairdressing establishment in New York, was an integral part of the entourage. Mary was marked on all official lists as "Princess Radziwill's secretary-maid." The cagey press caught on to her quickly. "The so-called secretary-maid," filed one scribe back to her paper, "carried around the latest portable hair dryer in her Government-issue typewriter case."

One must hasten to add that none of this entourage traveled at the taxpayer's expense.

Ambassador J. Kenneth Galbraith managed to redecorate and repaint the Gerold house in honor of Mrs. Kennedy's two-day occupancy, much to the owner's surprise when he peeked into it one day. The American Embassy wives engaged in a battle to see who could fill the house with the most flowers fastest, all of which I had to have removed. Mrs. Kennedy was not exactly crazy about the mausoleum look for an interior decor.

An entire press plane arrived, with correspondents from all over America and the world. Their lot was not to be an easy one. Many of the places Mrs. Kennedy was to visit were inaccessible to a mass movement of press. A pool operation had to be used often, and poor Jay Gildner had his hands full, trying to placate everyone from *Epoca* to *Paris Match,* from the *London Times* to the *Minnihaha Gazette.* Barbara Walters of NBC's "Today" show was along with a large crew, and close friends of mine appeared in the press caravan, including Molly Thayer covering events for the *Washington Post,* Joan Braden free-lancing for a magazine, and NBC's Sandy Vanocur. It was an impossible situation; the press could not be physically transported to cover the fascinating story of Mrs. Kennedy's travels in a fair manner, nor even in an efficient manner. Jay Gildner lost a great deal of weight and ruined a lot of his nerve fibers on this operation. He kept his cool; he was a real pro.

I was trying to keep above water, too, helping out with the press and sifting through a thousand pieces of mail a day. Requests for medical and financial assistance (everything from a new wooden leg to a four-year scholarship to Vassar) poured into my bedroom at the Economic Counselor's house. The chowkidar — by tradition a man who guards his master's gate at night — let several Indians slip into the house, with the result that all night long there would be gentle knocks at my door. Polite Indians would bow their way abjectly into my presence, making the Hindu salute from their foreheads, and then state their request. They either demanded an audience with Mrs. Kennedy or requested some of her money. One night at 2 A.M. I was going over the last sifting of mail from the Embassy courier, before attempting some desperately needed sleep. The last letter I had singled out from the pile to read — because of curiosity — was one written in an unusually dark shade of red, rather splotchy ink on parchment paper. It contained the usual pitiful request for money, then signed off with the following:

"To prove to you, oh fair white goddess of the world's greatest democracy, of the sincerity and the importance of my humble request, I have written this entire communication in my own blood."

I put the letter down, wondering if this would finally make a lasting impression on my publisher if I were writing another book. How many quarts of blood would it take per manuscript?

I did not have long to meditate on the subject. A knock at the door startled me once again, and in walked a family of five Hindus, with feet of a state of dirtiness to make me long for a vacuum cleaner on the spot. They stood by my bed bowing, saluting and smelling. I rushed out past them in my nightgown to the front gate, and hysterically grabbed the chowkidar by the arm.

"How much?" I shouted at the poor man, "how much are

you accepting in bribes from these people to make you let them in?"

He looked terribly abashed, then confessed his crime, and I somehow comprehended the pitiful amount of money involved.

"I'll raise it," I said, "I'll give you more — but you give me some peace at night, please let me sleep!"

That was at least one problem in India that was quickly solved.

I gave the helpful staff of servants in my house a picture of Mrs. Kennedy, and I was startled to see that back in their living compound, the Christian-Hindu worlds had been beautifully melded together by the First Lady. Three pictures were mounted on the crude walls, each with a burning votive candle in front. One depicted a Hindu god, one was of the Virgin Mary, and the third was the photograph of Jacqueline Kennedy.

+--+

The streets of New Delhi were a riot of blinding, psychedelic color, as though someone were constantly shaking confetti in front of one's eyes. The women's saris were a galaxy of color, pattern and fabric, no one like any other. The pastel Sikh turbans and the bright tangerine Rajput ones dotted the horizon everywhere. The streets were full of such intriguing sights and smells, I would gladly have walked through them. A car cuts one's senses off from a million impressions. The sacred cows — oh, yes, those dear sacred cows — ambled their unsanitary way along in the blended bouquet of dust, curry powder, incense, sweat and the odor of musty brass. Troops of scrappy performing monkeys popped up obscenely out of nowhere. Snake charmers with their inevitable lutes and baskets found me an easy target. After my first snake-mongoose fight on a street corner, I readily paid anyone who accosted me *not* to give me the show.

Mrs. Kennedy had bad luck, because when Prime Minister Nehru had the snake-mongoose fight performed for her in his gardens, the press pictures caused hundreds of angry letters to flood our offices back at the White House. The anti-cruelty-to-animals enthusiasts were furious, but what they would not realize, of course, is that had she refused to witness the fight, she would have been guilty of an open discourtesy to her official host.

The first lunch after Mrs. Kennedy's arrival in India was at Rashtrapati Bhavan, New Delhi's White House. We walked up a giant stairway lined on both sides with the presidential guards, all smartly uniformed, with shiny boots and towering striped turbans. They were each and every one 6'4" and over, and I was enchanted therefore by each and every one.

Our host, President Rajendra Prasad, a lovely, distinguished old gentleman, made us welcome at an enormous table, opulently set with china, silver and linen place mats. The menu read that we were eating Norwegian fish with Italian sauce (it tasted as though it had been dropped off by Leif Ericson on a Viking ship). This was followed by Chicken Korma with Almond Pullao (not even Julia Child could figure out the composition of this one), salad (an automatic "no-no" to Westerners in this part of the world), and then some goodies called Nana, Alu Mattar, Louki Raita, Pappad, and unpasteurized Coupe Royale for dessert. Before lunch, we had slipped canned soup and crackers to Mrs. Kennedy and Lee back at their little house, so they could pretend to eat, while just playing with their food. I had had nothing to eat, was starving, but knew this was not the place in which I wished to end my life.

Roast Chicken Tandoori seemed to be the staple party dish in India. It was in evidence on every menu, but only someone blessed with an ironclad digestive tract could handle all the spices it contains. When one realizes these spices are probably acting in a sterilizing capacity to the chicken, they become more acceptable. Since one could not drink the water — nor use ice made from Indian water, I would have had to drink my before-dinner Scotch straight. This was a hurdle I could not jump, so I pretended I had given up all alcohol for a year.

The Prime Minister and his daughter Indira Gandhi could not have been more gracious to all of us. They entertained our party at a dinner in their house followed by a concert of Indian folksinging and dancing in the garden. I died a thousand deaths for my Indian counterpart, as loudspeakers and the lighting system broke down with regularity. The Prime Minister shrugged and stroked his chin with resignation — no Irish temper had he. However, it really did not matter, as far as we were concerned.

The songs and dances, most of them from ancient times, were of such haunting sentiment and grace, so lilting and lyrical, it was like watching a whole series of Moghul miniature paintings sprung to life. I had already become a wild enthusiast of the decoration on the great Moghul buildings — intricate borders, moldings, tile floors and patterns on walls and ceilings that are copied everywhere today in our Western World, particularly in fabric and wallpaper designs.

In Delhi we stuck fairly close to our schedule. At the mere suggestion of a change, the Indian Government and our Secret Service went into acute manic-depression. Mrs. Kennedy visited the Cottage Industries to see the stunning fabrics and handicrafts for which this culture is so famous. She presented Mme. Gandhi with the "Children's Art Carnival from the Museum of Modern Art and Asia Society of New York," for the Indian children, and she visited the children's ward of the Medical Institute. These little trips and ceremonies lasted from fif-

Greeting the Girl Scouts on behalf of Caroline Kennedy and accepting a large doll for her

Receiving Japanese dolls for Mrs Kennedy, from a UNICEF representative and Danny Kaye

(*left*) Greeting the ladies from a women's organization with gifts for the Kennedys. (*below*) Arrival at Athens airport; Mrs Kennedy with Prime Minister and Madame Karamanlis, and Chargé d'Affaires William Tapley Bennett

teen to thirty minutes, but each one required at least three workdays of preparation by the Indians, the Secret Service, and myself.

The press began to chafe. They could not get near the object of their assignment. There was nothing Jay Gildner nor I could do about it. They had come a long, expensive journey, their papers and magazines expected something exclusive, yet Mrs. Kennedy could not be expected to grant each and every one a special interview. One could not discriminate in favor of anyone. Nor would she submit to the ordeal of an open press conference.

Then the schedule began to change, shifting like an escaped, naughty droplet of mercury. One never knew which was the most up-to-date piece of mimeographed paper, and perhaps fifteen totally different schedules were utilized by the innocents out in the field. Both Mrs. Kennedy and Ambassador Galbraith began hacking away at the complex arrangements. One reporter filed back to the United States the following piece of understatement:

> There is obvious tension among American officials concerned with arrangements for Mrs. Kennedy's visit. Everything is hush-hush to almost an absurd degree. Key persons are ungreetable. Lesser lights are terribly harassed. One feels that a too ambitious program was planned and that the postponements have created havoc with official nervous systems.

Finally Mrs. Kennedy, her sister and the Galbraiths took off on an exciting trip including Fatehpur Sikri, Agra, Benares, Udaipur and Jaipur. While they cruised sacred rivers, watched the Taj Mahal gleam in the eternal moonlight, dined in Maharajahs' palaces and rode on elephants that were painted and sequined like the Folies Bergère girls, I was padlocked to my typewriter, telephone and cable dispatcher. The schedule kept changing. I cried, "Oh, no, they can't!" Everyone in the Embassy and the Indian Government offices cried, "Oh, no, they can't!" And they did.

Another reporter wrote "What started out as a 'personal and private' tour has turned into an Asian caravan of such proportions as to make even a latter day Marco Polo bug-eyed."

I had figured out how much to tip the staff in the various Indian houses and palaces at which they spent the night, and had equipped the Secret Service with the cash. Signed photographs were also to be distributed. I had obtained a full list of household staffs ahead of time, and had hit what I hoped was a happy medium between what Queen Elizabeth had tipped these same staffs during her almost identical trip two years previously, and what the Indians would expect from "a rich American." Even this kind of decision was bound to rile tempers and hurt international feelings. One important Indian member of the Embassy staff said, "Mrs. Kennedy should not Out-Queen the Queen. She should, out of respect to the British Monarchy, tip less."

I would hate to have participated, even in a minor way, in out-queening the Queen. However, all along Mrs. Kennedy's way, our Signal Corpsmen would transmit pathetic little messages back to me in Delhi, "Secret Service says two extra footmen, pastry cook and hard-working gardener not on original staff list for this place. How much extra to them?"

One of the great unnecessary educations one receives as Social Secretary at home or abroad is that concerning domestic staff tipping. Sadly enough, the subject never comes up in my life on the shores of Lake Michigan today, so I fear I am becoming rusty.

In the meantime, I was being buffeted on the rocks of a diplomatic storm within our own Embassies. Mrs. Kennedy chopped more off the Pakistan than off the Indian schedules when she shortened her trip. The two countries, at each other's throats with drawn daggers on all issues, were very competitive for her time. The Paks wanted an equal number of days, but they were not to get them. To compound matters further, Ambassador Galbraith wanted to accompany Mrs. Kennedy on the trip to Pakistan, which sent every American official in Pakistan into orbit. They considered this a slap in their own Ambassador's face. By now, I was so accustomed to everyone being upset and offended, by the complaints from the press and officials in three countries (the U.S. included), I took the easy way out. I developed the "Delhi Belly" or the "Pakistan Ick," according to the country you wish to place the blame upon. Suffering from a high fever and an untold variety of complaints, I was flown out on a commercial airline to London, to convalesce for several days in the glorious confines of Ambassador and Mrs. David Bruce's beautiful Embassy Residence. There I could drink the water, delight in the salad, and forget the entire Middle East.

My own staff in Washington, sympathetically disturbed over their indestructible boss's having to "cop out," took heart in one bit of news that leaked out to them. I was not too sick at the Teheran stop-over to locomote myself from the plane into the airport to buy my full ration of fresh Iranian caviar.

↔

Leaving complaints and unhappy memories of these "non-official official trips" of Mrs. Kennedy aside, the major factor to be remembered is her incredible success with the crowds, and the thorough accomplishment of her mission — to create goodwill for the United States. She did that and more.

And if I tell but a part of my frenzied side of the story, it is only to warn future Social Secretary candidates that the pathway is not paved in gold.

※

There was always a minor civil war simmering between the East and West Wings, based on nothing less than sex. The West Wing, of course, represented the President's side of the White House, and our wing, except for the Military Aides and Arthur Schlesinger, was heavily weighted with Mrs. Kennedy's staff. It became apparent to me very early in the administration that our male colleagues would walk all over us unless we fought back. The Presidential Assistants tried to force decisions affecting Mrs. Kennedy on our office without consulting us. When my Scotch-Irish wrath fully articulated itself on these occasions, the men had to capitulate. I had the feeling Ken O'Donnell, the President's Appointments Secretary, disliked the idea of any woman in any office. There was nothing personal against me; I just happened to be a female in a man's world. Besides, he could not forgive me for having been a former Republican. I think I rattled him on several occasions. His Irish sense of humor finally forced him into a guarded truce with me. He was certainly one of the most cool, forceful and valuable men around JFK. Pierre Salinger, the Press Secretary, out of sheer impetuosity, would step into our ladies' territory with ease. He found our side's activities more interesting than his own at times. My father had always told me: "When you get into a tight spot and can't take any other action, holler." I therefore hollered often on behalf of the East Wing. After a year, Pierre treated us graciously as co-professionals, instead of silly children. He was blessed, of course, with one of the world's greatest senses of humor.

Our disputes with the President's Military Aides were inevitable, in that I was in charge of military ceremony, vis-à-vis State entertaining, and they quite naturally wanted to run this part of the show themselves. In spite of our heated encounters, the Military Aides were our great good friends and cohorts. I had very little to do with the President's Congressional Liaison, Larry O'Brien, except to receive his frequent exhortations to put more Senators and Congressmen on our party lists. I worked hand in glove with Arthur Schlesinger and Dick Goodwin on the cultural side of our party lists, and Arthur Schlesinger will go down in history as one of my heroes — simply because he could always tell when the Social Secretary was about to blow her stack from the pressure. He would rush me off to an expensive restaurant for a Bloody Mary luncheon just in time. Fred Holburn, the absent-minded professor on the President's team, sat in an office across the hall, littered with newspapers and magazines. He looked as though he were King of the Scrapmen. He worked on Presidential speeches, messages, and did research. When I had questions to ask of him, it was difficult to find him under piles of dusty newspapers. Perhaps because he was a bachelor, he always had the prettiest girls in the White House working for him. Ted Sorenson, another one of the Presidential Assistants in the West Wing, amazed me with his fantastic loyalty to JFK and his seven-day-a-week working schedule. When I teased him about still working in his office Sunday night at nine o'clock, he answered very seriously that he was doing a job for the President, and that frankly there wasn't anything he would rather be doing. McGeorge Bundy was my real soulmate in the West Wing. The activities of the ladies continually amused and delighted him. His eyes twinkled when I ran into him. "What are you girls up to now?" was his inevitable question. Mike Feldman, the Presidential Legal Counsel, and Dr. Janet Travell, the President's charming lady doctor, were my tennis playmates on the White House court. We would sneak down to the bottom of the South Lawn with a fourth at the end of the day for a doubles game, betting on who would be called first to the telephone. My old friend and European traveling companion from Paris days, Michael Forrestal, was perhaps the most eligible bachelor on the White House staff. When Michael would invite me to dinner and forget he had done so, in his absent-minded way, I always enjoyed the retribution: something delightful like a whole pound of fresh caviar. It was well worth being stood up for.

↔

The Kennedys both shared two innate gifts — a sense of style and a sense of history. Both of these gifts live on in the White House — in their entertaining innovations which have by now become a tradition, and in the metamorphosis of the White House itself into a museum of American Presidential history. The whole story of the formation of the White House Fine Arts Committee and its activities is so personally identified with Mrs. Kennedy, she should tell it herself in detail someday. It is an absolutely fascinating one. Great names in the fields of American philanthropy, education and art formed her committee, headed by Henry F. du Pont of Winterthur. There was also a healthy sprinkling of "the very rich," without whose generosity in acquiring specific treasures, the house would never have the value it has today.

Because of my own interest in antiques and in American decorative arts of the eighteenth and nineteenth centuries, the gradual restoration of the house was a constant source of intellectual and visual delight. The White House Police, who handle the special tours around the house, found themselves learning complicated new foreign terms and names of designers for the furnishings; their lives had become very exciting, too, after years of the same rather desiccated spiel on the interior. Our mail problems jumped ten-fold, with everyone in the country writing to suggest or sell something, but we dealt with it all gladly. The Mail Room and later the Curator's Office became a repository of "old everythings," that had been sent unsolicited to the First Lady, either for the committee's purchase, or to be donated as a present. These packages would reveal Aunt Mabel's pincushion, circa 1909, Uncle Joe's brass spittoon, circa 1919, a lace garter thought to have been worn once by Mary Todd Lincoln, and a nineteenth century shaving brush. Rarely, very rarely, an item of authentic historic interest would appear.

The press went wild, trying to keep up with the subtle changes in the house. Every time they covered a party, there would be a new piece of furniture to discover, a new rug, cachepot, pair of girandoles, and a constant game of musical chairs with the portrait hangings. Mrs. Calvin Coolidge, for example, changed her place on the walls five times in four weeks, as committee members argued to and fro about the bright red color of her dress and where it would look best.

Nothing was without controversy. We had learned by now that the kitchen could not even make a peanut butter sandwich without making someone upset. The N.S.I.D. (National Society of Interior Designers) finished, as their handsome gift to the White House, the famous oval Diplomatic Reception Room, filling it with dark polished mahogany, rich yellow damask, a custom-made sculptured oval rug, and magnificent examples of Federal furniture. An official of the A.I.D. (American Institute of Interior Designers) then felt compelled to pooh-pooh in front of the press the fact that the N.S.I.D. had spent $12,500 to purchase the "Scenic America" antique wallpaper used in the room. The paper, made from the original early nineteenth century Alsatian blocks, had been purchased by a Washington collector for $50.00 from an old Maryland house. Besides, said the A.I.D. officer, the paper was being beautifully reproduced at a good price by an American wallpaper firm, A. L. Diament & Co.

I held my breath when the A.I.D. completed their gift, the ground floor Library, with its exceptional Aubusson rug, delicate chandelier, Indian paintings and superb examples of Duncan Phyfe's cabinetry. Luckily, no one from the N.S.I.D. made a crack — in print. Both rooms are very well done, leaving one with a justifiable pride in the American taste and know-how of the late eighteenth and early nineteenth centuries.

One of the prized examples of furniture — loved by every-one, and valued at $20,000 — was a graceful little inlaid Baltimore desk, displayed in the Green Room. It turned out to be a fake. When the Red Room had the damask of its walls changed to a rich scarlet-fuchsia of the 1812 period, with matching up-holstered Empire furniture, complaints poured in about the strong color. Another reporter quoted a noted Washingtonian who described the new watered green silk moiré walls of the Green Room as "a bilious color, that makes one want to be sick." When the Blue Room was redone predominately in an off-white striped silk, with minor accents of blue, one would have thought that the American Declaration of Independence had been violated. No good deed goes unpunished.

The first Curator, Lorraine Pearce, succeeded by Bill Elder and then by young, gregarious Jim Ketcham, was housed in an old storeroom, surrounded by musty books, enough furnishings and incoming junk to fill three antique stores, and an assembly of constantly ringing phones. President Chester A. Arthur had compounded the difficulty of Mrs. Kennedy's task in making the house a truly historic one by having undertaken a massive redecoration program of his own during his administration. He solved his problem of dispensing with the "old-fashioned look" and of ringing in the new simply by dumping at a public sale twenty-four truckloads of historic furnishings, used by our earlier Presidents. By now such a tragedy will not be allowed to re-occur.

Indeed, it would take more than one volume to cover the "Re-birth of the White House" under Mrs. Kennedy's guidance — and it was tremendously exciting to be part of it. The President admired and encouraged his wife's role in this field, because of his own respect for the past — a respect that was emotional and sentimental as well as intellectual. When he was engaged in a major undertaking, he wanted it recorded — but also for his team's benefit.

Right after those fateful days of October, 1962, when he had stood up to the Russians on the Cuban missile episode — and won hands down — the President called me over to his office. His team of White House, State and Pentagon officials had literally been living at the White House the entire time. They had not gone home to see their families; they had slept on cots and subsisted on sandwiches and coffee behind locked doors.

The President told me how deeply moved he was by their loyalty and support — and asked me to have Tiffany's design for him a paperweight made of lucite mounted on a small silver base. The lucite was to reveal the regular October 1962 calendar month, with the days of the blockade crisis marked off with heavier numerals, so that they would stand out.

I carried the message to my former boss, Walter Hoving, who promptly replied Tiffany never had and never would compromise on such a matter. Tiffany's would never use lucite, or any plastic, synthetic material. It would be a sin to combine it with a precious metal like sterling. I argued that this was a moment of history, not a time for quibbling, and that the President was asking him. Hoving replied he would not do it for anyone.

I was quaking when I reported back to the President. After all, Tiffany's had had so much business from the White House in State Gifts. This was terribly embarrassing. Hoving strongly suggested an engraved sterling plaque, depicting the October calendar and mounted on a wooden base, as the appropriate trophy. The price was well over what JFK wanted to pay. After all, he had quite a few of them to purchase, and all from his own pocket.

The President reacted as I knew he would. He stormed and raged, so I ducked quickly out of his office. It always seemed to me I was in the middle of crises between my present and past bosses. If it wasn't Clare Luce, it was Walter Hoving.

The President called me over again a couple of days later. He had asked his friend Lem Billings to get several samples of what he wanted from the plastics manufacturers. They were well-designed, inexpensive objects, but hardly a precious item. "There!" he said in triumph. "If Tiffany's won't make what I want, these men will — and in less than a week. And inexpensively, too!"

He stood with one hand in his pocket, the other nervously fidgeting with his tie. He was waiting for me to pick up my cue. I was supposed to say, "They're great." I paused, then said, "I guess they're all right." He was anything but pleased with this reaction, and I quickly left his office before we had a knock-down, drag-out argument.

Two nights later, a Saturday, my White House phone rang at midnight. It was Camp David. The President came on the telephone. "Order the Tiffany silver ones. Go ahead. You and

Hoving won." The receiver clicked before I had an opportunity to react.

The recipients of these historic paperweights were so delighted, they turned around and presented their chief with one of the famous October calendars engraved on top of a large vermeil box.

As I look back over these exhilarating, funny, exhausting White House days, my impressions make a collage — of bits and pieces of warm history. Those days of the funeral weekend, and the days immediately following are not part of the collage. The memories that cling to the canvas are only the most alive ones, for death is not to be held in the same breath as the name of John F. Kennedy.

There is the annual giant fir Christmas tree in my collage, set up in the Blue Room, ablaze with twinkling lights, garlands and tiny characters from "The Nutcracker Suite" — all to delight the eyes of Caroline and John, Jr., as well as the eyes of the Filipino Navy mess stewards' children. There is the President giving me a firm going-over for putting all the State Dinner menus in French — because Congressmen had complained to him that the White House was getting "too Frenchified" — and then backing down completely when I read to him specialties in English that sounded so tacky (O.K., Mr. President, how does "Chocolate Pudding" sound instead of "Mousse au Chocolat"?).

There is Mrs. Kennedy handing a round crystal ball with a shiny gold angel inside to each wide-eyed child in the Children's Hospital wards. There is the President tasting and retasting the spiked punch with the butler and me in the back pantry, because he so eagerly wanted it to be right for his Congressional Reception friends. There is Mrs. Kennedy chattering away in French to a shy, nervous African President, completely putting him at ease in what were terrifying surroundings for him. There are the Kennedy children squealing with joyous laughter as they feed the Quack-quacks in the fountains of the South Grounds. There is the President, filling in for his wife when she was pregnant or not feeling well at ladies' gatherings, like the Congressional Wives' Brunch, or the reception for the Sacred Heart Alumnae — charming hundreds of ladies simultaneously with deft, masterful strokes.

There are the two of them together, man and wife, laughing, teasing each other, striking through the pages of history with their handsome children in tow, like a quick silver beam of light piercing the darkness of any place they land.

There is no assassin's bullet that can penetrate my own collage. I only hope, along with every other member of the staff from "those days," that many a student of history hundreds of years hence will stop at what will then be a short entry on the short happy life of John F. Kennedy, and say to himself, "Now *there* must have been a great guy. It would have been interesting to have lived in *his* time."

PART V

Mater Familias in Chicago!

V

To me, there are only three things wrong with Chicago: its wind, its overly-masculine orientation, and its inhabitants who keep apologizing for it. Chicago did not seem a logical progression after Washington, New York, Rome and Paris, but here I am. Here I will stay.

Ambassador Kennedy, in one of his conversations in my White House office, sitting on the green sofa, had asked what I was going to do after Washington days were over. Anything would be such a come-down, he said, smiling, so just what would my next move be?

"Obviously New York," was my answer.

He frowned at this. "Why be a little fish in a big sea and swim around unnoticed? Why not go to a city where a big girl can be a big girl?"

He was, of course, referring to the fact that New York is crammed with glamorous, gifted females with excellent backgrounds. The competition would always be rough, he added. Girls are often stepped on, or worse still, stepped over. Was that what I wanted?

Most certainly not, I had replied. All right then, he said, think about Chicago. He described it as a "great throbbing city, a masculine place in need of feminine touches in its business world."

He told me about his own property, the Merchandise Mart,

which happens to be the largest commercial building in the world. He described the enormous home furnishings wholesale markets that take place regularly, and how the showrooms are the showcases for every item of interior design that embellishes our homes or places of business or recreation. Informally, he offered me a job.

We were never able to discuss the Merchandise Mart or Chicago again. The next month, he suffered a severe, crippling stroke. I took his advice, however, and when White House days were over, I moved to Chicago with the position of "Consultant to the Office of the Merchandise Mart". It was Mrs. Kennedy herself who kindly wrote Wallace O. Ollman, General Manager of The Mart, asking him to see me to discuss if there was anything of interest for me. I flew out to see him one day for two hours, the job offer was extended, and I left the White House the following summer. My decision was reinforced by Sargent Shriver, who had spent several years on the executive staff of the Mart before coming to Washington as head of the Peace Corps.

My new boss was Wally Ollman, himself, tall, amiable and acutely perceptive. Joseph Kennedy had noticed the young accountant in 1945 and had hired him when he purchased the building from the Marshall Field interests. Manager of the Mart undoubtedly is the most complex landlord's job in the world. Not only does he have to oversee the rental and maintenance of more than four million square feet of space, but he also has to organize and promote the buyers' markets for his tenants.

I knew it would be a drastic readjustment after life in Washington, but the challenge involved in moving to such a big and unfamiliar city was a plus factor. I would be too busy to be lonesome. I had no close friends in Chicago and arrived feeling like a hick from the non-sticks. I knew the Drake Hotel, because I had given a benefit lecture on Schlumberger's jewels there three

In the ancient theatre in Athens. First row, left to right: head of Greek Theatre, Madame Karamanlis, Mrs Kennedy, the Prime Minister, Princess Radziwill, Chargé d'Affaires Bennett, the author and Prince Radziwill

Party given by Mrs Kennedy on her last night in Greece. The author on far left. Princess Radziwill, Mrs Kennedy's sister seated centre. Prince Radziwill standing far right

Dinner given by the Kennedys for President Ayub Khan of Pakistan in specially-decorated tent on Mount Vernon

The author chatting with a social aide at a military review held at the White House for the visit of the President of Tunisia

Mater Familias in Chicago! · 279

years previously. I also knew the toy department of Marshall Field's, because that is where my mother had always taken me as a little girl between trains. This was the sum total of my familiarity with the city. I did not even know Chicago possessed a baseball team, much less two, nor did I know what game the Chicago Bears and the Chicago Black Hawks played.

I know now. I became a fan in self-defense. This is a city of sports fans, and the local teams are as much a part of our lives as the wind we inhale. Although Chicago is a big city, it is one that completely involves its citizens, encompassing their lives with its problems, successes and controversies. When the super-sized, rust-colored, could-be-anything sculpture by Picasso was installed in the Civic Center Plaza, the blood pressure of the local citizenry went up a hundred points, as they either condemned or praised it. Like the Italians who are famous for their knowledge of their own art, everyone in Chicago knew about the sculpture and just had to express an opinion.

The city is an ever-widening pool of handsome buildings, exceptional parks and depressing slums. Urban renewal will hopefully catch up with the latter one day. The mercuric growth of brightly colored suburban developments is proof of the health of the industrial complexes around the city. The Chicago Symphony and the Lyric Opera Company, although beset with constant labor troubles, bring the sound of truly magnificent music to the population, and the Chicago Art Institute has as fine a group of treasures as any museum in the world.

Everyone seems to know what is going on in the local scene, whether it's the latest civil rights protest at City Hall, the topping off of a skyscraper, the addition of a porpoise to the Shedd Aquarium, the gangland stuffing of a body into an automobile trunk, the drive to combat lake pollution, or the latest pinching of a Playboy Bunny cottontail. The action is everybody's action, and it is discussed incessantly, person-to-person, over an imaginary back fence. Perhaps the reason is that the population is media-happy. Chicagoans are avid newspaper readers and television spectators. The TV and radio stars and daily columnists are idolized — Irv Kupcinet, Norman Ross, Herb Lyon, Maggie Daly, Mike Royko, Jack Mabley, Sydney J. Harris, Virginia Kay, Jim Conway, Lee Phillip, Jack Eigen, Mal Bellairs, Howard Miller and Wally Phillips. With a rich opportunity to make oneself heard on radio or television on major issues, a Chicago citizen can sound off in any number of ways, as though he were addressing the town hall.

I was soon to find that in a city tightly wrapped in civic pride, one cannot escape the extra work load. A business woman with a family is expected to perform for her city every bit as much as the wealthy suburbanite whose main project is giving orders to her household staff. Many is the time I would long for the good old New York days, when serving on the board of an agency or a benefit committee exacted only one piece of tribute: to allow oneself to be photographed with two other ladies, lunching at a chic restaurant or having tea in someone's apartment, while supposedly going over plans. The plans, of course, were never on hand, nor did one have to attend the benefit. The photograph duly appeared in the society section of the New York papers, and one's deed for humanity was done.

Ambassador Kennedy had referred to Chicago as a "virile town." I discovered what this meant. The city is masculine in its nature, aggressive, pulsing with the rhythm of business, success and energy to build for the future. What the President's father had not mentioned were the physical aspects of the city. There is great natural beauty in the long, winding lakefront trimmed in sandy or tree-dotted beaches. There is man-made beauty in the remnants of the first Chicago School of Architecture, such as The Rookery office building or the magnificent Auditorium Theatre, built by Adler and Sullivan in 1889. There is also man-made beauty in the examples of the modern Chicago School of Architecture, and in the experiments by Mies Van der Rohe with his glass apartment buildings on Lake Shore Drive. There is excitement and diversity in the buildings on the University of Chicago campus, and the Illinois Circle campus, in the gigantic Hancock Building, and in that small jewel in Glencoe, Yamasaki's synagogue. To most people Michigan Avenue has many more aesthetic values than New York's Fifth Avenue, and the coastline of Lake Michigan is far more spectacular than the Hudson or the East Rivers. In the summertime the sun-splashed beaches easily accommodate the city's millions of inhabitants. A Riviera tan may be effective, but an Oak Street Beach tan is just as good, and it's free.

In the winter one can walk along the dramatic spray-splashed lakefront and imagine he is listening to the pounding waves of Cape Cod. Sweeping vistas of the city's parks, beaches, luxury buildings and industrial complexes make striking patchwork quilt patterns from atop the tall buildings.

Chicago is even a friendly city, where Middle-western hospitality turns out not to be a fable after all. Those of us who move here become quickly incensed at the inferiority complex displayed by the natives. This is not a "Second City." It is totally different from New York and is a First City in many respects. If the women here do not have the courage to wear nude midriff harem pajamas to the opera, it does not follow that they are totally without chic. They are beautifully, tastefully dressed. The kookiness is left to the very young, as it should be. The carbon copy, tweedy look of the suburbs is no more prevalent than in any other set of suburbs. The Chicago woman entertains at home, so her elegant attire is not sprinkled around the restaurants for the benefit of the *Women's Wear Daily* columns.

The furnishing of apartments and homes is magnificent in the dwellings of the rich, amusing and inventive in the dwellings of the non-affluent young.

Most important of all, and New York can take note, when an old lady falls in the street in Mayor Daley's town, someone actually picks her up. The city is, however, made for the men. A woman bursting with creative abilities might as well pack her bags for New York. She will not earn in Chicago a salary commensurate to her abilities. The fact that I have learned to live with this injustice means I am far more fortunate than my lady colleagues.

✦✦

I found a small apartment on North State Parkway, an address that sounded as though it were a gasoline station on a superhighway. Instead, it was a tree-lined avenue bordering Lincoln Park and the lake, and was graced with any number of historic dwellings, including the Cardinal's red brick, multi-chimneyed nineteenth century mansion. Ours was a great old building itself, with an aura of a gracious gray-clad princess to it. It had been constructed in the early part of this century, modeled after the elegant apartments of Paris' Avenue Foch. Even the landlord, George Nixon, was charming. He was an expert on Chicago history and had fascinating tales to weave of the growth of the area from the days of Fort Dearborn, the earliest settlement on the Chicago River. My first day there I sat on my packing cases and happily surveyed the view. Although there was no longer a Washington Monument pointing up to the clouds, the scene below me of Lincoln Park, festooned with fluffy green trees, flowers and baby carriages, would have delighted a Seurat or a Renoir at his easel.

My furniture fit the new apartment beautifully, and there was even a distinct flavor of Washington around. My White House memorabilia were everywhere: photo albums, the oil sketch of Bernard Lamotte's mural of the Virgin Islands for President Kennedy's swimming pool, a sterling frame embellished with the Presidential seal which contained an autographed photo of the Kennedys, and a round table with its top covered in white parchment. It had been made by the White House carpenters, and it was signed in ink by the President and his family and by all the White House staff. In my cupboard sat beautiful crystal wine glasses, the gift of the White House Social Aides. Over my desk hung a framed motto, presented to me by my staff after a victory over the Presidential Aides in the West Wing: "Gentle when stroked; fierce when provoked." On the semainier sat a gift of great sentiment, a graceful sterling silver bowl, engraved with kind words from the White House press ladies. They had always been good to me. It should have been I who sent them a silver bowl.

Of course I missed 1600 Pennsylvania Avenue and all that went with it. I could hardly wait until the first trip back to see everyone. I had been in Chicago only three months, Nancy Tuckerman having most capably taken over my Social Secretary duties, when the chance came. On November 22, I sat with Henry Sell, then Editor-in-Chief of *Town & Country* magazine, having a Bloody Mary before lunch on the 39th floor of the Prudential Building. We were surrounded by thick gray clouds. The waiter brought us the menu for lunch and said quietly, "Someone has just shot President Kennedy in Dallas."

I got through to Nancy Tuckerman at the White House immediately. Then I talked to Sarge Shriver. It was at his suggestion that I took the next plane for Washington. I would have anyway. Sarge had been put in charge of the ceremonial arrangements for the funeral, so I worked under him specifically to implement Mrs. Kennedy's wishes for the funeral. Bobby was in charge of holding things together in the Presidential family quarters. I had to contact him constantly for two days. His strength and gentleness were superhuman. (I had thought many times what a great President he would make. It was impossible to realize then that the surrealism of the atmosphere after the President's murder would be repeated four and a half years later when Bobby too would fall to an assassin's bullet. Once again the noble cloak of tragedy would enfold a remarkable family.)

Mrs. Johnson asked me to stay during the first two weeks of the new administration, to work with her staff on the transition. It had not been the homecoming to the White House I had so looked forward to during those first weeks in Chicago.

The biggest adjustment in leaving Washington was the mere fact of moving away from the center of the world's most exciting political stimuli. There would be no more endless bull sessions on the polished floors of narrow Georgetown living rooms, where great wits and facile tempers embroiled everyone in international crises and politics. No other city but Washington can boast of such an atmosphere. It is, after all, the center of government, politics and power. If one possesses even a tiny piece of the big governmental jigsaw, then one feels important, necessary, related to every other part.

This part of the world, however, was politically conservative in its business circles, even distrustful of Washington in principle. One of the first things I would have to do was to ignore the anti-liberal tirades fired at me from across the dinner table at North Shore dinner parties. Even Bill Buckley would be considered a touch liberal in some of these circles. The hardest lesson of all to learn was that often the least-informed people make the most noise. In conversations with my family on the telephone, I would blow off steam on the subject of these dinner party conversations. My father, as a former Republican

Congressman, would calm me down. "Remember, Tish," he said, "in this case, you don't either lick 'em or join 'em. You learn to shut up." It was sage advice.

My new job was so different from the previous one, it was as though I had zipped myself into somebody else's skin. On all my prior jobs, I had existed as a hothouse flower without realizing it. My working environment had been sheltered, even insulated from a normal office way of life. Embassy Residences, a plush Fifth Avenue jeweler's and the house of the President of the United States hardly constitute the typical office milieu.

In Washington every morning a chatty Army sergeant, driving a black Ford and wearing a black uniform, had picked me up and deposited me at my office; he had also taken me home every night. Before that, I had driven my own car to work at the Embassies in Paris and Rome, and had parked it in their private driveways.

Going to work now meant standing like everyone else and being buffeted around, totally deprived of oxygen, on a bus. My suggestion to the Chicago Transit Authority that they either open a window on each bus or furnish their customers with oxygen masks has never met with an enthusiastic response.

At first, just the actual physical act of entering the Merchandise Mart proved to be a daily hazard. I can now meet it with ease. It merely takes athletic training and perfect timing. One is catapulted into the building at rush hour with one's 22,000 fellow workers through revolving doors with a magnetic force that would roughen up a Chicago Bear in his football padding. A decision to change direction during one of these encounters with the revolving doors would mean a listing in the obituary section of the paper as death by suicide.

The Merchandise Mart sits like an overly plump and pretentious hen on her nest on the banks of the Chicago River. Any compliments hitherto cast in the direction of Lake Michigan are rescinded in the case of this filthy river, criss-crossed by the world's ugliest bridges. The facade of the Mart is covered with a soot that all of the famous Parisian sandblasters could probably never remove. The grime from the regime of Louis XIV in the seventeenth century has proved to be far less stubborn than the grime of less than forty years in Chicago's air.

My new job on the Mart staff put me smack in the middle of the frenetic world of buyers and sellers and of designers and manufacturers engaged in the home furnishings business. It was another whole new world to learn all over again. My knowledge of antiques proved not to be a basic plus except in regard to my own personal satisfaction. It prompts the syllogism that knowing antiques is to the furniture industry what a small caviar hors d'oeuvre is to the entire meal.

The major business of the Merchandise Mart is home furnishings for the interior. Since everyone lives in an interior of some kind, this is as important an industry as furnishing the clothes for one's back, although there is not so much built-in obsolescence. The Mart is the central marketplace for this industry, where manufacturers show what they have to offer, where designers exchange ideas and gain inspiration for their next lines, and where buyers from big and little stores come to order their stock. The marketplace thus becomes the meetingplace twice a year for everyone involved in the home furnishings industry.

From the minute I walked in the door, I kept hearing the words "the market," as though it were the biggest event in history. I did not even know what "the market" was, other than in terms of the local butcher or the marketplace of ancient Athens and Rome.

Every January and June, thousands of people crowd our building and our sister building on Lake Shore Drive (The

American Furniture Mart) for four or five days during "the market." The presidents of the furniture companies are on hand to see that the lines are properly introduced. The big companies like Burlington, Celanese, Monsanto, Avisco, Allied Chemical and Du Pont send experts to Chicago to introduce their latest fiber stories with shows, displays and elaborate promotions. The lamp manufacturers arrive to show how their new lines adapt to the latest styles in interiors. The carpet salesmen beat the drums for their new colors; the curtain and drapery showrooms show the latest in window treatments, bedspreads and decorator pillows; the fabrics designers display and cross-promote their new fabrics in conjunction with the furniture on which they are used as upholstery material. The salesmen for all these companies come from the entire country to "learn the new lines" they will be selling, and to pick up salesmanship hints. The most welcome visitor of all to market is, of course, the buyer. He comes from Key West, Florida, or Fairbanks, Alaska, and can represent the buying powers of a B. Altman & Co. in New York right on down to a "Ye Old Gift Shoppe" in Kansas.

He wants to see what is new, predict what will sell (the two are not necessarily in harmony), and make the best deal he can get. The amount of fiscal conniving that is carried on in "the back room" of the showrooms reminds one of an Arab bazaar, except for the fact that the protagonists are not sitting on their haunches.

"The market" also means an exchange of ideas and the gathering of information about the entire industry. Experts address seminars over early breakfast meetings. Luncheon panels hassle over everything from how to crate merchandise to how one switches with great speed from a blue and beige inventory to an olive green and gold inventory, in order to keep pace with the capricious taste of the American housewife. There are endless gab-fests about the state of the economy. Price structures seem to wax and wane with the optimism or pessimism of *The Wall Street Journal*. It only takes the move of one major fiber producer to change prices on their carpeting to cause the entire eighteenth, thirteenth and tenth floors of carpet showrooms to shudder from the impact and immediately discuss changing their own prices.

Along with the home furnishings markets, there are other smaller ones scheduled on a regular basis throughout the year for the other tenants, for the china and giftwares industry, the men's, women's and children's wear industries, and the contract and office equipment industries. Whether a market is in progress or not, the lower corridors of the building make an intricate honeycomb of unbelievable vitality. The complex of showrooms is sliced through by seven and a half miles of corridors. These showrooms sparkle like brilliantly lit stage sets on either side of the purposely darkened hallways. Some of the showrooms are breathtakingly beautiful and tasteful, looking as though the interiors magazine editors had just stepped in to set them up for photography. The designers spare no costs in making the architectural background of these displays striking. Other showrooms look like the alleyways in the Casbah, where "things" hang from the ceiling and up the walls like cuts of meat at the butcher's.

Dotting these vast ranches of wholesale operations are little cities of somber, conservative offices, like the Quaker Oats Company, with its own kitchens tantalizingly testing batches of Aunt Jemima pancakes and oatmeal cookies during office hours. The intellectuals with books in their arms inevitably head for the World Book Division of Field Enterprises offices. The celebrities are dashing for the NBC television studios. Advertising men, bankers, investment brokers and public relations executives on their way to their offices mingle in the elevators with interior designers laden with sample books and lamps. If one smells a strange odor wafting through a ventilator above or below the Toni offices, it means they are at work again brewing a new hair product. There is often an element of cheesecake in the corridors, too, particularly during one of the markets. A good looking pair of legs is supposed to make a tufted carpet more salable.

The only aspect of calm to the Mart at the busy times of year is the area in front of the building, where Freddie the Doorman supervises the taxi line. He has been coping with this problem since the early thirties. He is an accurate source of who's in town and for how long, and he can spot celebrities faster than Irv Kupcinet in the Pump Room. If he catches someone cheating on his taxi line, he will put him in his place, whether the line breaker is a prize fighter or a multi-millionaire, just with his tone of voice and his choice of vocabulary.

At nighttime, when the building (equal in size to ninety-seven acres of land) begins to prepare for slumber and to rid itself of the bees in the honeycombs, the security men fly around the halls like mischievous witches on battery-powered scooters to check and recheck all the doors.

✢

I may have been newly arrived from a great seat of power, the White House, but I was just a little school girl in the Chicago business world of home furnishings. My title was "Consultant to the Merchandise Mart." In order to "consult," one is supposed to have some knowledge of the subject.

The big boss, Wallace Ollman, obviously did not have time to hold school classes for his newly arrived staff. He and his able young Assistant Manager, Tom King, were always enmeshed in some top level space rental deal, involving thousands of square feet of space, and thousands of dollars. It did not take me long to observe that Wally Ollman worked seven days a week. On Sundays he could be found checking over his vast empire to see if the fire stairways were being properly maintained, and if the rest room cleaners had been doing their jobs. He roams the acreage of the building like a general checking on the front lines before the attack. The building shows it.

My closest staff colleagues, Harry Finkel and his assistant, Dorothy Eastline, always seemed to be running on the double. Harry, a dynamic young man, was in charge of promotion and advertising, which is another way of saying in charge of crises. Dorothy Eastline, his slim blond sidekick, is a walking repository of information on the markets. She would be very difficult to computerize. I trotted behind them both like an admiring puppy dog for a while, hoping I could learn from them how to swing the lingo of the trade and know every luminary in the business.

Another of our colleagues on the staff, Ray Simon, fast with a cigar and very amusing quips, patiently explained the floors he supervises in the Mart, the fashion showrooms. They constitute a mini garment district in many respects.

I realized I could absorb a good deal through meeting the tenants, so I began visiting the showrooms. There are about a thousand in all. Some were brief stick-the-head-in-the-door encounters, but in some of the spaces I stayed to chat awhile. (Someone who noticed my excursions accused me of running for office.) If there were no customers around, the managers and salesmen were relaxed and easy to engage in conversation. We would chat about what was selling, and what colors, textures, fabrics, carpets, and wood finishes were "coming on strong." They would even discuss with amazing candor their business problems and their company's future plans. The most difficult part of this educational process was accepting the fact that my own taste was neither universal nor praiseworthy from a business point of view. I stopped enthusing over objects in the showroom, because my rapture would be met with an inevitable frown and the statement "It doesn't sell." The only important questions in the minds of buyers and sellers in this industry were, "What will sell, how fast can we get it, in what shape will it arrive, and how quickly can we move it?"

My personal judgment of design in the meantime would have to lie cold and lonely in a dark drawer of my mind, unstated and unappreciated. It was a humbling experience to pass a showroom jammed with furniture I considered in outrageously bad taste, only to see it jammed with enthusiastic buyers at market time.

It was interesting to observe an interior designer order one breakfront costing about $2,000 from Baker in five minutes, and then to observe a department store buyer order five hundred of a $2.95 child's garment in three minutes on one of the fashion floors. Supplying Mrs. America with her luxurious extravagance or with her child's basic romper suit looks easier than it is. Years of experience and know-how lie behind every rapid decision.

Those early days on the new job in the Mart were not without problems. I kept wondering if I had made the right decision. I had no secretary, no benefits that were readily recognizable. I even figured out that one was required to walk the equivalent of one and a half New York City blocks to reach the powder room on our floor, a far cry from my private shower-bathroom in the White House.

Gradually the power of merchandising began to excite me, and I began to feel at ease in this new milieu. I began to know everyone, from the blue-uniformed elevator operators to the

Presidents of large corporations. This was Chicago; it could not have been New York. Everyone smiled a greeting when passing in the hall or sharing an elevator. My job as Consultant grew in scope. My brother described my duties as "eclectic . . . Don't ask her to tell you what she does. It will take her all night." A consultant operates in two ways, I found. He takes projects assigned to him, but even more important, thinks up his own. Everyone on the Mart staff shared the same goal, to enhance the property and to promote the markets. The Mart must remain a place the buyers cannot bypass, a place where not only will they find what they want for their stores, but where they will also pick up selling techniques and aids.

I was given the job of coordinating the decoration of the sixth floor corridors, which was a joint project between Brock Arms, representing the N.S.I.D. designers group, and Lucile Knoche, representing the A.I.D. The project was also rather historic, in that the two competing organizations cooperated with each other. (Their fees were donated to their scholarship funds.) It was impossible not to remember back to the rivalry involved in the redecoration of the two White House rooms undertaken by the A.I.D. and the N.S.I.D.

I married the fashion and furniture floors together at the Casual and Summer Furniture Markets in October, by staging fashion shows of summer sportswear in conjunction with displays of wrought iron, rattan, aluminum and wood furniture. There was admittedly more buyer interest in a webbed poolside lounging chair when a blond wearing a bikini was reclining on it.

This kind of fashion show had a purpose other than just to entertain the buyer. It was a promotion he could imitate in his own store, to draw traffic to his terrace and patio shop. Once we installed a large Doughboy plastic swimming pool in the middle of the M & M Club for this buyers' party, as a realistic background for the swimsuit models. By the time the inevitable unplanned fall-ins had occurred, and the carpet on the club floor was sopping wet, building engineer Bill Abraham stated he hoped my creativity would veer in other directions, just anywhere away from his building. After I had finished commentating one of these shows, my voice rising in volume to compete with the noise and whistles of the happy party guests, a buyer from a small town in Kansas came up to me. "Is this very different from your White House life, Miss Baldrige?" he asked. "No," I replied, "Plus ça change, plus c'est la même chose."

"Gosh, Miss Baldrige," he said, his eyes brimming with emotion and admiration, "the things you learn in Washington!"

Thinking up lobby displays was another of my consulting projects for the Mart. I drew on my Tiffany table setting experience and pulled together room settings that featured different kinds of parties. We invited leading Chicago interior designers to do their own vignettes, using merchandise from the Mart, of course. I was a perfectionist about these displays, caring about even a speck of dust on a crystal goblet. We had a display of summer furniture in gardens, which featured over a thousand plants and trees lent by A. Lange, the florist. They were supposedly taken care of by professionals, but every morning on my way to work, I lovingly sprinkled the thirsty-looking ones with a giant watering can I hid in a broom closet. I had learned long ago that when one implements a project, the responsibility for every part of it lies with oneself. If a rug in a display is dirty, I will vacuum it, and if the silver on a table setting looks tarnished, if I don't polish it, it will remain tarnished.

Months before the big home furnishings market took place,

I would climb into my tower to work on an overall theme, in which the tenants could participate, and which would lend cohesiveness to the market. When my scheme of "Live Color" was implemented one June, we managed to involve the entire industry with our efforts. The Interchemical Corporation constructed a mammoth twenty-five-foot-tall "Color Fair" in the middle of the lobby on top of a multi-striped wall-to-wall carpet. Interchem's Color Fair demonstrated the intrinsic nature of color superbly; spectators could push buttons and pull knobs to their hearts' content, setting off more fascinating experiments than an overdose of LSD could create. My little scheme once again incurred the wrath of the building engineer, because in order to permit the parts of the structure to pass through the front of the building, the glass facade had to be dismantled. Fire regulations complicated matters further, extra power generators had to be brought in, and the logistics turmoil caused in all of the maintenance departments of the Mart did not subside during the entire market.

From the minute one stepped from a taxi onto the terrace in front of the Mart (covered in many shades of outdoor carpeting), and viewed Valspar Paint's eighteen-foot-tall "Color Pylon," the building was a carnival of color. Forty pretty young girls, who handle registration and information duties for the Mart, were clad in identical Monsanto dresses of brilliant patterns of color. *House & Garden* magazine constructed its "Color Carousel" in the lobby, demonstrating their new colors and fabric combinations in well-designed interiors. I even got the United States Government into the act, when the U.S. Bureau of Standards lent us their electric rotating "Munsell Color Solid" apparatus. Du Pont produced special shows on the subject of color in their closed circuit television programs; Allied Chemical and Alcoa demonstrated color in decorated rooms constructed in the lobby. Seminars were held in the M & M Club by the National Retail Furniture Association, the most amusing of which featured Dr. Isay Balinkin, professor of experimental physics at the University of Cincinnati. He taught color the way a magician performs his act. His only request of me before his program was to procure a nice ripe watermelon. I found a papier-mâché one on the Accessories floor of the Mart, which he gladly used. He admonished me to keep it well chilled in the refrigerator for him. Interchem also displayed their "color illusions" lining one whole wall corridor, which left the buyers rubbing their eyes at optical tricks. Monsanto hung color displays in the corridors, and Magee Carpets played games with the buyers by giving them Dr. Joyce Brothers' color psychology test.

A lot of planning goes into such a market. "Live Color" marked the first time my own blood, sweat and tears flowed in every hue of the rainbow.

+-+

The really enjoyable part of consulting for the Merchandise Mart is the "think-up-oneself project," which has a goal of generating goodwill and increasing the familiarity of the public with the Mart. Since the showrooms are closed to the public, except for guided tours, most of the citizens are confused about what takes place in that large structure with the dirty face on the banks of the Chicago River.

One of the ways to inform the public of the business of the Mart was through television. I went on local shows regularly, lugging home furnishings items with me, from wallpaper samples and ashtrays to heavy rugs and sofas. I set about attracting women's organizations to take guided tours of the Mart, and to lunch in the club while I lectured on decorating trends. My audiences would run the gamut from the national delegates to a Junior League Convention to the wives of the Consular Corps in Chicago.

One of my most satisfying projects was a clinic which took place every Saturday morning in the M & M Club throughout one whole winter, with an audience each week of approximately five hundred teen-aged girls. These girls were mostly from economically deprived backgrounds; some were from houses of juvenile correction and were allowed to attend with the matrons as "chaperones." The Mart benefited in its community public relations as a result of these clinics, but the personal rewards were far greater to all of us. I talked my friend Eppie Lederer into donating an hour of her precious time to speak to the girls one morning. They were spellbound as she spoke about their manners and their morals; since it was "Ann Landers" talking to them, they listened. For another session, I persuaded Eileen Ford, the head of the world's largest model agency, to fly out from New York with two of her top junior models to discuss grooming, posture and health. For another Saturday, Cora Campanella, a training director from Charles of the Ritz in New York, flew in with a leading hairdresser to demonstrate makeup, skin care and hair styling. The young girls themselves served as models. I discussed the subject of decorating another time, with tips on doing over one's bedroom on a very low budget. For this session I used slides from Joanna Window Shades and from *Seventeen* magazine.

Professor Helen Wheeler, my English teacher from Vassar, came to Chicago to lecture on the importance of proper speech and voice. This was perhaps the factor that needed the most attention for many of the Negro and Puerto Rican girls in attendance. Helen Wheeler recorded their voices, showed how important their speech was to their future careers, and brought her

Vassar-level ideas right down to their own understanding. When a young Negro Northwestern drama student read poetry over the microphone, the girls were transfixed. Here was a student in college, barely older than they, with a beautiful, mellifluous voice. She was an inspiration to the potential dropouts in the audience.

For each session, I borrowed clothes from the Mart showrooms and staged a fashion show, using the girls as models. As I guided each class to its successful conclusion and heard the girls state frankly what had been good, and what had been worthless, I felt I had received an education myself in communicating with their generation. They had an obvious thirst for what is right and what is beautiful, and for understanding why it is so.

This conclusion spurred me on to teaching history of art classes for the neighborhood kids from poor homes on Saturdays. I profited from teaching those courses, too. I learned, for instance, that one has to put the students through some arduous exercise outdoors on the playground before throwing culture at them in a stuffy auditorium. I also learned that when the lights go out for the projection of the colored slides on the screen, the boys have to be physically segregated from the girls. I also learned that even if their vocabulary seems to consist only of crude slang and swear words, these teenagers have a distinct feeling for and love of art. When my first group of students admitted sheepishly they had spent the previous Sunday down at the Chicago Art Institute, I knew victory was mine.

↔

The Mart sent me to Europe in November of 1966 on a mission that confused me almost as much as the audiences I was supposed to woo and win. The object of the exercise was to obtain foreign government assistance and foreign manufacturers' participation in a big contract furnishings market to be managed by the Merchandise Mart (called INTERCON I). The contract business is one of the largest industries in the world, for it includes the manufacture and the sale of all of the furnishings for places of business, commercial properties and institutions. In short, the contract market can involve everything from schools, hospitals and churches to offices, hotels and restaurants.

My schedule in Europe was a roller-coaster four weeks of dashing through ten countries. In each major capitol, I would base myself in some Embassy office, where a vacant desk was available, under the paternal eye of the Commercial or Economic Attaché. In most cases, I knew the attaché in question from my foreign service days, so he would add a measure of kindness to his assistance. Then, with the help of the Press Attaché, I would hold a major press conference, to explain INTERCON I and why that country's top manufacturers should take space to show their products. I would also explain why that country's top designers and architects should attend for their own prestige, international publicity and self-education. The next step was to hold a party in the leading hotel or restaurant, which would be attended by the top members of government engaged in the promotion of their own exports and by important figures in the home furnishings industry.

I had known Europe intimately as a student, as a young secretary in the diplomatic corps, and in the usual way, as a tourist. As a winged messenger for INTERCON, I was abroad in a new role. Suddenly, I was a woman in business, playing a man's game. My mission was so complicated and difficult, it took a great deal of private conversation with my psyche to maintain the courage to continue.

If Americans did not understand what the contract market was, how would the Europeans? How could I persuade governments and foreign businessmen to sink money into exhibiting wares hitherto never exported to the United States at a market never held before, in a place they had never visited? My contacts with designers and architects would be easy, I knew, because their role in this market was to observe, to participate in panels and discussions, and to meet their fellow luminaries in the field of good design. They understood my mission at once, and wholeheartedly supported it. In Cologne, I had to wait until the wine had been passed through three courses during lunch in a dining room overlooking the great cathedral. Only then did the dour Germanic expressions soften in my direction. I had to speak through an interpreter whenever the German language was used. It was very unpleasant. I could hear the interpreter using expressions I knew were incorrect in describing the nature of the market. I tried to charm my audience, to make them laugh; I attempted to appeal to their sense of chivalry. Nothing worked. It was like addressing the Presidents carved on the face of Mt. Rushmore. I longed for the security of standing up there as an official United States representative. This was the first time in my beloved Europe that I was courting the Europeans, seeking *their* money. Before, I had always been part of a team giving money away to them. The old world charm of life abroad rather evaporates in such circumstances.

In Vienna, the press conference was held in the Hotel Imperial, which had been Soviet headquarters during the post-World War II occupation of Austria. I had been detained for a short while in this hotel by Soviet authorities in 1952. Now, suddenly, in the overly-gilded rococo reception room, I stood under the crystal chandeliers addressing one hundred press, government officials and manufacturers. Again, the audience was all men, and I was the only woman in the room. I noticed that a good portion of my audience, holding their aperitif glasses, was hidden behind the pillars of the room, on purpose. They were probably embarrassed to be confronted by an American businesswoman. I began my presentation by saying, "Good afternoon. It is such a pleasure to be back in your beautiful city again. I have such happy memories of Vienna."

The interpreter put my remarks into German, and I noticed a rash of shy smiles coming forth. I grew bolder and took some poetic license.

"In our country, we have an old expression, which applies here: 'I am not going to shoot until I see the whites of your eyes.'"

A masculine titter, not unlike that heard in a ladies' lecture hall, ran like mercury around the room. The men moved out from the pillars, and into my full view. They had to stand, as there were very few ballroom chairs, and I had been told by the Embassy they preferred standing at functions like this. I regained my poise, strode like a verbal warrior into my subject, and suddenly felt confident I could win the battle of communication. After Austria, language was no problem. I used English in London, of course, and in all four Scandinavian countries. I spouted Italian in Rome, and spoke French in France and Spain. In Madrid, the Chamber of Commerce held a meeting and a champagne reception for me in their beautiful palace. The long conference table was lined with tiny American flags, and the room was crowded with over a hundred Spanish government and industry leaders. I stood up to speak after being introduced, and every man in the room sprang to his feet automatically. I motioned them to sit down, so I could begin my presentation. They remained standing, and motioned me to sit down. The President then explained they would not sit down while I, a woman, stood. They requested that I make my presentation seated. I explained to the group that I could not see all their faces, nor could I be heard if I sat down in such a crowded room. The lady won, but it was obviously an exercise in self-control for the Spaniards to sit patiently while I addressed them from on high. I inwardly blessed them for their delightful chivalry.

In Paris, the press conference was held in a beautiful salon that had been used in the days of the Louis, in the Hotel Crillon overlooking the fountains of the Place de la Concorde. The hotel concierge recognized me when I walked into the hotel from the days of President Kennedy's trip to Paris. I found the same upstairs maid I had known in my days as the David Bruces' Social Secretary. At the end of the press conference, a girl reporter whispered good-bye to me and put a bottle of French perfume in my hand. "That's to say thanks for helping me out so nicely at Malmaison in 1961 when you were there with Madame Kennedy and Madame Malraux." She slipped away before I could speak to her. I do not to this day remember what I did to help her.

It was an adventure to run around Europe with a tightly packed briefcase, cajoling millionaire industrialists and high government officials to go along with INTERCON I. I, of course, prevailed upon friends like the David Bruces at the Embassy in London and the Angier Biddle Dukes at the Embassy in Madrid wherever I could for bed, board and moral encouragement. My mission was a success. Several foreign countries organized exhibits.

INTERCON I headed toward its successful fruition. Then came the total destruction of the major display and meeting facility for exhibitors, including all the foreign ones. McCormick Place burned to the ground one cold early morning, two months before INTERCON I was to take place. The market was, of course, canceled, as no other proper space could be found on short notice. The only silver lining salvaged from the smoking ruins was that the international contract market began to bubble with renewed fervor, and we began to plan again.

⊷

Everyone in Chicago is proud of the fact that the largest retailing giant in the world has headquarters here, Sears, Roebuck and Company. Every family in town seems to have a member who either charges everything at Sears, is on Sears' payroll, or who has been trained by Sears somewhere along the way.

My work for the Mart often took me out the Eisenhower Expressway to the Sears headquarters on the West Side. It is a confused maze of buildings, rambling over a large area. Each building seems to have its own special type of architecture, running the gamut from brown Victorian, complete with turrets, to modern red cracker-box. The company has a definite tinge of the Pentagon to its organization, even if architecturally it resembles an artist's nightmare.

My main contact at Sears was the late George H. Struthers, Vice President in Charge of Merchandising. He was a silver-haired, handsome genius in the merchant's world; he had fought his way up a very difficult ladder. One day I sat in his office, feeling slightly restless about my career in general. I decided to ask him for some fatherly advice, even perhaps for a job.

"So you want to make more money, Tish?"

I had to laugh. One can talk about restlessness all one wants, but it almost always boils down to economics, and he did not have the time to skirt the issue.

"If you weren't a girl, you would be making a lot more by now," he said. "You have it in you."

His words were comforting to my ego, but I could not exactly change my sex at this point.

"If you want my advice," he said, tapping his silver pencil on the brightly polished desk, "you'll go into business for yourself."

Such an idea had never occurred to me. I had no financial security, no capital, no experience. He was talking in superlatives.

"Ask the Mart to release you from their staff full-time. Take a big cut in salary from them. But ask them to retain you as a consultant, because you need them for experience and for contacts. Besides, you will be much more valuable to them if you work more on the outside."

I remained silent. This was all coming too fast.

"I'll even give you a job with Sears. We will be one of your accounts, your major account. You'll be more valuable to us by having other duties on the outside, too, that are pertinent to your talents. Set up your own office. Let's see. Why don't you call it 'Letitia Baldrige Enterprises'?" He paused while he reflected on the sound of it. Then he asked with a smile, "What other girl has had the life you've led?"

In two weeks' time, thanks to George Struthers and his assistant, Vincent Graham, the new enterprises were a fact, not a plan. I had an office at Sears, and retained my niche in the main office of the Mart, too. I thus had two offices, two major accounts, no secretary, and lots of boxes of very expensive engraved stationery that announced my firm in bright red letters as "Letitia Baldrige Enterprises." I used the European symbol of the telephone with the office telephone number on the engraving plate, a small detail that impressed no one but me.

My little office at Sears overlooked the main avenue of buildings, but I had the good fortune to look down on the brilliant flower garden. It is backed by a pseudo-Grecian colonnade of white pillars, and by an impressive row of foreign flags. The garden is incongruously filled with strollers and picnickers on nice days, lending a note of a college campus to the otherwise hopelessly austere surroundings.

The executive offices, the catalog operations, the advertising and display departments, the quality testing labs and the central headquarters of all buying departments (except for fashion) are housed here and in Skokie, a nearby suburb. The fashion departments, of course, have to be in New York City, snuggled close to the garment district. My own cubbyhole was distinguished from the others in a long military row in the Merchandise Headquarters by its furniture, upholstered in a large sherbet-colored plaid. Such frivolity is very non-standard for the offices of this company, but my idiosyncrasy was chalked off with a "She's our Lady consultant, you know."

I was greeted by my colleagues on all levels in my new niche with great curiosity and skepticism, but finally with affection. Sears, like most companies outside of New York, is not used to lady executives.

The company is so large, so far-reaching, so frantically busy keeping up with trends, fashions, supply and quality control problems all over the world, there is no time in anyone's day for dawdling and gossiping. If a buyer makes a mistake on a ski sweater, it can be a many-thousand-sweaters mistake. Items are usually purchased by the thousands for catalog use. "Will it sell?" is an important phrase in the Mart. "Will it sell?" has cataclysmic ramifications in an operation like Sears.

My new boss when George Struthers died was the dynamic young head of Sears' flourishing Canadian operation, James W. Button. He became the company's first senior vice president. When one is the "first" anything at Sears, it is monumental.

My main partners in the Sears business of consulting were Vincent Price and his witty, charming wife Mary. We collaborated on a program of reproducing historic American objects

Mater Familias in Chicago! · 305

for the home. Vincent was, I soon found, the perfect embodiment of the Renaissance Man. He is an expert on art, a gourmet cook, an accomplished actor of everything from Shakespeare to horror monsters, a brilliant conversationalist, and a lusty connoisseur of the joys of living. When I was giving a talk one day to a group of Sears' lady employees on the subject of decorating, Vincent dropped in to say hello. "You're wonderful," he said, addressing the group in an almost purring, sensuous tone. "Isn't Sears lucky to have you working for them?"

One smitten typist of hefty proportions sighed to me after he had left the room, "He's the only man in the world who can tell me to work harder for the company and make me feel I've just been kissed all in the same sentence!"

Ted Williams and his sport staff were other consultants, but unfortunately my preoccupation with interior design and fashion did not criss-cross with their fishing expeditions, mountain climbs and campouts in the wilderness.

I began helping structure the classes for John Terrell and Liz Reed in New York for the Sears' Charm School program. The Charm Schools consisted of a series of classes on grooming, fashion and comportment which were held in major stores across the country. I persuaded the experts on these subjects, all old friends from New York days, to lend their names and guidance for the course. I also found myself on lecture platforms across the country for Sears, confronting teen-aged audiences.

Like a political candidate, I had to learn to field the loaded question. A sixteen-year-old girl, for example, came up to me and said, "Miss Baldrige, you claim a girl's mother has a lot to do with teaching her manners and taste. You said we should listen to our mothers. Well, my mother doesn't happen to know anything about manners. And I don't like her taste. I don't even respect her. So what do I do now?" Perhaps she was being sarcastic with good reason. I told her to find a teacher or anyone she admired and looked up to and to study the way that woman spoke, dressed and behaved in general.

Another girl asked me in front of several hundred girls why I didn't teach sex education instead of manners. Wasn't it much more important? Her question, of course, initiated a wave of excited tittering in the room. It is a great way to lose an audience.

"One teaches what one knows well," I replied, laughing to carry on her joke for one second. "But since we are on the subject, you know, don't you, that it's a breach of good manners to pose that smart-aleck question just to draw laughs for yourself?"

The company puts great store in the public service factor of these courses for the benefit of the consumer. More and more classes on "the subject of becoming a lady" are being held in the major stores for the very young; for the more mature woman, courses on grooming, entertaining and decorating are being offered. I found it a challenge to write in the Sears' textbook "how to" do a party by oneself on a tight budget, in a small space. It would have been easier to write directions for a woman with an unlimited purse and with a large staff at her disposal.

It is true that the girls attending the classes buy more Sears' merchandise because they are "on the spot." However, these are minor benefits when compared to the polish given the company image when a mother drops a remark in the supermarket about her daughter's "having learned that in her Sears class."

The women employees of the company heard about my lectures and wanted the classes themselves, so I took them on — almost two thousand of them — in a series of one-hour sessions in the largest conference room. It was hard on me to initiate my working day at 8:15 A.M. by addressing 450 women on "the real meaning of elegance." It was a lot harder on Bill Holland of Personnel who had to sit gamely through the entire program, helping me with my visual aids and equipment. His embarrassment mercifully did not show in the dark when slides were being shown and we discussed fat thighs and garters showing under short skirts. However, when I invited Elizabeth Arden's exercise teacher, Antoinette Haass, to perform on a platform in a skimpy leotard, his eyes shouted for help more than once. "Ladies," Antoinette's voice would ring through the conference room, "Lift up your rib cage. Lift! Lift! Tuck your derrière under. Don't stand like that! You over there. You have one breast up and one breast down. Such posture!"

Messrs. Sears and Roebuck must have shuddered in their graves at such goings-on in their mail order house.

I was fortunate to have had interior design experience before beginning the consulting work for Sears. As the company's representative, I plunged into the preparation of decorating lectures, using Sears' slides and a few that were borrowed from Celanese and Burlington. I showed high school girls how to redo their bedrooms, how to make coordinated accessories, if they did not have the money to buy them. I lectured and wrote articles on "Entertaining is a question of taste and know-how, not money." I found myself addressing groups on interior design principles, everyone from clubs of elderly ladies to meetings of fresh-faced, 4-H Club leaders. There were also table-setting exhibitions to design as models that could be implemented by the big "A" stores in the Sears system. The fact that it was Sears' merchandise on these tables and not Tiffany's was immaterial. The design principles, the uses of color and elements are exactly the same.

As a part of my consulting duties, I also led Sears' buyers into the showrooms of the Mart to see significant new merchandise. I initiated home furnishings projects aimed at the youth market, and managed to introduce prominent figures in the home furnishings industry to their counterparts in Sears.

It did not take too long a time to become a member of the family. This was a triumph, however, for Sears is a sprawling giant and difficult to embrace. There is not a day that goes by, of course, that a consultant such as I does not experience pangs of envy at the profit-sharing benefits gained by the nineteen-year-old secretaries, to which we non-regulars have no right. These girls can retire when they're an elderly thirty-five with enough money to buy their own businesses.

I must be an enigma in the company. I have never learned the "numbers racket." Sears lives by the numbers, but I stubbornly refuse to. Departments in this gargantuan club have no names; they are numbers. Sears people from Alaska to Hong Kong talk a snobby sort of universal code system. I still call Clem Stein's department "Rugs" instead of 637; Doug Odell's 621 is "Accessories" to me, and Fred Hecht's department is "Furniture," not 601. This is considered a heresy. Colleagues such as Ed Menninger of Public Relations and Dick Butler, head of the interior design staff, have to stop their speeches at meetings to give me the translations of the numbers; otherwise I am left totally in the dark.

I cannot help observing that in many ways the early history of this giant company ran parallel to Tiffany's. Both companies started with young men of great vision engaged in the watch business. Both mushroomed, miraculously on no capital, in the nineteenth century. However, Tiffany's business was always directed to the rich, urbane carriage trade, and Sears answered a desperate need of the rural family.

Richard Sears was just a young, impecunious railroad station agent in North Redwood, Minnesota, in 1886, when a Chicago shipment of gold-filled watches was refused by the local jeweler. Sears decided to gamble on selling the watches and proceeded to sell every one of them, quickly and at a profit, to station agents all up and down the line. He began to handle more and more of them, and soon needed to take in someone to service the watches of his many customers. Another impoverished young man, Alvah C. Roebuck, answered an ad for a watch repairer in the *Chicago Daily News*. Thus began a partnership in watch catalogs, which by 1895 had grown to a mail order catalog operation over five hundred pages in length, offering merchandise in many categories, from ladies' steel braces to "pink pills for pale people." Today there are almost 1,700 catalog sales offices around the country, and the catalog weighs enough to give one a serious back problem if carried around too much. Other names contributed to the jet-propelled success of the firm. Julius Rosenwald was the foresighted genius who handled the company's financial and management development; and, of course, Sears is synonymous with one of Chicago's most revered gentlemen and philanthropists, General Robert E. Wood. His snow-white head and erect figure are immediately recognized wherever he goes. In 1925, he experimented with one retail store, opened out at the Chicago headquarters on the West Side. Everyone at the time said he was crazy, and that the Sears organization was crazy to listen to him. He was just crazy enough to give the impetus to an idea that adds up today to over 800 retail stores in America and abroad, doing over $8 billion gross sales. General Wood brought Sears to the cities and their suburbs.

Thanks to Sears, I have now seen my own country. Before Chicago days, I knew my way around Greek mountains and Finnish fishing villages better than I knew life in the United States. I have now visited every kind of American city and hamlet for promotions and new store openings. These trips can entail anything from an elegant champagne reception for the state governor and the mayor to a peanuts and balloon jamboree right out of "seventy-six trombones led the big parade." I never quite know what I am supposed to do at these openings, except that I must remain chic and well-groomed. At a moment's notice, I can find myself meeting countless press, appearing on every kind of TV show, crowning local queens of this-and-that, and addressing either large groups of middle-aged women or restless young girls on subjects that range from, "Ladies, wake up your tired home with a budget decorating plan" to "Girls, boys want you to have good manners." No matter what the subject of my discourse may be, the first question invariably asked at the Question-and-Answer period is, "What was Jackie Kennedy *really* like?"

Actually, I am astounded at the interest shown by female audiences of all ages when I leap into the subjects of etiquette, manners or protocol. There seems to be a national sense of insecurity in our women today on this subject; and they know it's important.

I often have to address employees at mass meetings in the store. I talk about taste and self-education. It is a definite challenge to entice a lawnmower salesman into reading magazines that will teach him what women like and need to know. Any vestiges of victory taste very sweet indeed.

If I see America when I travel for Sears, it is because the trite expression often applied to the company is true: Sears *is* America. After a steady diet of European intellectuals, New York taste-shapers for the very rich, and high-powered politicians in Washington, this was exactly what Letitia Baldrige Enterprises needed.

✦

There is nothing more scintillating and challenging than sticking a female nose into the maelstrom of Chicago's business life. Hundreds of major corporations have headquarters in this city, adding the sweet smell of vitality, affluence, and creativity to the polluted air. With two major accounts under my belt, Sears and the Merchandise Mart, I was ready to take on more. Business began to come, and all by word of mouth. I would not have known how to go after accounts. Luckily, they came to me. A telephone call would come, "Tish, can you handle this for me?" The "this" could be anything from the opening of the new Knoll furniture showroom in the Mart or the new Knapp and Tubbs furniture showroom in New York, to overseeing the press arrangements for the touring graphic art exhibit sponsored by Champion Papers. Miss Elizabeth Arden asked me to handle the opening of her new building in Chicago; I did some consulting work for the Quaker Oats Company and helped launch the new branch of Tiffany's in Chicago. I was called on for advice on the launching of the Swedish Contract Design Exhibit in the Mart; and Roberta Church asked me to oversee publicity stories on her jewels.

It was easy to mesh several accounts into one publicity release. For example, in the interests of promoting hominy grits for Quaker, I had a high-fashion photograph taken of a hostess serving grits at her supper party. The purpose of the picture was simple: to make this typically Southern dish an elegant adjunct to a buffet supper. The photograph's destination was the women's pages across the country. I dressed the model in an Elizabeth Arden exclusive hostess gown; we shot the picture in a dining room setting of the Baker Furniture showroom in the Mart, and used Tiffany table accessories. Everyone received credit in the picture caption, which was accompanied by a recipe for hominy grits. Starring front and center in the picture, of course, was "a delicious mess of grits," as one colleague phrased it, filling the center of an oversized, elegant silver chafing dish.

As the number of my accounts grew, so did Chicago curiosity

about my little office. Women as a rule just do not set themselves up in business in this male-oriented town. "How many on your staff?" I was asked constantly. "Myself" was the answer for many months. I was accused of running a CIA cover operation or of being a Johnsonian White House spy in Mayor Daley's Elysian Fields. I was long on offices and short on personnel. I had a nook at Sears, a cranny in the Management Office of the Mart, and an office at home. A friend, Jane Dunne, handled the secretarial chores several afternoons a week at the apartment. Sears gave me a part-time secretary to help out at their headquarters, and I was fortunate to have a pert blond named Sue Purtell assigned to me at Quaker Oats. Sue had a sunny disposition and a warm telephone voice that could mellow any crank in the business world.

It soon became apparent, since I spent more time en route to my offices in taxis than I did in the offices, that I needed one central downtown location, as well as the one at home, where I could work on all accounts at once.

The fifteenth floor of the Mart, housing the giftwares industry and looking like an Arab bazaar, found a spot in one corner for Letitia Baldrige Enterprises. My office, furnished in a contemporary style, was incongruously tucked away in the middle of corridors of showrooms jammed with Christmas decorations, pottery and ceramics, boudoir accessories, candles, fake flowers and straw baskets. There was only one thing missing in my life, a full-time secretary who would do the work of three people for the salary of one.

I found the Good Samaritan, and put her on the payroll. Angela Gillespie, a tall, slim, honey-blond of unending calm and serenity, was the opposite of her boss in temperament. She was a superbly competent secretary, but had always worked for a man in a large office. Now, suddenly she was working for a noisy woman in a small modern, red, black and chrome world, festooned with clippings and unrelated artwork. She became the right hand, left hand and the tail wagging the Enterprises. Her boss was often on the road, and in the course of one morning, she would be charged with getting a mimeographed press release out in the mail "to all media," contacting the local society editors on an opening we were handling, overseeing a fashion photography sitting in Charles Bacon's studio, lugging furniture props down to the Jim Conway television show for her boss's interior decorating segment, and covering the office telephone. It is physically impossible to do all of this simultaneously unless one is a constantly-dividing paramecium. Angela therefore learned to be a paramecium.

Letitia Baldrige Enterprises had to become a jack-of-all-trades in the Public Relations world. I am first a public relations consultant, in that I advise companies or individuals on their overall program and plans, leaving said programs to be carried out by the company's staff. I am a publicist also, in that I handle product publicity for certain clients, take photographs, caption them, write press releases and press kits for them when they have something newsworthy to get out to the media. When I send out a release for the International Rattan Manufacturers and Importers' Association, showing rattan furniture draped with lovely models, and the story reads "Rattan is the glamour of leisure living," I am wearing a publicist's hat.

My work obligated me to rejoin professional groups to which I had belonged in my New York days, namely, the Fashion Group and National Home Fashions League. The professional women in these organizations are like women anywhere else, very noisy and impossible in large doses. However, they help each other very effectively in their business dealings. The groups put on excellent fashion shows for the public and home furnishings programs at market. They undertake civic projects of all kinds. Fashion Group, for example, helps the Chicago Historical Society with its growing costume collection, and the National Home Fashions League raises scholarship funds by giving decorating clinics for the public.

I found myself working closely again with the two professional designers' associations, the A.I.D. and the N.S.I.D. The activities of these groups, outside of serving their clients as professional decorators, are many. They help preserve America's historic shrines, raise money to educate design students, and instigate series of conferences for the enlightenment of students and of themselves. It was fascinating to observe them in action in the Mart showrooms. A designer would recover the most delicate Louis XVI antique chair in a contemporary cotton fabric, splashed in bright red poppies, then turn right around and cover a modern, low-slung, chrome-based chair in a seventeenth century flamestitch pattern. Nothing is sacred. Grandmother's Victorian rocker can end up being covered in kelly-green fake fur as well as anything else. There seems to be no rhyme or reason to the choices. After the first shock wave, one begins to see the amusement in it, then the good looks of it. Finally the eye adjusts and is pleased. After all, the new, the untried and the experimental are blessed with merit for someone.

The more work Letitia Baldrige Enterprises absorbed, the more we seemed capable of doing. I captured the services of my old friend René Verdon when he left the kitchens of the White House for Hamilton-Beach, a division of my brother Mac's Scovill Manufacturing Co. I had interviewed and hired René as the White House chef in 1961. Now I was helping plan his tour of major markets, demonstrating the use of Hamilton-Beach electrical appliances in gourmet cooking. The irony of it all now is that when René comes to Chicago, it is I who cook dinner for him. This would unnerve most housewives, to be making dinner for the White House chef. It is small recompense, however, for the hospitality of his kitchen during White House days. René is, as always, a great diplomat. When I left out two major ingredients of the chocolate pie recipe from his new cookbook, he smiled gamely through the entire disaster of eating it.

I was not engaged in "the oldest profession in the world." Yet, Letitia Baldrige Enterprises meant selling Letitia Baldrige, as well as her services. I began to appear more and more on Chicago television, and began making more and more public appearances for clients around the country. I would be asked to speak on "The Arts," "The Role of Youth Today," "Careers in Retailing," and "The World of Antiques," as well as on the usual topics of fashion and interior design. I began to feel somewhat like a walking machine of lecture topics. When it was time to speak, I simply flicked the switch, and turned myself on, always hoping I was speaking on the right subject to the right group.

Institutions like First Federal Savings and Loan asked me to give my course for their women employees, as I had done for Sears on the "polishing of the many facets of womanhood." I used slides, movies, a tape recorder and double talk to get my points across. Business institutions, of course, wanted me to emphasize voice and telephone manners. A company can spend hundreds of thousands of dollars on its corporate image and ruin its public relations aspect in one badly handled telephone conversation between a secretary and a customer, or potential customer.

My audiences at these classes for large companies would range from nineteen-year-olds with spray-cemented hairdos the size of old Queen Mary's hats, to women in their early sixties who "don't care" anymore. There is tremendous satisfaction reaped in getting through to any of them. It may be the girl with the greasy charcoaled eyes in the front row, who snaps gum insistently in my face while I talk, but who finally appears at class one morning with a minimum of eyeliner and a quiet jaw. It may be the grandmother with the bagging stockings and uneven hemline in the back row who suddenly turns up in class with a good girdle, a new well-cut hairdo, and a straightened-up posture.

In a city like Chicago, a public relations consultant can be of value even to a large corporation with its own public relations staff. A consultant can bring new and fresh ideas to that firm, and present corporate plans that would then be carried out by the regular public relations personnel. Being free-lance and "on the outside" is a plus factor, because it means being exposed to many currents, an asset which someone specializing in just one aspect of the business cannot share. The more I learned about what the public likes to look at and listen to, as well as what the press likes to report, the easier it became to switch from one business to another in making plans for different companies. Whether it entails drawing up a schedule to send someone around the United States, promoting his product to the press, or whether it involves the presenting of a corporation's new national award at a banquet attended by a thousand prominent people, the inspiration is the same. "Make your product known to everyone and *sell it*" is the key phrase. If you have to sell it by throwing a champagne press party in the stockyards or by staging a fashion show with elephants in a museum, the whole success of the project in either case depends on pre-planning, detail-watching, flair and good luck.

The imaginative ideas come only when one is aware of what is "in" in the worlds of fashion, decorating, food, sports and leisure pursuits. A professional working in New York inhales much of this information by natural osmosis, without even seeking it. There is an endless flow of Manhattan gossip in the trade, tales of what's new in the marketplace, who the "hot" new designers are, and what is percolating in the major "think" factories. One can absorb a mountain of information while sitting at a Madison Avenue lunch counter.

In Chicago, such a natural process does not take place. One has to keep up regardless. Awareness is a necessity, not a furbelow, in the public relations business. The solution is to read insatiably. One perhaps retains only one kernel from a magazine or a trade paper. But that one kernel can serve a very important purpose later. It may be a tipoff on a hem length that will be fashion-right for a photograph to be taken today but one that will be used six months from now. It may be which international jet-setters, artists, automobiles, sailboats, sun glasses and big beat bands will still be important status symbols next season. The trends in the premium business are important, too (the coupon giveaways in drug stores and food markets). The publicist first has to know the audience he is speaking to, which means its age, sex, region and financial status. He has to attract his audience by speaking its lingo, and by capitalizing on its aspirations.

Both in my office and at home, the piles of reading materials become endless. There are trade publications on every subject, fashion magazines, shelter magazines, literary and art magazines, and all the news and women's feature magazines. I carry them around with me on buses and in taxis, in order to utilize every free second to scan them. If people on the bus think I look silly reading a pre-teen magazine or a bridal issue, they should see some of my other reading material. Six daily newspapers do not help the incinerator problem either. I thank heaven every day for my rapid reading course. One must skim, learn to clip what is a new trend or a newsy nugget, and save photographs that inspire new photographic tricks. One must keep a file on the leading designers and products. A woman in business is never a voice of authority unless she is a walking encyclopedia of information.

When Tiffany's opened its branch on Michigan Avenue, another old friend from the Fifth Avenue store, Tony Ostrom, appeared on the scene to manage it. We busily planned table-setting exhibitions, television publicity, and tie-ins with important Chicago charities. We amassed an impressive pile of clippings for the gala champagne opening, but nothing in comparison to an unplanned event that hit every front page in the country a few days later.

One morning, three weeks after the opening, heavily armed bandits overtook Tony and some of his staff as they reported for work. The big safe was opened and cleared of its entire contents; the staff was made to lie on the floor, and the criminals had the impertinence to ask the whereabouts of the "big stuff" they had seen on television a few days previously. Our crooked television buffs had made a list of the big jewels they admired on the screen and had expected to acquire on this early-morning escapade. Luckily, these oversized rocks had already gone on to be exhibited in another city. The Chicago press, of course, was agog over the robbery, and I had to meet them during the entire day of the crime with firm instructions from the police not to tell them anything. They grew angrier and angrier with their uninteresting spokesman, and one of them sourly remarked, "Heh, Tish, you were around for the New York window robbery a few years back, and now this. Any tie-in there?" I thanked him for his chivalrous suggestion. It reminded me that on the occasion of the first robbery, I had received a telegram

Mater Familias in Chicago! · 319

from a thoughtful friend that read, "There isn't anything you wouldn't stoop to for a little publicity." The afternoon of the Tiffany Chicago robbery, I received another telegram, from the same person, which read, "There isn't anything you wouldn't stoop to for a little publicity."

⊷⊶

When the late Elizabeth Arden personally christened her new building on Michigan Avenue, I had a field day handling the arrangements. (This, incidentally, was the building into which Tiffany's later moved.) The handsome white marble building contained the Arden face, hair and body treatment operations, as well as a fashion salon. The entire ambience was one of romantic pinks and reds, crystal chandeliers, and lovely fragrances wafting everywhere. This was an easy story to insert into any part of the papers. It was an architectural one, a business and financial one, a home furnishings, beauty, hairstyling, fashion and accessories story. It was even a health story.

For women's page news while the building was still going up, we perched models in Elizabeth Arden's thousand-dollar evening gowns, dripping glittery earrings, up on the girders with burly men in steel helmets. We placed one model in a slinky lamé dress in an electrical tunnel, where she was almost electrocuted but the lighting effects were sensational. We put a model in evening pajamas astride an oversized heating pipe, like an equestrienne on her horse, reassuring her all the time the heat would not be turned on. Little Miss Arden herself, over whom I towered a full foot, was a dynamo in her eighties. She glided around on her tiny legs all over the building before the opening, usually on the efficient arm of the Chicago manager of the salon, Janette Marr, trying to change everything from the basic decor and the architectural structure of the building to the color of the lighting. ("I want a soft pink light right here," she would say firmly. "Women look prettiest in a pink light, and they shall look their prettiest here.") The fact that this was the day before the opening was immaterial. She was a fabulous woman, full of wit and spice, with a blade-sharp tongue and a mammoth heart. She was an astute businesswoman and a perfectionist. "What are all those men doing here, darling?" she asked me at the opening, "I mean, at a party for women?"

"They're plain clothes detectives, Miss Arden," I replied, "to guard the valuables of your guests."

"Oh dear," she sighed, "they aren't very decorative, are they? Don't you think my clients and friends know how to take care of themselves?"

I took the hint. The problem was solved by banishing them into the background. One of them seemed to disappear under a hair dryer in the "Drying Garden," and another peered apprehensively out at the world from a steam cabinet room. Miss Arden then stopped a young Andy Frain usher in his familiar bright blue uniform and white gloves. (He had been hired to help control the direction of the crowds.) She looked at him compassionately, as a deep blush spread over his adolescent, acne-marked face.

"Young man, are you having a lot of trouble with that skin of yours?"

He toed the carpet, obviously wishing there was room for him under it. The blush deepened.

"Wait here one minute." Miss Arden was off at a fast clip and returned with a small pink jar of Eight Hour Cream in her hands. "Put this on every night before you go to sleep. Rub it in well, now. In two weeks that skin problem will clear up. Just remember, every night. And you'll be all right. It's the hard part of growing up, you know."

Mater Familias in Chicago! · 321

And with a comforting pat on his arm, she was off again, to greet her friends from New York, Colonel Serge Obolensky and fashion editor, Connie Woodworth, who had flown out for her opening. She was firmly convinced the boy's psyche would be rehabilitated.

The Andy Frain usher stood looking after her, a transfixed statue with a small pink jar of cream in his white-gloved hand.

My number one reason for liking Chicago concerns a story of boy meets girl. I was the girl. Considering my past life, this phenomenon logically should have occurred in the Bois de Boulogne, on an Austrian Alp, in the Borghese Gardens of Rome, or at least in a horse-drawn carriage in Central Park.

I had frankly reached the conclusion that marriage was not in the cards for me. I had dominated the men in my life with boring regularity, and could never find anyone who had the stamina to control the reins. I had met so many men, fallen in love so many times, and had been disappointed so often by the actions of the opposite sex, I had quite accepted the fact of my spinsterhood. In fact, I was quite thriving on it.

There was nothing more enjoyable than the solitude of my apartment at the end of a pulverizing day, or at the end of a pulverizing social schedule at night. The gay facial mask would drop at the front door of the apartment, the door would shut, and then the blessed relief of solitude would fill the vacuum. I had a demanding job, interesting friends, and a so-called "glamorous life." There was not enough time to feel lonely. As the years went on and I had reached my mid-thirties, I had heard the questions asked sotto voce too often: "What do you think is wrong with her?" "Why do you suppose she's not married?" It all left me untouched and unperturbed. I did not need a head-shrinker. I had plenty of married friends who did, however. It seemed everyone was wishing me unhappily married, just for the sake of the wedding ring.

I suppose I was fortunate that there had been plenty of men around from the time I outgrew my teens and overcame my feelings of inferiority over being so tall. However, the unmarried girl's role in her thirties seems to become that of a compassionate listening post. Night after night she must listen soothingly and lovingly to a man's stories of how badly his ex-wife treated him, or to a bachelor's lament about everything from the calf muscle strained on the tennis court to the injustice of his roommate's handling of the liquor bill. It never seems to occur to the unmarried man to ask if the girl might just once have a complaint herself. In defense, the single girl learns to bottle it all up inside. (Some learn to "bottle it up" on the outside, with a glass in hand, which is no solution either.)

By the time I reached Chicago, I felt that the unmarried girl who was happily working in a job, with good friends, and who was secure in the knowledge she was making the best of her mind and of her appearance, was really a very well-adjusted person. In fact, she was fortunate. I was not even embarrassed by the fact that I had not as yet changed a baby's diaper. My friends, however, were still optimistically expecting me to marry, momentarily, someone with the rank of an Ambassador, Senator, or Cabinet officer. He would, they all agreed, most certainly be very rich.

One evening the John Greenes asked a young man named Bob Hollensteiner who worked for the real estate firm of Sudler & Co. to bring me out to their home in Lake Forest for dinner. His father, amazingly enough, worked in the Merchandise Mart, for A. L. Diament & Co. I could not remember the Hollensteiner name, finally had to write it down on a piece of paper and practice it. The man in question turned out to be quite a bit taller than I, an amazing fact in itself. The qualifications for resembling my ideal man stopped there. He was not even rich. However, he pleased me very much by refraining from asking "What was Jackie really like?" Nor did he say he needed an appointment with "Bob" or "Teddy" and would I please arrange it. In fact, he could not have cared less about any part of my background. He never spoke to me during the entire party until he had to drive me into the city again. I found him rude and aloof. Besides, our interests were totally different. His passions were hockey games, football and the sports page. Mine were opera, concerts and international politics.

We were married exactly ninety days later in the French church of St. Jean Baptiste at 75th Street and Lexington Avenue in New York.

We attend the Black Hawks hockey games two nights a week, including nights when we have been asked to the season's best parties, and we rarely attend an opera. The radio blares Cub baseball games all summer. On autumn Sundays he goes to the Bear football games and I read magazines on international politics at home. We are totally, completely happy. Perhaps a psychiatrist could figure that one out.

⊷⊷

I thought having babies was something that happened to other people. I also used to complain about my overly-charged schedule in my spinster days. I soon discovered that no matter how much stress exists in the responsibilities and career of an unmarried girl, nothing compares to the task of running a household. The Hollensteiner household thrives on chaos. We will always live consistently beyond our income. Our apartment was built for another era and another style of living. It boasts of a defunct architectural fantasy called "rooms for domestic help" in back of the kitchen. We have filled them with empty boxes and assorted junk, since they will never be inhabited by living bodies. When we moved into the place, little Clare, then just over two years in age, went around constantly ringing the bells on the walls in every room and in every hallway. Her little face was full of intellectual struggle and doubt as she asked the same question for each bell, and always received the same answer.

"What are the bells for, Mommie?"

"To ring for servants, Clare."

"What are servants, Mommie?"

"That's something I can't explain, Clare."

She will never know, *poverina*. It is a word that cannot possibly survive in the vocabulary of her generation.

We do have a cleaning lady. I am the *chef de cuisine* for all evening and weekend meals, including dinner parties in our grand dining room. It is blessed with paneled walls that Louis XV's courtiers would have found very suitable. In candlelight, with a lot of imagination, there is a liveried footman behind every chair. One must admit, however, that the care and feeding of a hungry husband, children and a nannie, all on separate menus, is enough to depress a well-organized staff, let alone a working mother. My grocery bills in my unmarried days averaged seven dollars a week. Now they look as though we were subsisting on champagne and caviar only. The very particular male stomach in our house does not like to live from a freezer, so marketing to buy fresh produce is a regular chore. As I wait impatiently in the check-out line three or four times a week at the martini hour, there is a certain masochistic pleasure in realizing I could be spending that same amount of time home in my tub, soaking in warm bubble bath with lotion-drenched cotton pads on my eyes. This is what the magazines say I should be doing.

The ebb and flow of laundry and cleaning that goes with an overly clean male, an overly clean nannie and a cavernous apartment makes me feel I am mistress of a hospital. As hampers fill, I long for the days when there used to be a small pile of nylon nothings sitting in my bathroom, with an adjacent box of soap flakes to solve my week's laundry problem with alacrity. Nannie keeps one soap company solvent by hand-washing her charges' underthings and overthings several times a day. Small pairs of white gloves decorate strung-up laundry lines over the bathtubs like birds chatting on telephone wires. One cannot enter the nursery through her bathroom; it is impossible to pass through the barricade of misty wet clouds of small people's laundry. It is as impenetrable as a Chicago fog-bank in November.

I am fortunate in having an office in the apartment, because it enables me to carry on my work at home on weekends and when someone is sick. One remains forever grateful to secretarial training that keeps the electric typewriter humming efficiently wherever one is. Unfortunately there is no toy dearer to a child than an electric typewriter. When Clare was born, my office was in the back part of her large nursery room. The first noises she heard were the hum of my IBM and the click of the Sears file cabinets in my office. She learned at a very precocious age how to start "Mommie's tightwriter" by flicking the key. She also became entranced with the festoons of carbon ribbon that can come out of that fascinating machine. She learned manual dexterity in lifting Mommie's files out of all the lower file drawers and refiling all of the material in her own special way.

Nice as it is to conduct business at home, there is always a certain lack of poise accompanying it. A little voice chimes in non-stop on the nursery extension during an incoming long-distance call on a business matter. The voice is husky, breathy, emphatic. "Hello, I'm Clare. I have a baby brother. I'm three. How old are you?"

Fortunately I am a morning girl. I arise happily at 6 A.M. to start the household running. One has to keep ahead of the milkman, the diaper service, the dry cleaning and laundry pick-up, and the inevitable repairmen. It is a lovely, restful way to start the day. I get breakfast started, bring in the morning papers and read them while standing, cooking, or working on lists and notes for the household. I am also paymaster for any and all services, and every morning there is a variety of envelopes to pay whoever is coming in to do something that day. I will never see any of them. Our only contact is an envelope. Perhaps it is a fortunate arrangement.

At seven I spend one and a half minutes trying to awaken my husband. If psychological torture does not work, there is always the physical. At seven-thirty Clare bursts forth from the nursery, which is my signal to read the comic strips in the paper to her, plus a challenging, sexy novel like "Sleeping Beauty." Nannie brings her breakfast down, I say hello to Malcolm exercising on his mat, and by eight-fifteen I am out of the house. Behind me I have left a litter of notes, and have stashed a quantity of others in my husband's briefcase. (He does not speak before 9 A.M. One must communicate with him by writing. He is not a morning person.)

I swing out the door, laden with a bulging red velvet briefcase and inevitable packages (repairing jobs, props for photographs, etc.). I cannot help but cast an immense sigh of relief into the cold morning air. I adore my husband and children. I am proud of our home. I am also very glad to get away from all of it for a while.

I must have read fifty articles about how dangerous it is to have children after the age of thirty-five. When I first became pregnant, my obstetrician, Dr. Byford Heskett, ceased reciting rules and regulations governing slowed-down behavior for the pregnant lady. I did not smoke, I consumed his iron pills faithfully, and I gained only fourteen pounds. However, never once could I manage a rest period or a nap. I worked up through the day each baby was born, including lecturing (lecterns are excellent camouflage equipment) and television shows (one can always find a piece of furniture to stand behind). The women of the Presbyterian St. Luke's Fashion Show Committee were so nervous, having me as their very expectant commentator for the show, they had a standby commentator sitting directly behind me to take over, in case labor pains would dare to come during the evening gown sequence in the show. The weekend Malcolm was due, I ran a series of receptions and press conferences for famed Paris couturière Madame Grès, and organized a benefit dinner dance featuring her clothes for the Junior League. With both babies, the eighteen-year-old mothers, my fellow inhabitants of the Maternity Ward of Wesley Hospital, looked on me as being rather obscene. I was the same age as their mothers. What was *I* doing having a baby? Each time it became my turn to snicker. I sprang faster from my bed, walked the corridors with more energy, executed my exercises with more devotion, and was back in circulation way ahead of time. When Malcolm began to arrive, Dr. Heskett found me in the Labor Room, writing an article on a large yellow legal pad, trying to meet my deadline. Five nights later, with hair freshly done at Arden's, I joined my husband at the Thatcher Wallers' dinner party at the Racquet Club.

As I think back on serving my "term" twice at Wesley, I can only remember that there is no more beautiful music in the world than the merry tinkle of that little bell, rung down the hall by the nurse to announce that the newborn babies are on their way in their little plastic carts to be fed. This is the music I would wish for each and every woman — at least once in her lifetime.

From adolescence onward, I had had a very romantic concept of marriage. Every evening, I planned to be waiting at the front door for my husband, dressed in a flowing hostess gown, bathed, scented and lovely. The front hall would be lit with candles; exotic canapes would be cozily warming themselves in the silver chafing dish; champagne would be icing itself in the silver bucket; and my solicitous greeting of my husband would remove all of his worldly cares at once.

I am indeed waiting for my husband every night, eagerly, but hardly in a glamorous context. Against the advice issued regularly by the women's magazines, I can hardly wait for him to walk in that door to communicate my problems. He has no chance to doff his hat and coat before I let loose with a blast that would make Maria Callas' loudest, most screeching high C sound like a gentle raindrop in comparison. Staunch male that he is, he takes it like a man, stands fast in the onrush, and then gets us both a drink before I become any more hysterical.

In my single days, I used to come home to the apartment in the same mental state, and kick a well-worn piece of furniture in my anger. It is much nicer to take it out on one's husband. What the husband then proceeds to kick in reprisal for bearing his wife's woes I have not yet discovered.

The question I am most often asked is, "How do you do it?" Women can't understand how one can find time to run a house, participate in civic events, work all day, raise children, do the cooking, write, play tennis and brush one's teeth in the morning.

The answer is simple. One has to have a saint of an understanding husband, a loyal hairdresser, and a superb nurse for

Mater Familias in Chicago! · 329

the children. If a working mother has these three human beings in her life, she can sail through every emergency.

Take the husband, for instance. It is imperative that he be blessed with very strong psychological health. It is not easy for just any man to toss on a robe, emerge from his shower on Saturday morning and unexpectedly find a photographer in his bedroom. The photographer, of course, is in the process of rearranging all the furniture under hot studio lights. The husband retrieves his underwear, which had been draped over one of the chairs about to be photographed, and finds the morning mail torn to shreds by his daughter and tucked into his bedroom slipper. He flees to the hallway and fights his way into the kitchen for breakfast past something else he was unprepared for, a women's charity board, having a coffee meeting on an upcoming project in the living room. In the kitchen, his only hope for privacy, two deliverymen are struggling through the service door with a hulking piece of furniture he has never seen before. It is to be placed in the library for a photographic prop. When he protests there is not room in the library for this piece, the deliverymen dump it in the hall, blocking the doorway. He opens the refrigerator and discovers all the breakfast delicacies he had been contemplating by now with desperate relish have been moved to the children's side, with a stern warning from Nannie written on labels: "Do Not Touch. For Children." The telephone rings three times consecutively while his eggs are cooking. A Sears stylist asks him to please report to the photographer in the bedroom at once that a live shaggy dog is on its way to be photographed in the library setting; a reporter calls from O'Hare to ask Miss Baldrige if she can confirm a rumor that the whole Kennedy family is on its way to Chicago for a secret meeting; and a foreign voice says in a thick accent that, since he had a letter to Mrs. Hollensteiner from a mutual friend, could he drop by today during his few hours in Chicago, around lunchtime?

When the husband finally fights his way back into the library with the morning papers, he discovers his absent wife has clipped out five or six things on the woman's page, all of which are backed by articles he wanted to read. There's a note on the table by his favorite chair from his wife, saying they would have to forego the hockey game tonight and attend an important black tie dinner in honor of some leading industry figures. Would he also remember please to mail a heavily censored version of *Playboy* to his nieces Megan and Molly in Connecticut as he had promised? And would he please feed the goldfish?

The husband writes a note back to his wife, using unprintable expletives to make his point clear that she can go to her dinner by herself. He will go to the hockey game. Off he goes in his tennis clothes to take out any unexploded wrath on a white rubber ball. He does not file suit for divorce, although the grounds are there. He must somehow realize that he is the pole holding up the tent.

The second most important man in a woman's life has got to be her hairdresser. Most women spend half a day getting themselves "done." Some spend the entire day. I devote all of forty-five minutes once a week to the deed, blowing into Elizabeth Arden's on a ninety-mile-an-hour wind. The job is done with alacrity. A woman in business is on show every day of the week, so she has to keep the coiffure looking well. There is no mercy extended to a badly groomed woman. Unlike a man, she cannot afford one minute of frowsiness in public. A man with an unpressed suit is forgiven as being "too busy." A woman with an unpressed suit loses the account.

There is no question but that children create a major dilemma for the career girl. Leaving them with a succession of babysitters or cleaning women who are concentrating on their household chores is not the answer. Any working mother who leaves her little ones all day suffers guilt pangs. However, if she leaves them with someone they love and trust, and who also stimulates their minds, then she has done the best she can. I am constantly being confronted by the question, inevitably posed with malice over after-dinner coffee in the bedroom, "Tish, just how *can* you stand another woman bringing up your children?"

The truth is that if I were home all day, we would *all* be under psychiatric care, children and parents alike. Another undeniable fact of life is that if one needs money, one needs money. We all feel that the problem of leaving the children has been handled in our case as best it can be. Ruth Lee, a successful free-lance publicist in Chicago, a fellow Vassar-graduate, and a fellow working mother, often discusses this subject with me. We have decided a working mother has to be a horse. She has to be healthier, stronger and work harder at her office than any man. The competition is rougher. She also has to concentrate more on her mother's job than the mother who is at home all the time. Ruth is ahead of me in the marriage game. The Lees celebrated their fiftieth wedding anniversary this year when we celebrated our fourth. She has had more experience in facing the career-children problem. It is basically a balancing act.

At times I have to cheat on doing the right thing by my husband, at other times by my children, at other times by my job. As long as the cheating is not too intense or regular in any one direction, a happy equilibrium can be maintained. As far as children go, the quality of time a working woman spends with them has to be as important as the quantity of time stay-at-home mothers give them. My weekends belong to the children. So do the early morning and evening story hours. It is a precious commitment we all have to each other.

There is never a day that goes by in the office that I am not aware of motherhood. The press releases I take from my briefcase to be mailed are covered with colored crayon marks. My jammed office calendar is interrupted all over with red jottings: "Call Helene Cummings about nursery tea party" and "Order baby jellies for Malcolm." If I am missing important reference material for my clients, I know enough to look in the nursery. Each day in my office Angela puts through a call from Clare, regardless of the visitor by my desk. It usually concerns something earth-shaking. "Mommie, I'm very brave. I picked up the plastic spider all by myself. I touched it! I touched it!" I rejoice in her triumph. In the background, one hears the very satisfying baby noises of young Malcolm, playing with his playpen toys in competition with the nursery rhymes on the phonograph. I have yet to have a client sitting opposite me in my office become angry at such an intrusion. If I am in the middle of photographing a fashion story on jewelry and receive a call from Nannie, everything stops. I meet her at the pediatrician's with the children and keep the photographer waiting half an hour. I usually find upon my return that he has enhanced his lighting effects with the extra time.

I know I am fortunate. I am in business for myself. Although this entails working even harder, it also means that if a child needs me, I can cover myself with a white lie and absent myself from the job. I will never have to miss an appearance in the school play. I think our children are fortunate, too. They will become a part of our adult lives far ahead of the normal child. They will also know the meaning of money, and how difficult it is to earn. When my children grow up, I hope they will understand why "Mommie" is always at the office. If they do not, then it marks a true failure on my part.

Our "Nannie," imported from Ireland and trained in the old

British tradition, is quite a sight in Lincoln Park with her official gray nannie's coat. She keeps the children immaculately, teaches them at four months to put their hands to their mouths in order to stifle yawns politely, and has a voice which can rise in volume to that of a hog caller's. Grace is said after every meal, followed by the stern admonition, "Go on your pot!" in the same breath. Prayers are said diligently morning and evening, and holy water is dispensed lavishly when the slightest sniffle appears. Diapers in our house are nappies; bibs are feeders; and anyone calling the Sol Whitby pram, imported from London at an incredible price, a "buggy" rates forty strokes of Nannie's tongue. An Irish Nannie is always easily recognizable. She is the one with the hood of the pram all the way down, regardless of the weather. American prams, according to Nannie, are unbearably bad, and American baby clothes are inferior, because "they don't even have any decent smocking, fore and aft." I would love to have Nannie work with the Sears buyers on a collection of "Nannie Approved" equipment for babies and children. However, she would probably cause me to lose the account. If our children suffer fewer colds in winter than their contemporaries, it is due entirely to the British and Irish woolies they wear, and to the fact that they are out walking and "perambulating" five hours every day, whether in floods, snowstorms, tornadoes, or locust plagues. I cannot tell whether the children's pediatrician, Dr. Martin Hardy, is impressed by Nannie or amused by her. He has never crossed her yet, even when she "potted" both babies from birth.

We all manage to survive this "Irish Britannia Rules the Waves" atmosphere in the house because Nannie is such a pro. I found her by advertising in the London magazine all the nannies covet, *The Nursery World*. She has had thirty years of experience with little ones, whereas her employers had never held a baby before they were blessed with a pair of them. She feeds both children simultaneously and reads to them, which I find impossible to accomplish. The drone of her Irish voice at mealtime wafts from the nursery all through the apartment. When she tells a story, she is as dramatic in her reading as a Shakespearean actor. In an atmosphere punctuated by baby Malcolm's burps (referred to more delicately in nannies' language as "passing wind"), her voice admonishes little Clare:

"And Cinderella looked down sadly at her rags. How could she go to the ball dressed like . . . PUT YOUR FEEDER UP! CHEW WHAT'S IN YOUR MOUTH! . . . dressed like this? The fairy godmother, of course, knew just what to do. With her magic wand she . . . DRINK EVERY LAST BIT OF THAT MILK, DO YOU HEAR ME? NO, YOU CAN'T GET DOWN, NOT UNTIL I SAY SO . . . waved it over Cinderella, and there she was, transformed from rags into a splendid gold and white dress, ready for the ball . . ."

The atmosphere in our household is at all times intellectually stimulating.

―――

One's values in life are like a bas relief carving. The values of the present are sculpted in strong relief, because one can reach out at any time and touch the present. There are not so many nuances, however, in the values of things past. My scrapbooks and albums stimulate specific strong memories, not subtle details, of life in foreign capitals and in the service of the White House.

One forgets many things, usually the unpleasantnesses. As one matures, the girlish enthusiasm that is lost is replaced with a degree of prejudice and impatience. In other words, the things I hold important today from those adventuresome days are not what I held important then. It is only logical. The solid, lasting values that shape one's life are a gift of experience, the result of a very precious process of continuous selection.

The glitter and the glamor of the White House parties are insignificant beside the fact that I was part of the John F. Kennedy Administration, and that I was a member of his team. To be a part of a precious moment of history is perhaps one of the greatest privileges in life.

I never used to be a champion of my own sex. Quite the opposite. I always preferred men as *people*. I still despise large groups of women and the cackle of female voices when they are banished to the bedroom after dinner to discuss food prices and child care over their demitasses. I resent being sequestered with the ladies and being deprived of the companionship of the best hour of any man's day, when he is well fed and enjoying his after-dinner smoke, drink and conversation. My attitude toward the ladies in general has changed, however. Working for and knowing well remarkable women all over the world who live under pressure, and who produce, influence and inspire has made me proud of today's woman, and especially of today's American woman. She is unjustly a consistent target of criticism in all of our media. Whether she is the heroine of a television soap opera, a labored novel, or a ladies' magazine, she is usually portrayed as a male castrator, a nincompoop, a neurotic disaster, or a conniving villainess.

One of the women I admire, Rose Kennedy, the late President's mother, ranks high on my list. Like everyone else, I was struck by her chic, youthful appearance in pre-White House days. Like almost everyone else, I thought she was probably a wealthy, pampered butterfly. The real woman emerged very quickly to those of us on the White House staff. She is an aggressive fighter on mental retardation; she is concrete-willed, persevering, witty, sentimental, a perfectionist, and above all a lesson to anyone who has to suffer. She has been hit so hard so often with personal tragedy, she has earned the right to be a paragon of self-pity. She is the opposite. Her iron-buttressed religious faith is perhaps the key. Whatever it is, she is extraordinary, and my idea of a real "trouper."

Another woman who has not been given proper credit in our time is Jacqueline Kennedy's mother, soft-spoken Janet Auchincloss. Far from seeking public acclaim, she shuns it. She is not an organizer, a stateswoman, a joiner. I have known her since I was a very young girl, and have looked up to her as a model of kindness, loveliness and exquisite manners. She is an inspiration to any girl possessed of an interest in "growing up to be a lady" in the true sense of the term. She is the epitome of femininity, a quality that seems to be rapidly disappearing from the American scene. She also raised a daughter who had the poise and the instinctive manners to become a very fine First Lady.

My debts to Evangeline Bruce, my first professional teacher as the American Ambassadress in Paris, and to Clare Luce, who has given me inspiration and guidance since Rome days, are immeasurable. There are no strident, aggressive, masculine women of accomplishment on my list. In fact, in my opinion, those qualities do not exist in any of the women who have earned a special niche of womanly distinction for themselves in our society today.

To any young girl who wants to pursue a career, I can only say it can be a wonderfully exciting and satisfying experience. I admit from personal experience that a perfect culmination to that career is a happy marriage and children, whether or not the career continues. However, if the right man does not come along, there are many fates far worse. One is to have the wrong man come along.

The American woman has more opportunity to develop her inner self and to contribute to her society than any other woman in any other time or place. She is therefore almost morally obligated to develop that inner self. I cannot help but remember some advice one of my college professors gave us over a cup of tea one Sunday afternoon. I wrote it in my diary, because she used to speak in such a colorful way. I always found her very quotable. "Your main job in life, girls," she said, "is to be happy. And to be happy you must push to the farthest of your capabilities in all things, whether it's work or play, war or peace. Above all, keep your eyes open, look *up* as well as straight ahead, and for God's sake, know when to get off your tail!"